What others are saying

Eric Taylor has written delightful short stories reminiscing on childhood experiences in West Texas during the depression and his maturing years in Texas and Wyoming. A lifetime of experiences is encapsulated in these stories on discoveries in life as one matures. You will laugh at events described in stories like "When I Was Five," where his fifth birthday is full of misadventures. Eric Tells of his brother's collecting Toad Frogs (Ribbit!) in his mother's flower beds and how, unhappily for the frogs, his mother failed to search all of this brother's overall pockets on washday! The author also describes a deep friendship with a hunting buddy in the story "Remembering Frank." In the story "The Sheriff's Wife," Eric describes an experience nearly all of us have had in crossing paths with someone we knew many years before in a different place and a different time. Reading these stories will not only be entertaining, but will bring back your own fond memories of times gone by. As Eric states, "Some things you never forget…"

Phyllis Kennon, Professor,
South Plains College, Levelland, Texas.

Eric Taylor is a story teller who has been accumulating tales for decades. In this collection of short stories and essays, he shares years of recollections and wisdom. His tales take the reader across a lifetime of experiences and memories from the sandy plains of West Texas to the sunny land of opportunity in California on to the rough hills and mountains of Colorado and Wyoming. While the settings change, his stories cover a full range of human experiences and emotions. Some are sad and some are funny. Some will evoke memories while others will document a more simple era when family was everything and friends were forever. We invite you to join us in sharing Taylor's tales from yesteryear.

(s) Stephen Henry, editor/owner/publisher
Levelland News Press, Levelland, Texas.

THE BOOK:
COUNTING *to* 100

ERIC C. TAYLOR

THE BOOK:
COUNTING *to* 100

TATE PUBLISHING
AND ENTERPRISES, LLC

Published by Tate Publishing & Enterprises, LLC
127 E. Trade Center Terrace | Mustang, Oklahoma 73064 USA
1.888.361.9473 | www.tatepublishing.com

Tate Publishing is committed to excellence in the publishing industry. The company reflects the philosophy established by the founders, based on Psalm 68:11,
"The Lord gave the word and great was the company of those who published it."

Book design copyright © 2015 by Tate Publishing, LLC. All rights reserved.
Cover design by Samson Lim
Interior design by Mary Jean Archival

Published in the United States of America
ISBN: 978-1-68097-326-6
Biography & Autobiography / Personal Memoirs
15.05.15

After my wife, Nancy, read the very first article I wrote, she became my most dedicated fan.

As I became more aware of my calling as a writer, I elected her to edit my efforts. She has suffered through the editing of the two novels I have previously published and the very difficult editing of all the non-fiction short stories within the cover of this book. I owe her much that can never be repaid with anything but love…in my forever.

An explanation...
well, sort of...

When choosing the order of assembly in a collection of short stories there are a couple of things that must be taken under consideration. The first consideration, of course, is what importance each story gives to the collection. The second, the subject of each story as it gives the most significance to the things the other stories try to demonstrate.

In the early years of my own and my brother's life, two very significant things happened. These occurrences, one his and one mine, set the separate stages for our entire lives. Mine happened a few years earlier than my brothers which I will write about shortly. But my brother's...

He was around eight years old when our father took the family to our great uncle's cabin just east of Taos, New Mexico. While there, the family took the short trip into Taos and we visited a tourist curio shop. In a display case in that shop, my brother discovered a double-twined selenite crystal in a shape similar to a double cross. He was so fascinated by this oddity of nature that it took a very important place in his mind. Because of that crystal, he studied geology and graduated with a PhD in that field. He has spent his life chasing that field and is still involved in trying to figure out how God made the world He made.

My significant thing happened a few years earlier than that. It gave me a love of literature that did not come to full blossom until I was many years grown. The first story of this collection tells that tale; the tale that for me culminated in mid-life and continues to inspire me to this very day. Some things you never forget...

Contents

Part 1: The Younger Years

Part 2: The Top Of The Hill

PART 1

The Younger Years

Counting To One Hundred

The tall, slender gray-haired woman standing in front of about fifteen or so of us six-year olds told us her name was Mrs. DeShazo. Well, she made an impression on us all, especially me. She was closer to me in proximity than any woman other than my mother had ever been. And, I didn't like any of this, my first day of school, even though my home was only just across the dirt road going by the two-room school building.

Topping all that off, I didn't know a single soul in the one room we were in. The boys were mostly wearing pin-striped bib overalls, the girls had on simple cotton dresses, mostly homemade. Most of us were barefoot, partly because the weather was plenty warm, partly because Texas was still in the lingering effects of the depression and most folks were just plain poor. All of us were squeaky clean and neat.

The schoolroom had a bare creaky pine floor with built-in splinters, a pot-bellied cast iron stove in the center of the room. Two or three small-paned windows looked out on the sandy playground, and one door led to freedom.

Some fifty-odd years later it's kind of hard to remember all the details. I suppose the first thing we had to learn was to print our given name: Monkey-see, monkey-do fashion. Somewhere along there we must have learned to count to twelve, because I do remember a big white cardboard clock with big black numbers in a circle and "hands" that could be moved, one big hand, the other smaller. Learning to tell time wasn't too bad, though. Everyone needs to know if it really is bedtime when Daddy says it is.

In these first few days of this first school year I caught chicken pox from someone; I don't recall who. I had more red spots on me than freckles, and I have got a lot of freckles. Now back then when you had chicken pox, you had to stay in bed and lay real still so chicken pox wouldn't have any lasting effects in a certain unmentionable place. Since everyone knows every young boy likes to lie real still, having chicken pox is really a lot of fun for all in the near proximity.

The postmaster's daughter, Jean Witte, heard about my situation and gave my Dad a box of old books for me to read. She must have thought I was really old because most of the books were. One of the books was Zane Grey's "Thundering Herd." The title fascinated me so much that I learned to read it with my mother helping me over the hard spots. Grey's words of buffalo and the smell of sage held my attention as nothing else ever had in my short span of cognizant memory.

Having finally recovered from the chicken pox, I was back to attending school. After a few days I was made to be aware that most everyone else could already count to one hundred having learned while I was recuperating from the pox. So, for me came the really hard part: Learning to count to one hundred. For some reason I procrastinated. At the end of each school day just as we were leaving for our separate homes, I remember Mrs. DeShazo telling those of us who had not yet learned to count to one hundred that we all were going to have to learn. But by the time I had accomplished my long walk home across the road, I had forgotten all about school and was thinking of stacking big flat thick dirt cakes from the road pretending they were adobe bricks. For some reason I just did not want to learn to count really big. I just really wasn't interested in learning to count. Maybe it was the long span of concentration memorization took, or the mental energy required. To this day I don't like to memorize things I am not particularly interested in.

One day a most terrible thing happened. Mrs. DeShazo told me since I had not learned to count to one hundred as everyone else; I was going to have to stay after school until I learned. So, there I sat all alone except for her after the other kids left. Then out came the twelve-inch ruler and my hand was extended in front of me, palm up, with this lady holding onto my fingertips. After about two whacks of the ruler I was counting to one hundred so fast you could not believe it.

Learning to read was a lot different. Mrs. DeShazo pointed out everyone needed to learn to read so they could read the Sunday funny paper without having to wait for Daddy to find the time. At this time, I pointed out to her I could already read. She did not seem too impressed until I read "See Spot Run" to her on my first opening of the little reader with no problem whatsoever. As for the rest of the class, in just a few days most everyone was reading up a storm in no time at all.

Well, all of us-as I remember-survived the first grade and eventually went on to bigger and better things. World War II ended, my Dad moved us to another town, and I gradually pushed the small two-room schoolhouse and Mrs. DeShazo into the dark corners of my mind. A lot of her teaching stayed with me, though. I mostly stopped procrastinating because of that twelve-inch ruler.

Through her beginning influence, I graduated a little above average from high school. I attended Texas Tech College until interrupted by the U.S. Marine Corps and Korea, and much later, retired as a first level supervisor with a large public utility company.

A few years ago, my wife and I traveled to the land of my childhood. The town is still small, quiet and really very pretty in my grown up mind. The house we lived in by the school grounds is still there but it sure has shrunk over the years. The road between the house and school is paved and curbed now; no more adobe bricks. The white two-room school building is no longer there and nothing remains to indicate it ever existed. As my wife and I continued to drive around looking over the town, odds and ends of memories dimmed by years flashed through my mind. I had once been there; some of us played mumblety-peg under that big elm tree. Billy King, who died in a sand hill cave-in a short time later, lost his left eye that day, throwing his pocketknife into the trunk of that tree. Instead of sticking in the tree, the knife bounced back and the blade point struck him in his eye.

Preparing to drive back to the highway to leave this place of my young memories, I stopped at a "T" intersection in order to turn left. Suddenly, I became aware we had stopped in front of a fairly new large, very pretty single-story tan brick building with a freshly mowed lawn divided by a wide concrete walk leading to the entryway. Suddenly, memories came back. This building had been constructed over our sandlot baseball field. Where, while batting during a game one hot summer afternoon, I accidentally hit the catcher on the side of his head when I took a mighty swing at the pitched ball. Scared? I threw the bat down and ran home, just as fast as I could. I do not now remember badly the catcher was hurt.

As I looked closely at the building that sat on top of the sandlot ball field, I realized that unforgettable person of my childhood had made an unforgettable impression on a few other people, too. For over the building's entryway in large shiny steel letters was the name: Mary DeShazo Elementary School. In Muleshoe, Texas, that is.

Somehow, all these years later, I still have the book "Thundering Herd." Reading still fascinates me, gives me Heroes in White Hats on White Stallions, Perfect Lives and Perfect Worlds. As an adult, one of my first major purchases was all of Grey's published westerns; I have read each many times. And, I can still count to One Hundred when pressed.

Foozy

The time of the year was early spring. I was three years and eight months old. My parents had just brought home my baby brother from the clinic/hospital where he was born. Even at the very young age I was, I remember exactly what happened to this day. I have an excellent memory. I did not understand why he had not been born here at home like I had been told I was. Anyhow, I was not at all happy; in fact I was pretty mad. If they had told me they were going to get me a baby brother I sure as heck didn't remember it.

I had been standing just inside the kitchen door looking at him in his bassinet. I went outside through the kitchen door. I grabbed a handful of coal dust and sand, went back inside the kitchen door and threw the handful in his face. There. I felt I had started to get even for him disrupting my life.

However, I did get a licking. It was not my first, and it sure wasn't going to be my last. Not that I was mistreated or anything. I was just a really active boy. Yessir, I was active. I got into anything and everything I could and then some. But, I really didn't mind the licking after the fact. After it quit hurting, that is.

A few days pass. My father brought home a small black wire-haired terrier puppy for me. Really fuzzy. All black. I decided to name him Foozy after Alley Oop's buddy in the Sunday newspaper comics. I knew about Alley Oop because my dad read the comics to me every Sunday. The real comic strip Foozy wore fuzzy black short pants. Just like the ones I wore only mine weren't black or fuzzy. And nothing else, like I also wore. Bare chested, that is. But the real Foozy's short black fuzzy pants look real curly just like the puppy's black fur coat.

Foozy and I became great buddies. He followed me everywhere I went. Mostly he followed me because there was no one else for him to play with except the barnyard chickens. And, he didn't like them because most times they ignored him when he barked at them; othertimes they pecked his nose. He learned to stay out of their reach.

We lived in a small rectangular white frame house my father built on the family's one-hundred-eighty acre farm. That was the house I was born in. There was a barn, corral, and windmill with an elevated water tank set on a wood framed enclosure so the cool inside could be used as a creamery.

During the time of the drought, only two things grew on the entire farm: An elm tree on the south side of the house; and a grape arbor on the southeast side of the house. Nothing else. Not even weeds. We did have a bunch of chickens. And, a milk cow. And a flock of pigeons lived in the barn loft.

My dad put a rope swing with a board seat on one of the larger tree limbs. But the wind blew sand just about every other day. There was a big sand hill that would be created by the wind on the north side of the house when the wind blew from the south. On the day that the wind blew from the north, the sand hill would almost cover the tree up to its bottom limbs and I could not use the swing. Our house was like a block for the sand no matter whether the wind came from the north or the south. The sand would hit the house and fly over, the wind losing its energy causing the sand to fall on the side of the house away from the direction of the wind.

In order to sleep reasonably sand free at night, mother draped a sheet over our beds to keep the sand from drifting on us. Even though the house was fairly new and very well-built to modern standards for the time, it leaked sand. Older houses leaked sand really badly. So, really, by the amount of sand that leaked into the house, I knew that my throwing the sand and coal dust in my brother's face was no big deal. I felt I really didn't deserve the spanking, but at the time, I decided I would take a licking anytime for a puppy.

The cow would sometimes stand still and let me get a squirt of milk or two. The cow didn't like Foozy. He didn't bark at her or pester her some other way; she just didn't like him. Nor was the cow afraid of Foozy. When he was around, she would give him funny looks and drag her feet back and forth on the ground.

My father's parents lived with us. My grandmother had been sick a long time. She had a bed in the kitchen so my mother could be with her most all the time. After a while, she went away. At the time, I did not know where. Then a while later, they brought my brother home and put his small bed in the kitchen.

Right after my brother arrived, my grandfather got sick. He stayed in his room and never got out of bed anymore. My dad built a bathroom inside the house so he could give my grandfather a bath. My dad would carry him into the bathroom and help him with his bath.

My grandfather and I were great buddies. We used to take walks, talk and kill rattlesnakes and everything. So I was really lonesome after he went to bed. But right after my brother was born, Dad got Foozy for me and he and I went mostly all over the farm together.

Soon after I got Foozy, my grandfather left. I couldn't understand why everybody left and no one ever comes back.

A whole bunch of men came to the house and sat around in the front room with the door shut. My mother wouldn't let me go in there. But, someone left the door open a little by accident. I was there and I peeked in the room and saw the men sitting around a big long box with a candle on the top of it. At the time I thought it had something to do with my grandfather but I was not sure. Today I know it was my grandfather in a plain pine coffin and those men were there for his wake.

A few days later, my folks started putting things in boxes and told me we were going to the city. My dad put a bunch of stuff in our cellar out behind the house and filled it full of dirt. Today I know it was mostly my grandfather's personal possessions. My dad kept only his father's Bible, cane, and .410 shotgun. Everything else he buried. He did not talk to me of my grandfather for many years.

The day we left for the city, I could not find Foozy. I was told he had to go stay with a farmer. Because we could not take him with us to the city. At the time, I did not understand. As we started to drive off I looked around everywhere for Foozy. I didn't see him. He was gone.

I was forty years old before I was able to have another dog. It was a black Lab; a hunter. I thought at the time about naming him Foozy. I finally decided to call him Pepper.

The Sandhill Swing

You might think this story's title is strange. Well, it was a strange swing so it deserves an unusual title. It hung in an elm tree on the south side of my parent's house. And, the tree wasn't very big, and neither was I. So it all evened out. But to this day, I remember that swing very vividly, and a kid named Jimmy. I'm pretty sure Jimmy remembers that swing just as I do.

I was born in the southwest bedroom of the house my dad built. It wasn't very fancy, but in the 1930s very few houses were in this part of Texas. The house was located at that time on what is now the corner of Popular and College Avenue in Levelland. That area was the northwestern corner of the Taylor farm: One-hundred eighty acres, some of which is now occupied by the South Plains College. At that time, there really wasn't much of this place called Levelland. Looking toward the west, you could see forever with the view unobstructed by any type of building construction. Same thing looking east.

The construction of the house was completed without an indoor toilet. That part was left out back. A 'Chick Sales', it was called. The house did have a parlor, two bedrooms, and a large kitchen. The kitchen did not have running water for the sink at first, but it did have an icebox with real ice in it. In the center of the kitchen, there was a square of flattened gallon tin cans nailed to the floor. Sitting in the middle of the tin can square was a big iron pot-bellied stove that kept the house warm in the winter by the burning of coal. The kitchen also had a fairly large kerosene cook stove.

I reckon you could say by today's standards we were poor. Well, back then everyone was poor. Very few people lived any different from what I have described.

My father was fortunate enough to be employed. So many other men weren't. At that time, he was a lineman for Southwestern Public Service Company. Our house was wired for lights as a fringe benefit of employment at that time was free electricity.

This land I was born in, Texas, was not only in the midst of the great economic depression of the Thirties, it had not rained for most of that decade. It was so dry that not a single blade of grass or weeds grew on the land my folks owned and where we lived.

The only two green things I remember on that land were the elm tree and a large grape arbor just to the east of the house. I didn't pay too much attention to the grape arbor unless the grapes were ripe, but that elm tree meant a lot to me.

My dad had hung a rope swing with a board seat in that elm tree for me. And, I used the swing every day that I could, and swung as high as I could. As time passed that swing became most important to me; it turned out to be the only swing I ever had.

The only bad thing about the swing was the location of the tree it was hung on. That tree was located just off the south side of the house. On the north side of the house was a big sandhill. It did not belong there. It grew there gradually at first because there were no grass or weeds anywhere to hold the sand to prevent it from blowing around. One day when the wind got tired of blowing…temporarily…it just left the sand there. Well, left there part of the time. When the wind from a northern direction would start up again, it moved that sand hill to the south side of the house…to settle around the elm tree and partially cover my swing—or most of it, that is. It covered enough of it so you couldn't see the board seat; just the ropes going down into the sand. My swinging time stopped until the wind came from the south and moved the sand hill back to the north side of the house.

Somehow around this time, I found a friend. Or, perhaps we found each other. Jimmy lived a little to the southeast of our place; maybe he actually lived on our place. His folks lived in a house just about like ours except his house had no nearby tree.

Jimmy and I became good friends. I'm sure we became friends because my folks knew his folks…both families had lived around here for years. Jimmy and I would play together every chance we had. We played mostly at my place; I had a tree with a swing and he didn't.

On the days the wind had moved the sandhill to the north side of the house, Jimmy and I would take turns swinging. Sometimes we would take turns pushing each other in the swing, as high as we could go.

On the days we couldn't swing because of the sand hill, I would run off to Jimmy's house as soon as my dad left for work and I could get out of the house. My mother would see me go and scream at me "You are going to get a licking as soon as your dad comes home from work." I suppose I did get the licking at the end of the day when I would come home because my mother never lied. It must not have been much of a licking though; for one reason I don't remember any licking, and for another it never stopped me from running away to Jimmy's the next chance I got. I suppose he must have run off to my place, too, though I really don't remember how he got there, he would just show up.

I know we got together as often as we could until something happened that stopped our being together until years had gone by.

On the fateful day of our last time together, Jimmy had come over and we were swinging in the shade of the elm tree. It was his turn, and he was busy trying to see how high he could go. Now, you really couldn't swing high to be in jeopardy as the elms tree's branches were in the way. But you could swing high enough to touch the leaves with your big toes.

Somehow, Jimmy jammed one knee up against his chin really hard. I suppose at the time, he had his tongue sticking out in sheer ecstasy, trying to touch the end of his nose with the tip of his tongue. All of a sudden he stopped the swing, jumped down and started running home. I didn't understand what had happened that had made him run away like that, but it did scare me.

A while later that day, Jimmy and his mother stopped at our house on the way back from Dr. Dupree's office. It was then I found out why he had run home so suddenly. He had managed to jam his knee against his chin on the upswing and had bitten almost completely through the part of his tongue that was sticking out of his mouth. His mother was not very happy.

I didn't get in trouble for the accident, but my swing did. When my dad came home, he took the swing down. It really didn't make a whole lot of difference; summer was almost over, anyhow.

Not too many days after that, my grandfather, B.W. Taylor, died. My father sold the farm and we moved to Lubbock. Into a new house just barely finished. It was a nice enough house. New houses back then hardly ever had trees.

One really unusual thing happened that first winter in the big town. It snowed. Now, I had never yet seen rain in my short lifetime…but snow? Wow!

Years later, Jimmy and I both lived in Gresham Hall at Texas Tech. Occasionally we would get together in the evenings in front of the fire place in the common room. Some nights we would reminisce and talk about the dumb things we did together those years ago: Looking for rats in our barn; climbing in the rafters looking for pigeon squab.

One time I asked him if he remembered the swing in the elm tree. He told me he did.

Sour Pickles

Of all my preferred foods in the world, sour pickles have been my absolute favorite as long as I can remember. Now I really don't know why this is true, it just is. I don't mean dill pickles or old fashioned pickles or garlic pickles. I mean real sour pickles. The kind you can't find in most places I have been. I can't understand why…they put all other pickles to shame. Makes my mouth water just to think of them. And, because they are so hard to find, once in a while I will eat a big dill pickle just out of plain desperation.

When I was very young, my mother, Katherine Taylor and my grandmother, Mary Ola Conatser, used to make sour pickles. My grandmother's pickles were the very best you could eat. To this very day, I have never eaten a better home canned pickle. My fellow cousins all agreed that our grandmother's pickles were the very best.

In those many years ago, you could find sour pickles at most grocery stores in a big wooden barrel. When I was tall enough to lift the lid of the barrel, I would lift it and look at all the pickles inside in their sea of vinegar. And take a deep breath. Made my mouth water. But those pickles cost money, mother's and grandmother's pickles didn't and they tasted better, anyhow.

Back then, if I had my way, I would have a pickle in my fist every chance I got. In fact, sometimes I couldn't even wait until the freshly canned pickles were cured; temptation would get the best of me and I'd open the jar long before they were ready. I even raised cucumbers so my mother would have a ready supply for making pickles.

One time my intense fanatical craving for sour pickles got me in trouble. Well, not really spanking trouble, but I made a laughing stock out of myself. For years, my mother and cousins laughed about it whenever something reminded them of it.

My mother, my brother and I were spending a few days at my grandmother's house. I always enjoyed spending time there as she always had plenty of sour pickles. She usually would give me one just about any time I asked. My mother wouldn't. Mother was really stingy with her sour pickles.

During this one particular visit, we all went over to my aunt's farm house at the east end of the dirt road now called Cherry Street. Her husband, my mother's brother, Lloyd, had a dairy there, not too far from my grandmother's house. My aunt was going to give my both mother and my grandmother a hair permanent. This was about the time when home permanents were pretty new. It also took quite a bit of time which was alright with the ladies as they would talk up a blue streak while the permanents were curing, or whatever you call it.

Me? I was busy riding my cousin's tricycle around the perimeter of the farmhouse and at the same time, eating one of my grandmother's pickles from one jar of several she had given my aunt.

I was just as happy a kid as you ever saw, riding around and eating that sour pickle. That is, until the pickle was all eaten up. So I went back into the house and asked for another. Naturally, my mother said no. I really expected her to say no; mothers think it isn't good for kids to get everything they want, especially delicious homemade sour pickles.

I went back outside to figure some way to get another sour pickle. Pretty soon it came to my devious mind (plenty devious when it came to getting sour pickles) that I probably could sneak into the kitchen completely unnoticed and get into the pantry where the pickles were kept. The women were so busy gabbing I was sure they wouldn't notice me even though they were right there in the kitchen where the pantry was.

Well, I figured right. I was able to get into the kitchen and into the pantry completely unnoticed. But I couldn't pull the string to turn on the light for fear they would hear the snap of the light's switch. So I felt around in the dark until I found the pickle jar. I very quietly unscrewed the jar's lid, and stuck my hand into the jar. It took me about two seconds to realize what I stuck my hand into wasn't a pickle jar, so I started to pull my hand back out. Then I smelled it. I had stuck my hand into a partly full jar of home blackstrap sorghum molasses. The thickest, gooiest stickiest stuff you ever run into, anytime anywhere. Somehow I managed to get my hand out of the jar. I don't remember putting the jar's lid back on. I stuffed my molasses covered left hand into my overalls pocket and quietly snuck back out of the pantry, out of the kitchen and out of the house.

Now there was no way I was going to let my female cousin catch me molasses handed, so I kept it in my pocket and very casually crept back on the tricycle and resumed riding around the perimeter of the farm house. Just to the north of the farmhouse was a really neat, nice smooth hill, just right for riding over. So, every time I rode around the north side of the place, I rode over the hill. I'm doing all this one-handed, my left hand still hidden in my overall pocket. As I mentioned earlier, it was summertime. And, here in Texas in the summer time, it gets hot. But kids don't really notice the heat, being busy doing all sorts of outside stuff.

Just after riding over the hill for the umpteenth time, I felt the ground shake. I turned and looked back and the hill was gone; instead there was a big hole in the ground. I decided to ignore the hole and resumed riding away. However, the shaking of the ground had been felt in the house, or maybe there was a little noise. Anyhow, all the women in the house were out and looking at the hole in the ground and me on the tricycle. It didn't take too long for them to figure out how the hole got there. I probably looked about three shades of guilt anyway.

They saw I wasn't hurt or anything. They said it was a miracle I hadn't fallen into the hole when the top caved in; and I guess it was. Looking at me and noticing I had my left hand stuck in my overalls pocket, my mother wanted to know why I was keeping my hand in my pocket. About then, I discovered I couldn't have gotten it out of my pocket if I had wanted to. The heat had partially dried the already thick blackstrap sorghum molasses. I had to tell them I had somehow gotten molasses on my hand and it got stuck in my pocket. It didn't take any female geniuses to figure out where and how I got the molasses on my hand. That's when the laughter started, and didn't stop for years.

Except for my Uncle Lloyd, that is. He never did think it was funny, especially when he was sweating in the hot sun digging a new cesspool.

I always figured it this way, though. He was really lucky I showed him the boards that covered the old cesspool were all rotted. No telling who might have fallen in walking across the top. Also, he had a place to put the dirt from the new hole.

Sour pickles? I still crave them: My grandmother's. I haven't had one in years.

The Gallon Glass Jug

The important part of this whole story is the high water table and growing up in the swell town we lived in. I was not old enough to know much about the fact of World War II which was going on at the time; so everything to me was pretty rosy.

As I mentioned, I did not know very much about World War II and the terrible things that were going on as a result of it. Things we youngsters did know about were the things we heard our parents discussing very often. We knew certain things were rationed: Butter, gasoline, oil, tires, and tobacco, among other things. But the lack of those items did not particularly bother us kids.

Every evening the war news came on at six o'clock and whole families gathered around their radios to listen to war news announcers H.V. Kaltenborne or Gabriel Heater.

Vehicle traffic was pretty much limited. In fact, all the traffic was people walking or the use of horses and horse-pulled wagons.

But to continue with the main part of the story: In this very small town where I grew up, the doors of people's homes were almost never locked. The front and back doors of the homes did have locksets, but people never used them, except maybe when they went away for a long time. Then they probably used the locksets, locking the doors for security. But I'll bet they had to hunt for the keys in order to lock the doors even then. What I am trying to say is that I grew up in a much simpler time.

The only drugs, besides doctor prescribed medicine people used, were coffee, tea and tobacco; the use of any alcoholic beverage was pretty rare as there were none available legally in the immediate area.

And, everybody looked after everybody else's kids. You might as well have had a whole town full of parents; you couldn't get away with nothin'.

As I look back now, I realize it was the best way there is to grow up the way we did. We had a lot of fun; we could wander all over town and nobody would complain unless they got their window broke as a result of a clod fight or errant baseball.

An unusual thing about the area was that the water table under the ground was pretty high. In fact, it was so high if you dug a hole a foot or so deep and let it set overnight, in the morning an inch or so of water would have seeped up into the bottom of the hole.

Farmers did not have to depend on rain for their crops. The water also tasted good. Now that I am grown and have been educated I know that in that particular area the Oglala Aquifer just happened to be very close to the surface of the ground back then. Today, it probably is still pretty high even though I am sure modern day irrigation has lowered it some.

The ground was so damp all the time you could turn over just about any rock in that town and find a really big centipede. Sometimes a small snake might be there or some bugs. But, mostly centipedes. They were at least a foot long, or so they seemed to us kids. Not every rock would have a centipede under it, but two out of three was pretty much guaranteed. So, all of us were pretty careful when we decided to turn over rocks.

One day, my buddy Butch and I decided we were going to catch us a bunch of those centipedes. Or—maybe I decided. I was a year older than Butch, and he pretty well went along with whatever I wanted to do.

So, we scrounged up a big wide-mouthed gallon glass jug. I don't remember where we got it, we just got it. I do remember thinking it had to be a gallon jug. A quart just wasn't big enough. So off we went on our centipede hunt, each of us carrying a scooping stick and one of us had the gallon jug with its tin lid.

One of the first rocks we turned over had a big fat centipede beneath it. One of us held the jug, the other scooped with the stick, and into the jug went the centipede. We had our first trophy.

Now if you have ever observed centipedes, they do not move very fast. I guess you could compare them to badgers or skunks. With their defense systems, those two critters do not *have* to move very fast. Of course, centipedes were designed before kids came along. Centipedes just didn't have much of a defense system against kids with sticks and gallon glass jugs.

Before we had turned over too many rocks, we had a jug full of centipedes. Naturally, we had to be really careful each time we opened the jug's lid to stuff in another centipede. And, the inside of the jug got kind of muddy from all the centipede activity inside. Pretty soon we couldn't see what was going on in there, and we figured it was getting too scary to open the lid.

Finally, we decided we had to empty the jug, and we weren't about to just turn them loose. Old Granny (that's what everybody called her) Faulkner had a big round water tank next to a windmill inside a big corral. This tank was used to water the several horses kept inside the corral. We decided we would put them in the horse tough for safe keeping. We could also wash the jar at the windmill after we dumped out the centipedes. Then we could go get more centipedes, being able to see once more into the jug.

And, that's just what we did. We spent all the time we could that afternoon, collecting centipedes, dumping them in the horse tank and washing the jug at the windmill. I don't remember how many centipedes we collected but it was a bunch. I remember when we quit they were getting pretty scarce. Or rather, unturned rocks were. Small towns have a limited supply of rocks.

Every day or two after that, we would check on the centipedes to be sure they were still there, even though most had drowned the first day. Centipedes don't swim very well. They sort of float alright, but their legs aren't built for paddling, just stinging. One day we went to the horse tank and the water was all gone; the tank was empty. I guess Granny's son had found the centipedes. We didn't hang around there too long that day. The centipedes had all dried up, anyway.

The Galvanized Wash Tub

My poor mother was completely gray-haired by the time she was twenty-five years old. I never remembered seeing her any other way. And, I suppose in retrospect it was completely my fault. Not that I was really bad, you understand. Just that she thought I was. I always had the ability to get my fingers or toes in just about everything you could imagine. You know, really interesting stuff.

For instance, I was born in the kitchen of the house my dad built several years before my birth. It was situated on what is now the corner of Popular and College Avenue in Levelland. But, when I was born, it was the northwest corner of the family farm consisting of one-hundred-eighty acres.

Three and a half years later, my brother was born in the fairly new yellow brick clinic-hospital. Now, that was alright, him being born in a hospital instead of at home. I have never envied that of him, nor the fact that in later years, he achieved a PhD degree and became a teaching professor in a far-away college. I just didn't want my parents to bring him home from the hospital. Being almost four years old, I figured one boy in the family was enough.

So, on his arrival home, I went outside the kitchen door and carefully selected a handful of coal dust and sand and let him have it in the face where he lay in his crib in the kitchen. That must have been good for at least a half-dozen gray hairs. At least. After that incident, they kept me away from him for awhile.

And, some time later, there was the lake incident. My uncle, my mother's brother, felt the need for one reason or another to dig a new cesspool in the back yard of the house his family was living in.

This uncle had a daughter about my age who was my partner in the act of creating grey hair. Her mother, my aunt, was also pretty well gray-headed by this time. Anyway, to get back to the cesspool: Cesspools were used in the place of septic tank systems years ago. Cesspools have been outlawed for a long time. However, in those early years they were the only game in town. The cesspools were a hole dug into the ground usually about ten feet deep and square. Boards were used to cover the hole and dirt piled upon that, sealing the hole from the world. Most were vented so that water would have no problem flowing into the pool.

While this particular one was waiting for its lid, my cousin and I decided it would make a really good lake. We placed a garden hose into the excavation and turned it on full force. The ground the hole had been dug in was mostly of sand. People who are familiar with sand know that water flowing onto sand simply disappears. After a while, we got tired of waiting so we went on to do bigger and better things intending to come back later. Eventually we forgot the water was still flowing into the hole. After several hours, the hole finally filled with water. By that time, though, my uncle found our lake and turned the water off. That little incident was not only good for a least a dozen gray hairs for our respective mothers, it was also good for two individual lickings administered by her father and my uncle: One for me, one for her.

My mother gave me a bath most every morning in a galvanized wash tub situated in the center of the kitchen floor. My father had piped in water from the windmill overhead tank and put in a small sink. My mother would fill the tub with this kitchen water. She would then heat a little more on the kerosene cooking stove to pour into the tub to take the chill off the cold water and in I would go.

As soon as my bath was finished and I was dressed, out the door I would go running as fast as I could for parts unknown with my mother yelling after me to come back or I would get a licking when my father got home.

Now, don't take all this wrong. I was not mistreated by any means. But I did get a lot of lickings when my father got home in the evenings. That did not keep me from running away almost every morning for parts unknown.

However, I stopped after one very fateful morning. Not stopped completely, but sure 'nuff slowed down.

But, before this one fateful day, my mother took to delaying my getting dressed as long as possible in the hopes I would get interested in something else and forget about taking off each morning. Well, one time I fooled her. Boy, did I fool her. As soon as she got me out of the tub and mostly dried off, I took off in a run outside the kitchen door for parts unknown.

However…there was this really big red ant hill right in the path of the direction I was running, lickety-split. When I realized I was going to run across it, I tried to stop before I got there. I was able to stop my head-long run. Right on the top center of the ant hill.

Now, these Texas red ants are nothing to mess with even when they are not mad. Two big (to them) feet standing on the top of their house dripping water is not a soothing situation to red ants. All two million of them decided to do something about these two big feet standing on top of their house.

I stood there, screaming as loud as I could, hoping somebody would rescue me. My grandfather, my buddy came running out of the house, picked me up by a handful of my red hair and took me on a run back toward the house. Once there, he tried to tell the difference between freckles and red ants and just pick the ants off. When he finished, my mother coated me completely with a paste she made of baking soda and water.

As I remember, things were pretty quiet around the Taylor household for a while after that. As I mentioned earlier, I almost quit running away. For a few days, anyhow. I am not sure if my mother got any new gray hairs over that, but I almost did.

When I aged enough to have some intelligence, I went on a rampage against red ants. When I would find a hill, I would get a pint or so of kerosene, pour it down their front door and light it off with a match. This wasn't trying to get rid of the ants. This was revenge.

I never really admired galvanized wash tubs too much after that, either.

The Smell Of Christmas

When I was a small boy years ago in depression era Texas, Christmas had a magic all its own for me. It wasn't so much the receiving of gifts; it was the Douglas Fir tree with its magic of lights, hanging shiny bulbs and glistening lead foil icicles. Never had I seen anything so mysterious and beautiful. But the smell, the wonderful smell of the pitch from the needles of the tree. As soon as the newly cut and bought tree was brought into the house, the pungent smell saturated the air in every room with its wonderful mystic aroma.

The only fir trees I had ever seen were the ones brought into our town at Christmas time. My childhood part of Texas had trees of elm, oak and such. And those were planted by people who lived on the bare flat land of the Texas South Plains.

Well, now, the land wasn't really bare. It had plenty of mesquite, catclaw, sage and small scrub oak long with wild grass on the prairie. There were a few volunteer elm trees growing here and there. But the land still seemed bare and empty.

Getting back to the Douglas Fir Christmas tree…the first few Christmases of my knowing life, we didn't have a Christmas tree. Practically no one had one. They just weren't available. There were two reasons people didn't have Christmas trees. There was a terrible war in progress; people were dying in far-off lands. This situation I sort of comprehended; a life long friend of my folks was away overseas due to the war. This friend I called uncle, he was that close to my family and me.

In the beginning, he came home for a short visit several times, dressed in his somber looking uniform. After one visit, he left us for a place called Italy. I didn't see him for a long, long time after that last visit. When he finally did come home, he was different. He was quieter and didn't laugh as much as he used to. Maybe my insight of his difference was because he grew up while he was over there…or maybe I had grown more mature listening to the war news on the radio every night. My father would answer my questions over what I heard over the radio. Now in my grayer years, I know that this was a most terrible time for the entire world.

I remember lying on a throw rug in front of a Franklin gas stove in the living room. It had isinglass windows so you could see the heat from the burning natural gas cause the clay flame elements to glow cherry red. With the reflection of the lights on the Christmas tree visible in the heater windows, I would dream of the forest the tree came from and smell its wonderful aroma. I had never yet seen these forests, but I read wonderful descriptions of them in several of Zane Grey's novels. Naturally, I thought from that I knew exactly what those forests really looked like.

Gradually a few presents would appear under the tree. By today's standards those few presents weren't much. Maybe a book or a game for me, a new pair of overalls or a shirt, maybe some socks. And, the same for my brother.

In the year 1941, our family had a car. It was a 1937 Ford sedan. Right after the war started, our father jacked each wheel of the car up and set the axel on blocks, holding the tires above the ground. The reason he did this was gasoline for the engine was rationed due to the war effort so there was none for the car. In the early days of 1942, he sold the car. Our family did not have another vehicle until the summer of 1948.

At Christmas time, my mother, my brother and I would walk downtown to the stores and select some gift for our father. Around the same time, our father would take my brother and I downtown to select a gift for our mother. None of those presents cost very much. We were no different from anybody else living in the South Plains of Texas at that time. No one had money for presents. But the price of the love we gave with each present: It was all the love we could give.

Today I see the presents my grandchildren are given for Christmas. The number of presents each child receives is staggering. The cost of each present makes me catch my breath. For these reasons alone, not one of the presents has much meaning. And the number itself nullifies the love that is offered.

All these years later, I think back to the Christmases of my childhood and realize how fortunate we all were. Somewhere through the years it seems to me family love has changed. One thing I know. I look around and observe other families. Today family life and love is different. People have more money now to spend on present at Christmas. Maybe that's the problem. We no longer know how to appreciate our good fortune.

These years I lay on the carpet in front of our fireplace and look at our own Douglas Fir Christmas tree. Now there is only my wife and myself to enjoy it. Our children are grown. They have their own Christmas trees in their own homes with their own children in faraway towns.

At the writing of this message, I am living in a land that grows plenty of Christmas trees. I work in a forest of them. I see them most every day. I see them with raindrops on the tips of the needles; sometimes I see them covered with snow. When it is Christmas time we have one in the house. The smell of the pitch on the needles is strong throughout the house. It gives me an excuse to lie on the carpet in front of the fireplace to enjoy the warmth of the fire. An excuse to enjoy the wonderful smell of Christmas and dream.

When I Was Five

O n my fifth birthday, my great uncle and great aunt journeyed from their home in Amarillo to the farm of my birth near Levelland, Texas. The year was 1940, and the car they drove in was a new Pontiac Chief two door sedan. As I remember, it was a two-tone shade of brown and tan. The country was still in the great economic depression and our part of Texas was in a terrible drought which made local living conditions really harsh for all.

My great uncle could afford the new car as he was a locomotive engineer for Santa Fe Railway. He bought a new car just about every year. The town of Amarillo, where they lived, was a big railway shipping center back then. He was required to work so much he had trouble getting days off. Because of that heavy work schedule, he was able to afford a new car just about every year.

Even so, this would be his last new car for many years due to the world war that was about to begin.

When the United States entered the war every part of industry was dedicated to the war effort. Car axles went up on blocks so the tires did not touch the ground, everything concerning vehicles was rationed and could not be had even if a person had the required ration tickets. Horse buggies came out of retirement. People either rode in the buggies or rode a saddled horse…or walked. That's what my family did. Walked. We had no buggy or horse to pull it.

At this young and tender age, I was just becoming aware of birthdays and what they were supposed to mean. People would give you presents. The fact of being a year older was lost on me, but the present part wasn't.

So early that morning of my fifth birthday, my mother and father had given me a pair of pointy-toed boots. The first of many I would wear and wear out over the years to come. At that point in time, I do not remember even having shoes. I was always barefoot. So were the few friends I had that were my age. Nor did I recognize the significance of boots. We had no horse as I wrote earlier, but we did have a cow. I had ridden the cow a few times when my grandpa would lift me up and set me on her back. Playing cowboys and Indians was still a few years off for me. But I really liked to ride the cow. I could not get on myself, and the cow wouldn't squat. So my cow riding was pretty much dependent on my grandpa's help.

Back to birthdays. Specifically presents. My great aunt and uncle had brought a brand-new fire truck for me. The kind that had pedals and you could sit in and steer while you pedaled around in it looking for fires. It also had two white ladders, one fastened on each side. And, a big empty space in the back where you could store stuff you might need in case you did find a fire. All I needed was tumble weeds and matches. Weeds were out of the question. Because it had not rained for years, there were no weeds. So even if I could somehow get a hold of some matches, there was nothing to use them on to light up.

Now I did know what fire trucks were for. For several years there had been a roller skating rink in a Quonset hut building just a little ways away from our farm. It could be seen, looking out our front bedroom windows. One evening, it caught fire and burned all the way down to the ground. People with a fire truck tried to put it out. That's how I knew all about fire trucks. I watched the rink burn. I didn't know about roller skates or rinks, but now I knew what fire trucks were.

Since my birthday happened to be in July, I got pretty hot after a while, pedaling all around the farm. Somehow, I wound up stopping behind the right rear of the Pontiac. I decided I would put the fire truck in the shade underneath the right rear fender of the car. That way, when I cooled off and was ready to look for fires, the fire truck would be cool enough to ride around in. Actually, outside of one Elm tree on the farm, the car was about the only shade around.

Now that I was resting, my attention span focused on the new Pontiac. I really didn't comprehend the fact the car was new, it was a car. I had seen one or two before and even rode a short distance in one. My dad drove a pickup that belonged to the utility company he worked for. The pickup was only for work, though. He drove it home so when people's electricity went out at night for their homes, he could go fix the problem and turn their lights back on. By my next birthday, we would have electric lights and a refrigerator instead of the coal oil lanterns and icebox we now had.

I managed to get the passenger door of the car open and I crawled inside. It looked really nice: All kinds of shiny knobs and such. I had seen my great uncle use the cigarette lighter, so I decided I would use it the way he did. I pushed the lighter in, and after a short while it popped out, ready for use. I don't think at that particular period of time I knew that it got really hot; else I wouldn't have done what I did next. I took hold of the knob and pulled the lighter out the way I had seen my great uncle do it. My eyes and my mind were transfixed on the cherry red glow of the lighter. So I put it to my lips. Now that lighter being new, really lit up my lips. I started screaming, dropped the lighter, and continued screaming. I could scream pretty loud, and it was no time at all everyone was out of the house looking for me to see what monster I had managed to get aholt of. On finding me, I was carried into the house and lard...or something...was put on my lips.

Well, later that day, my great aunt and great uncle had to leave to go back to their home in Amarillo. Everyone told them goodbye out at the car as they prepared to drive off. And as they backed up to turn around and face the road, the right rear wheel of the Pontiac flattened my red fire truck with the two white ladders. And, I mean flattened. Flattened flat.

So, with the new pointy-toed boots, my cherry-red lips and my flat red fire truck I don't have too much trouble recalling my fifth birthday. Not even all these years later. What really hurts is the fact it was the only fire truck I ever had.

The Snow At The Foot Of The Bed

I love the snow. I have always loved the snow. Snow was one reason my wife and I first moved to Wyoming years ago. As the years go by and I age further, either my wife or I may not be able to tolerate the cold that is present with snow. However, if we leave this wonderful snowy country, it will be with deep regret.

Years ago when I was young and the weather was in one of its 'cold' cycles, my family was lucky enough to live in the small and wonderful town of Muleshoe, Texas. Each winter of my youngest years, there would be more than sufficient snow for making snowmen…and sledding. There happened to be sort of a problem with sledding. Muleshoe is mostly flat. But, if there had been some hills there was plenty of snow to sled around in.

Some of the bigger kids had homemade sleds they used to take turns pulling each other or maybe attach a rope to the back bumper of a car and slide around town that way.

All my brother and I could do was watch all those really great activities of the bigger kids. We were too young at that time to be able to build our own sled out of scrap lumber as the bigger kids had been able to accomplish.

But we did plenty of other things in the snow. It would usually be sunny after a big snowstorm, so we could play out in the snow without feeling the cold. Of course, young people hardly ever feel cold or rain or even the sun when they want to be outside having fun. But I know now that you can't make them want to go outside even on the most desirable day unless they themselves want to be out.

We made snowmen of sorts; threw snowballs at each other and anything else that would stand still long enough for us to aim at. Except big people. We left them alone. They either told on you or threw back harder and more accurately than we could.

Once we played so much and so long in the snow which reflected and magnified the bright sunlight that I became affected with snow blindness. My eyelids swelled completely shut and both the eyeballs, sockets and lids really hurt badly. Even after I had started to recover, they still hurt looking out through a window at the bright sun reflecting off the snow. So I stayed mostly in my bedroom that had indirect sunlight as the two casement windows faced north.

I had one window wide open and had the sheer gauze curtain pulled aside and was talking to my brother and feebly trying to watch him play in the snow. Only thing was, when all was done and night was near, I forgot to close the wide open window. This was hidden by the gauze curtain. And, there was no breeze. None. Never is when one is needed.

I slept in that bedroom by myself. My brother was two or three years old and for some reason he still slept in our parents' bedroom in a crib. That was okay with me. Maybe we only had the one bed for me and none for him.

During the winter nights, my folks turned the unvented open flame gas heaters off. My dad was afraid if left on, one of the two heaters might start a fire. Also, there was the danger we might asphyxiate due to lack of oxygen in an atmosphere of carbon dioxide and carbon monoxide those unvented gas heaters produced as they burned the natural gas fuel.

We did sleep warm with plenty of homemade quilts over us. However, my feet were usually a little cold.

During that night, it snowed again. A lot. And the wind blew from the north, right into my open bedroom window. The snow came in with the wind; sifted through the window screen. The snow made a really nice snow drift across the floor, filling the space between the window and my bed, and left a nice pile on my bed. Fortunately, I was short enough that it only reached my feet. Back then, I slept pretty soundly. And as my feet were usually cold, I just didn't notice anything unusual.

Sometime during the night, my dad came in to check on me. He was very upset when he found the snow on the foot of the bed and stacked level on the floor between the bed and the window. The noises he made talking and trying to get enough snow out of the window sill in order to close the open window woke me up. Shortly after being awakened, I realized I had forgotten to close the window. Wouldn't have done any good to try and tell him my brother did it; he was short enough yet so he couldn't have even reached the sill. So I just kept quiet.

However, I did get a sudden urge to cough. Turned out I had developed the most outstanding case of croup I have ever had.

My father spent the rest of that and the following night observing me as I slept. Making sure I was able to breathe and didn't choke because of the croup. He moved me onto a bed he made for me on the couch in the living room. He sat there in a chair near me with the open flame gas heater burning and throwing out heat you could feel the radiance of across the room. It seemed to me I hardly slept; I could remember looking at him in the dim light and seeing him sitting there, trying to read from a book.

By the time I was over the croup and the snow blindness and well enough to be back outside, the snow had all melted. In those wonderful days of my youth it was the best snow that I remember we had. And, I missed most of it.

I know that was not the first time my father sat up worrying about me. I am also sure it wasn't the last.

Fathers are like that.

The Day Of The Sandstorm

Everyone can tell you what they were doing the time certain worldly important events occur. For instance, I remember well what I was doing the day John F. Kennedy was killed. We were living in California at that time. I had worked a graveyard shift that early morning and had come home, gone to bed and was asleep. My wife, in tears, woke me just after she heard the news on television. She was crying uncontrollably. She was Catholic as he was and took his death more personal because of that fact. Me? My immediate reaction, being a Texan, was "My God, look who we have for a president now."

A few short years later, I finished my swing shift at the steam-electric generation power plant where I worked. The operator at the nearby power plant switching station had called me a few minutes before my shift ended and requested that I bring him a pack of cigarettes.

As I left the plant, I detoured to the switching station with the pack of cigarettes. He gave me entrance into the secure locked-down facility. We went into his office and sat at his desk, each enjoying a late-night cup of his fresh-perked coffee. We were talking as good friends do with a radio softly delivering recorded music in the background.

Suddenly the late-night disc jockey broke into the program with the news that Robert F. Kennedy had been shot and killed in a hotel kitchen in Los Angles. The operator and I were both so stunned by the news we simply sat there, looking at each other and concentrating on what the almost hysterical newscaster was saying. After a few minutes I bid him a very blunt goodbye. He remotely unlocked the exit door for me and I went home.

I arrived home to find it quiet and all in bed asleep. I went on to bed and did not wake my wife to tell her of the tragic event until we all had breakfast later in the morning.

Those two events, especially the first, made significant impacts and changes throughout the world. But mostly the changes in the parts of the world other than our homeland were reaction changes and limited in scope. I personally felt that our way of life would be severely impacted by both but primarily as a result of the second. These two events did bring subtle changes. In shock, our eyes were opened. No longer were we living in a perfect country. It seemed we were as vulnerable to political unrest as other minor countries of the world.

Let us now travel back in time to the early fall after my sixth birthday. An event occurred that brought significant changes to just about every person's life in the 'civilized' parts of the world. Some lives were ended as a direct and immediate result. Families were altered to never again be the same. My own life was changed in ways that I will never be able to recognize or comprehend. But those changes were as a result of the occurrence and probably not very significant since I am not able to point to any one thing and say "There! That's a change!"

My father, my great uncle and I were hunting Indian arrowheads and other small relics from the past in a sand 'blow' in a field just south of Amarillo, Texas. We had been hunting for an hour or so when a sandstorm came up and it progressively grew worse. It became very hard to see what we were doing.

Back in that era, hunting sand 'blows' for artifacts was a fairly common hobby. To hunt an area with the wind blowing helped; objects might be uncovered right before your eyes, so to speak. But before long it became impossible to even see due to the quantity of the sand in the air. The sand also got in our eyes making vision very uncomfortable and mostly impossible.

My dad and my great uncle agreed that it was time to quit, so the three of us went back to the car and we started out going north to my great uncle's house in Amarillo. We arrived there about one o'clock or so in the afternoon. My great aunt fixed us some sandwiches and we were sitting in the kitchen having a late lunch. About that time the wind and blowing sand had stopped. I was all for going back to continue hunting but neither my great uncle nor my father wanted to. And, as I was too young to drive and it was too far to walk, we stayed put.

Their son had joined the U. S. Army a few weeks earlier. He had finished his basic training and was home on leave and had been out visiting friends here and there. Suddenly he burst through the front door into the living room shouting, "Turn on the radio! The Japs have bombed Pearl Harbor!"

Of course, the radio was turned on and all of the adults present became victims of stunned silence listening to the very excited and almost incoherent announcer taking about something that had happened that I had no comprehension of at all, and would not really understand for years to come.

As I grew old enough to finally understand what happened that dark Sunday, it mystified me then and still does now. How one small nation consisting of islands and one crazy civilization occupying a land that would easily fit inside of Texas with room left over ever thought they could overcome by force the free will of the rest of the entire world. If you cannot get that picture, find a world globe and compare those two nations insignificant bits of land with the rest of the lands and waters that make up the entire globe. It is a certain example of the successful song hit "High Hopes" that Frank Sinatra recorded so many years ago. For those of you who are unfamiliar with that song, part of it was about the ability of ants to accomplish the impossible.

Later on that day we returned home to the small town of Muleshoe where we had previously enjoyed a very gentle way of life. A way of life that was to change in ways I would recognize and know. Adults listened daily to newscasts on a regular basis and let nothing interrupt until the report of the progress of the war was finished. Everything was dedicated to the war effort with no compliant from anyone even when cigarettes became rationed and almost impossible to get.

Smokers went to Bull Durham 'roll your own' when they could get it; others went back to pipes when some small quantities of tobacco was available from time to time.

The light heartedness of small town life was no more. Adult males I knew around town would suddenly disappear. Small rectangular flags with a blue star on a white background trimmed in red would be hung in those family's front room windows; some were displayed in store windows downtown.

These flags represented a son or father gone to war. Over time, some of the blue stars were changed to gold indicating the death of the person the flag represented.

I cannot sit here and write one-two-three of the way so many things were changed by that awful war. But from time to time I did become aware of many individual ways our world was changing due to that war. And the only thing I can truthfully say that the change for the better was the advances made in the medical field. Those changes came from the blood shed by our service personnel.

Every other advancement that occurred we could do without, and in some cases we would be better off without.

The one advancement we could have made, we didn't. We have not learned one real thing. Not one. Wars are continually being fought all over the world. Wars that have no real meaning. No real reason for occurring to begin with. Every once in a while, somewhere the sand blows again.

'Til It Thunders

Back when you were a little kid, your mother told you that if you played with turtles and one bit you, it held on 'til it thundered. Remember? And, it always seemed that if you played with turtles and got bit on the finger, it never thundered. And, when the turtle finally got tired or got hungry or something and finally did let go, you never told anyone that you got bit. I guess that was because you didn't want anyone to know that you 1) Didn't believe your mother or 2) That you were dumb enough to get bit in the first place.

Well, one summer in a very small town in Texas when I was also very small, I got bit by a turtle. I really wasn't being dumb. And, that time it never did thunder. At least, not in the part of Texas where I was that day. It wasn't that I was trying to prove my mother wrong about how long turtles hung on when they bit you, it was just that circumstances kind of got out of my control. Sort of.

You see, I had this pretty new American Flyer Red Wagon. It wasn't prettier than any other Red Flyer, it was just pretty new. I drug it behind me just about everywhere it would go. It was very handy for hauling stuff I would run across in my travels around this small town and decide to keep, at least keep for a while. I don't remember my dad ever complaining about the stuff I brought home, but he probably did. I was just too enthused about all the stuff to pay attention to any complaints by anybody at all. Bolts, nuts, washers, nails, a can or two, sometimes a used horseshoe…I picked it all up within a wide range of our house. The town really didn't need to hire a street picker-upper, I did it all for free.

Well, early one morning it rained. And, I mean rained. On the Texas Plains when it rained all the turtles that it rained over would dig themselves out of their nests so they could play in all the puddles and do all the stuff that turtles do in puddles when it rains.

Needless to say, that morning when I started my usual stroll with my pretty new red wagon, I saw turtles all over the place just crawling around. And, as I had not yet found anything to haul (pickings were really getting kind of slim) I started picking up turtles (desert box terrapins they were, I found out years later).

Well, I didn't have too awfully far to go before I had a wagon full of turtles. I was really pleased. I didn't exactly know what I was going to do with all those turtles, but, as I said, I was really pleased. But I began to see I had a problem. I observed I had more turtles than I had wagon. And there were more turtles in sight, crawling all over the place. So I started stacking them on top of each other. Pretty soon, I realized that this was a mistake. A single layer of turtles was alright; their legs were too short to reach the top edge of the wagon sides. But a double layer of turtles meant their legs were long enough for them in the top layer to be able to crawl out of the wagon and drop down to the ground. So, I was not only busy trying to pick up new turtles, I had to watch and pick up the escapers. This was where I got into trouble. I had so many turtles I had trouble knowing where all the turtles were in relation to my fingers. Finally one turtle got one finger.

Now, everyone knows when lightening finally strikes (with no thunder) you stand there, totally amazed, that what you knew was going to happen finally happened. It doesn't hurt. At least, it doesn't hurt while you are busy figuring how to get out of the mess you got yourself into. Or maybe you hear in a tiny corner of your mind your mother telling you "I told you so" before the fact of her knowing you were bit or else you are hoping it will suddenly thunder out of the clear blue sky overhead and you start looking for clouds.

At any rate, after standing there for a few seconds of eternity with a turtle hanging on my finger who showed not the slightest intention of letting go and no hope of thunder I took matters into my own fingers and threw that turtle as hard as I could in the hope he would come off leaving me my finger.

Come off he did and flew a short distance and landed with a thud… right in the bottom section of our neighbor's shiny black car door. Shocked,

I stood there for about a half-second and looked round to see if anyone heard the noise.

Seeing no one, I quickly abandoned that turtle and started off back toward home with the wagon trailing behind me losing turtle as I went. As soon as I sort of got out of sight of the car, I dumped what was left of the incriminating evidence in the nearby barrow ditch and continued on home pulling the now empty wagon.

Now that I was currently out of trouble, my finger started to hurt. By the time I got home, it was hurting pretty good even though I had sucked on it some on the way. I put my pretty new American Red Flyer wagon by the porch where I kept it and went into the house not noticing a little blood on me here and there from my finger.

Naturally my mother noticed the blood, and asked "Where are you bleeding?"

"From my finger."

"What did you do?"

"Skint it."

She looked at it. "Well, come here and I'll put some iodine on it.

"Ouch."

It never did thunder the rest of that day.

Ribbitt!!!

By age four my younger brother was able to be outside; mostly by himself. He was a very special little boy; a very private person. He enjoyed exploring the great outdoors; mostly by himself. He delighted in turning over rocks to look at the bugs or whatever creature happened to be under that particular rock seeking its own solitude much like my brother.

We lived in a very small town where each kid pretty much answered to every grown person as if that person were their parent. So we kids had the roam of the whole complete town. There were no off limits. This roaming behavior was pretty much encouraged; wondering around mostly alone. But, as I mentioned, every older person looked out for these wandering young ones. And you can be sure the natural parents were informed of any misbehaving adventure that occurred. And, when told of the misbehaving adventure, the natural parents rarely said "Not my kid!" They usually said they would clean his (or her) clock as soon as they could be found. It was that kind of world; back then.

Somewhere along here in my brother's life he discovered frogs. Not the California Angel's Camp Jumping Frog Type, just plain old frogs. Toad Frogs, in particular. Texas has a lot of Toad Frogs. These Toad Frogs enjoyed hopping around in the populated areas; mostly because that's where most of the water in puddles and such was back then. That is, our part of Texas was pretty dry most of the time. When it rained, it rained all at once. Two, three inches per cloud. Maybe more. Kind of depended on the size of the cloud. But not too often.

So if a Toad Frog was going to enjoy his part of life, he hung around where people watered gardens, grass, flower beds and such. This included hanging around the mud puddles produced by leaking stock tanks and trying to avoid getting stepped on by whatever big critter watered there.

But…let's get back to my brother and his concern with the Toad Frogs. Somehow in his wanderings he discovered that Toad Frogs liked mostly to hang out in flower beds where the ground was soft and damp.

It wasn't a whole lot of trouble for the frog to dig himself a nice hole and sort of cover himself up with dirt to stay cool, damp and out of sight. Mostly out of sight, that is. Until my brother discovered that underneath each one of those small piles of dirt was a very content frog. So he would dig the frog up. Then the frog was no longer content. As soon as my brother would get the frog out and pick it up it would 'wet' in the palm of my brother's hand. My brother learned to hold the frog out and away from himself until it ran dry, then stick it into a pocket of his bib overalls.

Bib overalls were everyday dress back then for most all kids. There were fairly cheap and very durable. They came in two colors: Blue stripes on white. And, they had a lot of pockets. Two in front, two in back and one great big one in the bib situated in the center of your chest.

As soon as my brother had his Toad Frog safely and dryly tucked away in his bib pocket, he would immediately start looking for another soft mound of dirt. If he was lucky and ran out of pockets, he would carry a frog or two around in his hands.

When my brother had his quota of frogs or when the sun went down (whichever came first) he would tote the frogs to the garage and pick out a nice box for them. He would put some dirt in the box and then empty the contents of his pockets into the box. Then the box would go sneakily into the house and under his bed for the night. Now Toad Frogs aren't too hot on croaking unless it rains. So they were pretty safe from Mon and Dad. This enforced overnight solitude probably helped the Toad Frog population around town. So I guess you could say my brother really did all those Toad Frogs a favor; this private enforced captivity of a lot of the local Toad Frogs.

Sometimes he would forget or maybe overlook a frog in one of the pockets of his bib overalls. Then Mother would wash the poor frog in the clothes washing machine with the dirty clothes. Not too many frogs survived this ordeal, so after a while she learned to carefully check each and every pocket in my brother's bib overalls to be certain there was no frog being extra still and quiet hidden in a pocket. Naturally, instead of giving the Toad Frog back to him, she would turn the poor frog loose in one of her flower beds. My mother thought she was doing herself and the Toad Frogs a favor by putting them into her flower beds where all the bugs were. Years went by before my mother finally figured out where my bother caught most all his Toad Frogs.

One night my mother came into our bedroom to check on us before she went to bed. She reached down to cover my brother with his blanket when she uttered a small scream as she discovered something sitting on his chest. Naturally it proved to be a Toad Frog that he had temporarily stowed in his pajama shirt packet. She picked it up and took it outside through the garage door and put it carefully…back in a flower bed.

The Toad Frog's habit of hiding in my mother's flower beds was both good and bad for the frogs. They had a nice cool damp place to hide; the flower beds also gave them their food supply as the flowers attracted bugs. It also aided in their departure from the beds once my brother figured out what those small mounds of dirt meant.

All those years of my brother's frog hunting my mother used to nag my father into hoeing the weeds from her flower beds each spring. And, she was always a little put out because of the empty spaces in the planted areas. Small pockets of bare dirt. She quietly blamed my father for not knowing the difference between a freshly sprouted weed and a flower. She never complained though; she knew if she did he wouldn't hoe weeds for her anymore. And nice flower beds were a matter of pride in the mostly barren Plains of Texas back then.

My brother's habit of frog hunting continued mostly through his years in elementary school. It did seem to taper off about the time he became a freshman in high school. Maybe he became aware of the lingering peculiar smell of frogs or on his hands or clothes; at any rate he finally gave up frog hunting.

My brother grew up, went off to college and earned a PhD in geology. Now he turns over rocks and digs holes in the ground for a living.

After my brother gave up on collecting Toad Frogs, the holes in the flower beds were no more. I don't think Mother ever made the connection between the Toad Frogs, my brother, and my father's weed-hoeing ability.

The Black Fan

The complete fan stands thirteen and a half inches high. Each of the four blades, encased in a wire cage for safety, measure five inches in length. On the top of the motor there is a gearbox with a brass knob. When this knob is tightened (clockwise), it causes the fan to oscillate in about a ten-inch arc. Loosened, the fan stays still.

Westinghouse Electric Company placed a brass label on it stating all the particulars of the fan, including the date of manufacture. It was a long time ago: November, 1929.

When the fan was completely assembled, the craftsmen copied Henry Ford. They painted it black. After the paint dried, they added green felt on the bottom to prevent scratching whatever the fan was sitting on.

Back in those early days, craftsmen and companies had real pride in their product. A pride that apparently disappeared for years and is now appearing to make a comeback, as far as the craftsmen are concerned. Most companies have yet to restore any part of that pride or to even admit they lost it.

My father had gone to work here in Levelland for the Texas-Oklahoma-New Mexico Public Utility Company about the same time the fan was manufactured. This company eventually became the Southwestern Public Service Company. He worked for them for over forty-six years and finally retired as district manager in Seagraves.

As an employee fringe benefit, he was given free electricity. In that day and time, this really didn't seem like a whole lot. About all people had to use electricity for was lights. And not many had facilities for those.

Even though the great world economic depression was a year or so off in the future, there was not a lot of money floating around Texas in those days. In the rural and less populated areas, refrigerators and electric stoves were yet to become popular in the South Plains. This was partly due to the cost of the items. Automobiles were scarce; riding horses and wagons were the dominant mode of transportation. And, the iceman brought the weekly ice delivery for the iceboxes in a horse-drawn wagon. So when you got right down to it, there really wasn't a whole lot of need for electricity. But the new industry was sprouting here and there, and after the conclusion of World War Two, this industry would soon change the way the world we would come to know existed.

My father's mother, my grandmother, was very sick in the early years of my life. The only memory I have of her is seeing her lying on a bed in the kitchen. Her long red hair was fanned out on each side of the pillow under her head.

It had not rained for many months. The wind would blow sand at night; our beds had dust covers stretched over us as we slept for protection from the dust. Daytime was hot and still. Grandmother suffered. In the hot still daytime my mother would fan her with a folding paper fan so popular during those days.

Her middle son, my Uncle Ben, had graduated from college. He also was lucky enough to have a regular job that paid him enough money to buy his mother a much-needed gift to aid in giving her some comfort in her illness. He brought her the black Westinghouse fan I have described. He got it to move the hot dry air in the room around, possibly giving her some very much needed relief from the heat.

The fan stayed with my grandmother until she died. Almost a year later, her husband and my grandfather died. Whatever the circumstances were at the time, the fan became my father's possession.

The fan was in occasional use over the years. The fan blades are made of some sort of composition material. During my young and dumb years, I used to poke a finger very carefully into and just touching the edge of the blades. The blades would make a brrr! sound as each in turn, struck my finger. But no blood.

After the time of my youth had been spent at home and I had left the nest, my father finally bought a refrigeration-type air conditioner. No longer needed, the black fan was retired to a storage place in the family garage. Years later, after my brother and I were away making the path of our own lives, my mother and father moved to Colorado, taking the fan with them, I suppose for the sentimental value. It was moved into the workshop behind the new house where it had occasional use. On one of my first trips to the new home, I saw the fan sitting there in the workshop, and for the most part, gathering dust.

One time in my own home I was watching a movie on television that portrayed those early years at the end of the thirties and the beginning of the forties. One scene displayed a fan. The exact fan in my dad's workshop in Colorado. The very next time I talked to him on the telephone, I asked if I might have the fan to bring it back to my own home. Without hesitation, he gave the fan to me. He knew that I would treasure and care for it as it should be. The very next trip east, I picked the fan up and stowed it in my truck to take home when we left.

At home, I took the fan apart and carefully cleaned the dust and lint from the motor; cleaned and oiled the bearings. I replaced the power supply cord; the fabric covering was frayed in several spots. I was able to find a new fabric covered cord that was an exact copy. The small section of cord that carried the current from the switch in the fan's base to the motor housing I did not replace. It was old but in pretty good shape so I decided to leave it as it was. In order to replace it, I would have to take the fan motor sections apart. I really didn't want to do that until it became absolutely necessary. I just would not run the fan in the oscillation mode; this would prevent flexing of the wire and help preserve it.

I have had and used the fan now for about four months. It runs very quietly. If you wanted to use it to cover background noise in order to sleep, you would be out of luck. It is much too quiet. For its' size, it moves considerable air.

A couple of years ago, the summer of 1994, my wife and I bought a small air circulation fan for our RV and occasional use in our home. It was painted white and very pretty. However, it made enough noise that you could use it to cover background noise in order to take a nap. It lasted one and a half seasons. The wiring failed in the motor.

I guess you could say that the durable-looking 1929 model Westinghouse fan sort of took the failed white fan's place. Only, as I mentioned: It's painted black.

This Is Progress

About thirteen miles or so west of the small town of Muleshoe, Texas, on U.S. Highway 64, a half-dozen or so nice looking fairly new homes are situated on either side of the divided four-lane highway leading to Clovis, New Mexico. This is how things were in the year 1998.

As you approach the area, a small road sign identifies the group of homes as a village called "Progress." It appears to be a peaceful place; the yards are neat, the houses well kept. There is, at present, no store or post office; maybe there will be in the years to come. In the beginning, there was a small school. Over the years, the village has grown from one small one-room tarpaper shack to its present size of a half-dozen families.

This small place called "Progress" was a place of one man's hopes and dreams. That one man put all he had into it; he fought and lost a weaponless war with the State of Texas over it. He did not want his town to be where it is. He planned it elsewhere, but the State of Texas eventually convinced him to move it to where it is now. The story began a lifetime ago…

Around 1910, a man by the name of Joshua Blocher came to this area. Somehow, he acquired title to a quarter section of land just south of what would eventually be the paved Highway 84, at that time a narrow dirt two-lane road. In any case, he built a small shack, which he used both as a small grocery store and his living quarters. Eventually, a small one-room brick school was built nearby.

In time, the State of Texas decided to pave the road, and to go by Josh Blocher's shack and the school would require paving a right angle turn in the road. The state was not too keen on this, so they re-routed the road and eliminated the turn. This also bypassed the school and Blocher's store by several hundred yards.

I am sure Joshua was not worried about the school, but it would probably mean the demise of his store for the benefit it was to him financially if the road bypassed him. So, each night after the roadworkers went home, Josh would move the survey stakes. Finally the roadworkers lay in wait for him this one night and arrested him as he started pulling up the re-set stakes of that day.

At that dire result, the workers would forgive Josh if he stopped interfering with—uh…progress. Reluctantly, to avoid jail time, Josh gave up and relocated his tarpaper shack to the present location of his town of Progress.

On the slanted roof of his tarpaper shack he put a large sign that was as long as the roof. The sign was easily read by any one passing on the road in either direction, and very boldly proclaimed "THIS IS PROGRESS."

Over time, Joshua became known around Muleshoe, the closest town, as sort of a recluse or hermit. No one knew much about him. It was said he told people that he come from North Dakota. That he had a wife up there and a small piece of ground. That one day he and his wife were going to town in a wagon. At the start of this journey, she had been nagging him about one thing or the other. They came upon a gate across the road; he stopped the wagon and she got down to open the gate. One the gate was open, Joshua drove the wagon through the gate without stopping for her or looking back…all the way to Texas.

At this time, Muleshoe was a fairly small town; its population was somewhere around fifteen hundred. It was a peaceful town. It was a very clean town. It, like every other small town in Texas, was a very patriotic town. When World War II started, the town took the War very seriously. Many of its sons volunteered right off and were shipped overseas, some to the South Pacific, some To England. Some never came back.

Joshua Blocher had no car, but that wasn't very unusual for that day and time. He walked most everywhere he went. People who knew him would pick him up on the highway as he journeyed from home to town or back. Most of us kids knew him. I guess he must have been a pretty friendly fellow as us kids were not scared of him.

He walked the streets of town with an empty feed sack slung over his shoulder. Any item of interest he might come across during his travels he put in the sack: Pop bottles, nails, whatever. It's not too likely he ever found anything of much value. Almost everything that could be used for the war effort was had already been salvaged for that purpose. Probably that's what Joshua did with whatever he found and picked up…give it up for the war effort. Or, at least try to.

Somehow, Joshua acquired the notoriety of having money…that he was rich and had the money hidden somewhere. Small towns need something mysterious to hold on to and talk about…a ghost who walks the streets of town in the moonlight; a buried treasure, or a notorious person once lived there. In this case, poor Joshua fit the bill. And, his reputation of having hidden treasure traveled much farther that the general area of the town of Muleshoe. Much farther.

One day around 1947 two ex-convicts came to town, looking for Joshua. They had heard of his reclusive nature and that he had a hidden treasure. And, they found him. They took him to a dry rainwater lake about a half-mile from his shack where they beat him, trying to get him to tell the location of his treasure. That is, if he even had any treasure. He never told them and they beat him to death trying to make him relate the treasure location.

It didn't take long to catch the two killers after Joshua's body was found. And, back then, Justice was swift. They were tried for his murder, found guilty, and sentenced to die in the electric chair in Huntsville. Their loot consisted of the contents of Joshua's pockets: One silver nickel, one copper penny and one used coke bottle cap.

Joshua's shack stood alone and empty for some time after his death. The sign on the roof faded and finally fell over sideways.

After a few years, the State of Texas decided a divided four-lane highway was needed between Muleshoe and Clovis, New Mexico. Joshua's shack, or what was left of it, was in the way of a different kind of progress. So the shack was torn down. Buried in the dirt floor were a few sealed Mason fruit jars. Full of paper money. Dollar bills. Old. Big. Some ones, a few fives, a few tens. Most in the large bills and of gold and silver certificates. Over ten thousand dollars face value. Joshua's hidden treasure. The secret treasure he died for without telling where it was hidden.

This is the story of Joshua Blocher as I best remember it. I was very young when it all happened. A while back, I drove through Muleshoe and west on U.S. Highway 84. As soon as I came onto the sign for the village of Progress, memories filled my mind. I could see that lonely red tarpaper shack with the sign on its slopped roof: "THIS IS PROGRESS."

The Sheriff's Wife

The year I was going on ten years old, my mother and father separated. My father moved my mother and my younger brother to Amarillo, Texas, into an apartment in a large four-plex house next door to our great uncle's home. I was required to stay with my father in a rooming house in the small town of Muleshoe, also in Texas, where we had lived before the tragedy of the separation. My parents sold the house the family owned and had lived in for several years.

A few years ago, I was back in the town of Muleshoe. Actually, I was on my way to somewhere else but as my route would take me fairly close, I decided to detour to the town and check out what it had turned out to be. Another reason for visiting the town was for my wife. She did not believe there was a town called Muleshoe, even after I showed her where the town was on a Texas Highways map. So, we bywayed to the town to prove its existence to my wife in addition of fulfilling my own curiosity.

Touring the town, I found this house with no trouble at all where my family lived before the separation that led to the divorce. It made me really sad to see it even though it was in very nice shape with a well-tended yard. In our travels through the town, I was very saddened to see it; the memories I still have of that really neat, nice town are still very sharp and hurtful.

I guess in my ten-year old way, I almost hated my father for the disruption of our family life. For some reason, I mostly blamed him. He was the father, and fathers don't let such things happen. So, somehow, it had to be his sole fault.

In the day and time this divorce occurred, it was a very uncommon and disgraceful thing. As a kid sensitive to the esteem the other kids had for you, you did not even venture to talk about it. You kept it a secret and hoped no one would catch on to what was going on. The teacher probably knew, but you didn't think of that. You kept as straight a face as possible and went on living.

When school was over for the year I rode the Santa Fe train from Muleshoe to Amarillo in order to spend at least the summer there with my brother and our mother. Going on a journey that far alone may seem kind of risky for a father to put his ten-year old son on the train all by himself. But it really was no big deal. My great uncle was driving the train and he had seated me on the tail end of the train in the caboose with the brakeman and the switchman. I had ridden in the engine a few times before for short distances. But the old coal-burners really weren't the safest place for a nosey kid. So for a long trip I was stuck in the rear.

Living in Amarillo was really exciting. They had more than one picture show, they had red and green traffic lights for the cars. I didn't see a single horse or wagon anywhere except in barnyards. They even had buses to take you where you needed or wanted to go. My mother didn't have a car; we rode the bus to downtown and walked to most other places.

Toward the end of summer my Aunt Muryl Mayfield came to visit us. She and her husband Frank had two children, an older boy named Mickey and a daughter, Mary Anne, a year younger than me. They had driven all the way from Guymon, Oklahoma in a Model A Ford two-door sedan. Now I wasn't all that familiar with cars, so this one seemed really neat. Naturally, being an earlier model Ford, it was black.

After they had stayed a few days, Mary Anne and I became fast friends. She was really a tomboy. When it came time for them to go home, she and I decided I should go with them, stay a few days and come back on the bus. My mother agreed. I had recently quit my job as dishwasher for the Santa Fe Jr. Railroad Café due to the drunken antics of the male owner. I was still suffering from the tragic effects of the incident that determined my resignation. I had really liked my job as dishwasher. This trip should help me overcome that entire situation.

Away we went, north to Guymon in the Model A. It was August, and this particular year, a really hot time. Aunt Muryl carried extra water in the "A" for its radiator. We had to stop several times to add water to it.

Home for them was a farmhouse a couple of miles north of town. It was big, wooden and two-storied. When we arrived with the extra person, I think Muryl's husband, Frank was a little surprised. However, he made me very welcome. I was a little afraid of him; he was blind in one eye and had a very obvious glass eye. I do not now remember which side. He worked as a water well spudder and was gone most every day, sunup to sundown.

I had been there a few days and was really enjoying life. One morning Aunt Muryl decided she was going to go to town for some reason or other, and she decided to walk. After she had been gone for a while, Mary Anne and I decided we should drive the Model A into town and give her a ride home, it being so hot now at mid-day.

As I write this, all these years later, I still cannot believe we did this. Somehow, we got the spark adjusted just right and crank started the Model A. Away down the road we went, south to town. Me driving, like I knew what I was doing.

About a quarter-mile from the farmhouse Mary Anne called home, I managed to kill the engine. The car stopped, naturally, right in the middle of the road, right in front of a farm house. So, after kicking the tires a few times, Mary Anne and I very uneasily went over toward the house. The lady of the house had been sitting in a rocker on the front porch, watching us. Back in those days, people were really big on rockers and large front porches, mostly screened. She very nicely came to our rescue, restarted the Model A and drove us home in it. But…after she parked it and left to walk home, she took the key with her. I guess she figured we might try it again.

When Aunt Muryl returned from town Mary Anne told her what we'd done; only she made it sound like it was all her idea. Aunt Muryl never said much as I recall. But she did go over to the Model A and put the key back in it. Later on at supper, Uncle Frank kind of laughed about it. Mostly because the lady happened to be the county sheriff's wife, and Mary Anne and I were really lucky we weren't spending time night in jail for 'car stealing'.

Soon after the 'car stealing' incident, it was time for me to leave for home on the bus.

Now quite properly, this story should end here. But…years later I moved into the town of Antioch in California; a town nearby to the place of my employment. At one period of time, I was assigned to work straight days, a break from my usual rotating shift duties.

At the end of a work day and on the way home one hot afternoon, I decided to stop at a kind of 'rickey-tick' saloon not too far from where I lived off Lone Tree Way. In fact, the name of the establishment was the Lone Tree Saloon. The past-middle aged lady called Willie, behind the bar, was very courteous and friendly. At that time, I was living by myself and sometimes felt a little lonesome. So I sort of made it a habit to stop on the way home for a good cold beer the duration of the time I was scheduled for the day shift.

One day I decided to pay particular attention to the pictures I had noticed a while back that were scattered around on the walls. Beer in hand, I made a tour, looking at all the various scenes captured in black and white format. I noticed a few of them had an old-fashioned city water tower in them with the name 'Guymon', Okla, painted on it the way some small towns still do. I made a comment to Willie about the aunt and uncle I had that lived in Guymon years ago, and where did all the pictures come from?

Willie told me the pictures were hers from years before when she and her first husband lived there. When he died she moved here to Antioch where a daughter lived.

She asked me the name of my aunt and uncle. I told her they were the Mayfields and lived a couple miles north of the town of Guymon. She smiled and told me she and her husband lived just south of the Mayfields; that her husband was the sheriff of the county for years until his death. I bought another beer; as I drank it I told her the Model A story.

After I finished with the tale, she smiled at me and said: "You had firey red hair back then."

Willie and I became fast friends. I would stop and visit her whenever I was able. One afternoon the door to the saloon was closed and locked with a black-ribbon bow on it. The next day I read her obituary in the local newspaper; her daughter was sending her home to Oklahoma.

The Saloon never re-opened. A year or so later some people bought the building, remodeled it into a home and moved in.

Not too long after Willie's death, the company I worked for transferred me to a plant distant from Lone Tree Way. So I had the necessity of moving closer to the place of my employment. It was just as well. It had made me sad each time I drove past the site where the Lone Tree Saloon had stood for many years.

Years later, I was passing nearby on the freeway. I decided to detour and take a look at the building that in those early years housed the Lone Tree Saloon. As I neared, I could see there was nothing there I could recognize. Nothing left to bring old memories to the light of day.

Ten Thousand Lakes

The summer of my fourteenth year three significant things happened to me: I was baptized, I got my first driver's license, and my folks took me on a vacation to Minnesota.

The first will last all my forever. The second I could only use to take my mother wherever she needed to go. The third…well, now that was an adventure.

I had heard some about Minnesota in school: How it had Ten Thousand Lakes (which I did not believe) and that it was stocked with a lot of fish and Scandinavians. The fish part was verified by a couple of friends of my father's.

These friends of my father's: The Moss brothers were dedicated fishermen. Dry fly, wet fly, bait, dynamite, they had done it all. They had nothing but good things to say about the land of Ten Thousand Lakes.

My dad had recently bought his first car since before World War Two. It was a 1948 Chrysler New Yorker. A really fancy car; only a year old. I'm sure my dad was able to afford it because he had not had the expenses of a car for the years of the war. Having the 'new' car, and I guess the reports of the fishing in Minnesota from the Moss brothers did it; he just had to take us on a trip there. Pelican Lake, to be exact. Near the small town of Ashby.

Well, all of us being Native born Texans, me especially, did not believe Minnesota had Ten Thousand Lakes. I was certain it had a least one lake, because the Moss brothers had talked about Pelican Lake. But to have more lakes than Texas? Say it ain't so, Joltin' Joe! So I decided to keep a closed mind about the whole thing and just count the lakes if we ever got there.

Get there we did. On the way we survived a night in Deadwood, Kansas, where they had old saloons, a Boot Hill Cemetery and a museum with history of Old West Outlaws. We spent a little time wandering around the town just like good tourists were supposed to; I don't think we spent much money except for food and lodging because we really didn't have a lot of extra money to spend.

Soon after the start of travel the second day, we entered the state of Minnesota. The small mountains were covered with trees; that was sort of new to me. I had seen forest in New Mexico but not as dense as this. As soon as we topped the first hill we looked down into a valley in front of us. There was a lake in that valley with the bluest water I had ever seen surrounded by white silver sands. We topped the next hill and there was another almost identical lake. It wasn't before too many more hills, valleys and lakes I was fairly well convinced that Minnesota might not have Ten Thousand Lakes but it did have a bunch.

At the end of the second day, we arrived at the Copple Fishing Resort on the north shore of Pelican Lake where we had a cabin reserved for a week. A small rowboat came with each cabin, so we were all set to fish as soon as we unpacked. Mr. Copple was raising his younger brother, Chuck, who was my age. Chuck and I got along like years-old buddies. He showed me around and told me all kinds of secrets and neat stuff I have long since forgotten.

Each morning and evening my father, my younger brother and I would go fishing on the lake using the small rowboat. I don't remember the lake being all that big, we caught enough fish each day for a good meal every suppertime. Except for one day, that is. We did catch a lot of fish this one particular day. Too many for the stringer we had, so we started using a piece of small diameter rope to string the fish on. But it had no end snap to attach to the boat so it was necessary to tie it to the oar rail on the top of either side of the boat.

In the excitement of all the fish we were catching my brother forgot to tie the makeshift stringer. All those fish (a dozen or more perch) slowly sank to the bottom of the lake. Of course, I felt that I had caught most of the fish and that my brother had been careless on purpose. As a result, I was pretty mad. Of course, it is usually pretty easy to get mad at your younger brother, anyhow.

The water was so clear I could look over the edge of the boat and see all those fish lying on the bottom, still on the makeshift rope stringer. My father and I tried snagging the fish with the hooks on the ends of our fishing lines…with no success.

There was a big barn on the edge of the lake that had a huge pile of sawdust on the floor. Half the barn was full of ice and covered with more sawdust. I was told by Chuck that the barn was used by the townspeople; during the winter the lake would freeze over and as soon as the ice was thick enough, most everyone in town would come out to the lake, cut the ice, haul it into the barn and cover it with the sawdust. Our last day to be in the camp, Chuck and I walked to the barn and went inside. Standing there in the half light and enjoying the cool air inside the barn, it smelled sawdusty and felt very magical.

I was very sad when our vacation days were up and we left the beautiful state of Ten Thousand Lakes. I had been required to buy a fishing license there: My very first. I still have the license; sometimes I take it out and look at it. It brings back memories of a very special time in my life.

I wonder sometimes, where the magical feeling of youth has gone as I get older. Nothing stays the same. Everything changes, yet the magic of newness of each change has gone away.

Even today, I can close my eyes and look over the side of that rowboat down into the crystal clear water of the lake and see the fish strung on that rope…their tails waving slightly in the gentle current there on the bottom of the lake.

The Santa Fe Jr. Railroad Café

The year I was to be eleven years old, my parents had a disagreement so serious it would up in a divorce and one-year separation for the family. As a result, my mother and younger brother moved to an apartment in Amarillo, Texas, next door to our great uncle's house. My father sold our family home; he and I moved into a boarding house in the same town where we had lived for several years.

I was to stay the school year with him, then spend the summer in Amarillo with my mother. It need not be said this situation was very traumatic on all of us, especially me. This was an important formative age for me physiologically. I now know that the effects of that situation have lasted for me to this very day. This occurred in a day and time when divorce was a family disgrace; it made outcasts of the people involved. It especially affected the younger ones at school.

This disruption of our family life lasted a little over a year. After the reconciliation, we moved to a new town with a new house and met new people. This new town became 'home' to me; it still is even though none of my family have lived there for many years.

My parents have read almost everything I have written. I have made an effort to see they had access to the stories; I have been proud of all that I have written, published or not. However, this story I do not ever want them to see. Their generation, if any ever did, has a pretty good set of excuses for their actions and behavior.

Not only did they live through the Great Depression that affected the entire world, they suffered through a drought at the same time that the

United States had never seen before or since, followed by a world war that they had to endure under mostly unknown situations and experiences. No generation since that of our own civil war had faced such disastrous situations. In my love for them I cannot find fault for this disruption of family life. It occurred, it was corrected; we all survived.

Most weekends I was put on a train that carried me from the town we lived in, my father and I, to Amarillo. This was really no big deal, even though the train ride was sometimes as long as three or four hours. You see, our great uncle was driving the train so he had the conductor pay special attention to me. Made me feel important in front of all those passengers to be singled out by the boss of the train.

My great uncle and many of my ancestors had, at one time or another, worked for Santa Fe. Now in my school associations this was a really big deal. Not too many kids can run around bragging their uncle was a real-life railroad locomotive engineer back when locomotives were real steam engines with a real mournful whistle that inspired all kinds of country-western songs. Especially inspiring for guys like the late Jimmy Rodgers and the very much alive Johnny Cash.

As soon as the school term ended and summer began, I was moved to Amarillo as my father could not adequately supervise me during his normal business hours. This was pretty much all right with me; it gave me new world to explore and master in the way of most ten-year old boys.

This fascination did not last long, however. I soon discovered that life in the city was very restrictive compared to the life I had enjoyed in the very small town I had left. My great aunt, on seeing my predicament, laughingly suggested I should get a job; idle hands and minds were the devil's workshop. So, being plenty stubborn as most country kids are, I started looking around for a job, not realizing there really wasn't much a ten-year old going on fifteen could do.

I wound up, somehow, at the back door of the Santa Fe Jr. Railroad Café, declaring I could do just about anything the owner, a Mr. Dunn, wanted me to do. For some weird reason, he decided I could skin and clean up about a bushel of over-ripe half rotten nectarines he had on hand. The cook, a very nice grandmotherly lady took a paring knife and a clean bucket and ushered me, dragging the fruit basket, to a stool out in the back under a shady elm tree. In a fairly short time I salvaged the fruit as best I could. Mr. Dunn was so impressed; he decided to try me out as a dishwasher.

The café drew its name from the railroad roundhouse occupying about a hundred acres of land, the southern edge of which began just across the street from the café. A great number of the railroad men took coffee breaks and meals in the café, open twenty-four hours a day, seven days a week including Christmas and New Year's Day.

I finished the day pleasing Mrs. Dunn to the point of a regular job filling the vacant evening dishwashing position. The hours were four o'clock p.m. to midnight. Mrs. Dunn took me home to talk it over with my mother. At first, my mother was very unsure of this situation. We all went back to the café where my mother had a talk with the cook and it was decided the cook would sort of look after me; at midnight my mother or one of my older cousins would come to the café and escort me home across the wide vacant block to our house which was in sight of the café.

The job paid twenty-two dollars for an eight-hour shift six days a week, and included supper each evening. Now, I really felt grownup. I was actually starting a work career that was to continue to the present day. Not washing dishes: Just working.

Things went well the whole summer. I spent the evening of my eleventh birthday washing dishes. The cook and waitress made a small cake for me with candles. The railroad men on supper break, the cook and the waitress, all sang Happy Birthday to me. They lit the candles on the cake which I promptly succeeded in blowing out and we all shared the cake. I was very pleased and surprised by this.

Towards the beginning of August one fateful evening, Mr. Dunn came to the café to chew out the cook for some minor infraction. He was drunk. Nasty drunk. I had seen 'drunk' before a few times in the café. But only happy-type drunk. And, at that I did not really understand 'drunk', coming from a very small conservative church-going town populace that sold no liquor within the city limits. But I had never seen a nasty drunk or had any idea concerning that type of drunkenness. In no time at all, his ranting, raving and throwing things around had both me and the cook crying. The cook threw her apron down and charged out toward the front of the café. Leaving my apron on, I scooted out the back door running for home. The dark of night had never scared me at all and did not now, but that violent drunk did. Because I had never seen a mean drunk before, I didn't know what was wrong. My mother, of course, guessed what was going on and soon soothed me.

The next morning, Mrs. Dunn came over to the house to beg my mother for my return to work. But I had been pretty badly scarred by the whole incident. There was no way I was ever going to go back to the café. And, during the remaining time we lived in Amarillo I never did go back to the café.

That's my story; the summer of my eleventh year. It was the start of my loss of innocence, my becoming aware of the real world.

Most stories I have written have funny or happy endings. This one doesn't.

Squirrels In High Places

My life began in the middle of a decade of terrible times for the people who lived in the middle section of the United States. A decade in which the central part of the country endured the effects of a drought not equaled in our country's modern existence. A decade in which a world-wide economic depression made the most simple basic existence a day-to-day struggle. This depression compounded the effects of the drought, destroying homes, families and lives.

I was born near the very small town of Levelland, Texas, on a farm that was a farm in name only because of the lack of rain. Irrigation on a scale larger than that of watering a tree or garden was not yet more than a dream. At that time, the only two things growing on our farm was an elm tree just south of house, and an adjacent grape arbor on the east. The rest of the land didn't have enough moisture on it to grow weeds.

This situation was of about a ten year duration. Families who had enough money to leave, packed up whatever meager belongings they could take and went west. My family, for whatever reason, stayed put.

So I grew up on the South Plains of Texas: The land named Llano Estacado by the Spanish Explorer, Francisco Coronado. Legend has it that he looked out across the land from the back of his horse, and saw the hundreds of prairie dogs standing like little sentinels by their holes. He compared them to small wooden stakes on a land so flat and treeless with air so clear you could see forever. The descriptive translation of 'Staked Plains' is still used today. That could have been changed to 'Baked Plains' during the term of that terrible drought.

Located a few yards south of our house was a windmill and elevated water tank sitting on an enclosed frame normally called a 'creamery'. This was of use to store milk from the family cows for later processing. Generally, the overhead tank leaked enough water to keep the creamery cool. This cooling effect helped preserve the milk for the short time it was kept in there. After this short time, the cream would separate from the milk and float to the top. Then it would be skimmed off to be used in making butter and butter milk.

The windmill's water tank was constructed of cypress wood with galvanized steel bands to hold it together and had a roof with a small access hole and an attached covering lid. This particular covering lid, normally closed, was accidentally left open and caused a great deal of trouble.

Several things contributed to the trouble that was soon to happen. There was only one tree available for the squirrel for several miles. There was only one windmill available for several miles. There was only one water tank with an open access cover. There were no mud puddles around the base of the windmill's water tank tower, so if the squirrel wanted water, he had to climb for it.

Simply because of the availability, a squirrel took up residence in our elm tree. His occasional appearance, when noticed by my grandpa, would be pointed out to me on the times he and I were together. I was fascinated by the presence of the squirrel.

We had a grey tiger stripped cat named Jiggs and a small wire-haired terrier named Foozy. Jiggs would occasionally come around looking for affection from me; Foozy was mine and went most everywhere I went. I was disappointed at not being able to pet the squirrel as I could the cat and the dog. I was just too young to understand about wild things. The chickens didn't run from me, so why should the squirrel?

After a while neither my grandfather nor I saw the squirrel, so it was no longer in my short attention span. But then the water in the house at the kitchen sink started tasting sort of funny and smelled pretty bad. In order to determine for sure the cause of the bad-tasting water, my father climbed up to the platform the water tank sat upon to be able to look inside the tank. Sure enough, there was the poor squirrel floating in the water.

I suppose the squirrel went up there for a drink and the water level happened to be down some probably due to a few windless days. He couldn't quite reach the water surface in order to get a drink, He must have stretched way out to try to get some water and fell in. Once down in the water inside the tank, there was nothing for him to grab onto in order to get out. As soon as he wore himself out scratching on the sides of the tank, he gave up and drowned. A few days later, his presence in the tank became known.

After removing the squirrel, my father emptied the tank. He scrubbed the inside of the tank with home-made lye soap. Then he thoroughly rinsed the tank with fresh water from the windmill. As soon as the wind blew enough for the windmill to pump, the tank was refilled with fresh clean water. This time when my father was finished, he made sure the access hole lid was closed.

Well, now that the squirrel had caused so much trouble, he was sometimes in the forefront of my mind. I missed seeing him scrambling around in the tree. A few weeks later, my grandfather died; my father sold the farm and we moved into the city. There were no trees in the new housing district where we moved. No squirrels.

By the time I saw another squirrel, I had just about forgotten what they looked like.

Years later, I had my own place with a yard large enough for several fruit trees and one almond tree among several other non-bearing trees of different types. Not long after we moved there, a squirrel took up residence in a huge old oak tree standing tall just off the edge of our property.

I noticed him one morning as I was sitting and reading the paper on the deck that extended across the entire back of our house.

That mid-summer as the almonds became ripe in our tree, I would see the small critter traveling on the power cable that passed through his oak-tree home and bordered the edge of our property. The cable was anchored on a utility pole right on the property line close enough to give him access to the almond tree and harvest the nuts.

Occasionally our Golden Retriever would notice the squirrel in his travels and stand down on the ground near the almond tree barking at the squirrel. The squirrel would stop short in his travels and give the dog heck just for noticing. Both satisfied with themselves, they would each go on about their business. The squirrel would continue to gather as many nuts as his mouth would hold and take them over to his cache somewhere in the big oak tree.

This went on for several summers. I would sit and read, anticipating the arrival of the squirrel each morning. We never once had any nuts off that tree. Not one nut. The squirrel hoarded them all.

Then, the last year we lived there, there was no small creature running down the power cable to harvest the almonds. After a few of the nuts started falling, I went down to the tree and gathered most of them. Lightly roasted, those nuts were really sweet.

I felt sad at the disappearance of this small busy creature. I did not envy him the nuts. I felt sure some disaster had taken his poor small life. So far, it has been a really dry summer. I guess he could have fallen into someone's water tank. Or swimming pool.

The Horse Jump

I don't remember the exact year it happened, but it makes little difference. There probably aren't two handfuls of people still alive who knew of it and would remember, it was so long ago. So, you see, the actual year of the occurrence makes little difference. What does make some difference is the fact that someone does remember.

World War II had just started. The great depression was still affecting my world of Texas. The dust bowl and drought that had ruined the Midwest and created California was just over. What I had heard of for all of my tender years and had known not had finally happened: It rained.

It rained a lot. It rained so much that there were rainwater puddles everywhere. Some deep enough to swim in. Swim. If you even knew what that was. That was something else some of us had heard of but never done nor seen done.

Toad frogs and box turtles appeared by the dozens seemingly from nowhere. All over the place. All of us kids had collections of either or both, and sore fingers from the many pinches of the hooked beaks of the turtles. Like the rain, most of us had never seen such wonderful creatures.

One early summer Saturday there was word of mouth advertisement going around town about an impending horse jump off a low tower, then a swim across a fairly large rainwater lake just east of town. Naturally, everyone was talking about it. That's how 'word of mouth' advertisement works. Really well. Spreads like a prairie fire in a stiff wind.

Hours before the appointed time, the people started gathering on the west side of the lake near the crusted reddish sand access road. As I recall, it was a pretty good sized lake of the same brownish-red color of the sand in the fields it flowed over on the way to the low spot it now occupied.

Years later, the term "tank" was applied to these water storage areas nature had provided or similar ones dug by farmers to hold runoff water. Usually those man-made tanks were in an area that interfered least with crops. Cattle would frequent the "tanks." The farmers had yet to have the mechanical ability to level out their fields for the entire growing capability. The "tanks" occupied quite a bit of the fields then and for quite a few years to come.

With the invention of the yards-long 'land plane' pulled by tractor, most of the unwanted tanks disappeared into the leveled fields. Cotton was planted and grew, filling up the previously empty space left by the summers-end evaporation of the water.

Now, back to the day of the exciting event. I remember sitting on the hot hood of the old Ford my Dad had. Sitting in the hot sun. Waiting for something to happen. Looking in the hot sun. Waiting for something to happen. Looking at the low wooden tower that had been constructed with an access ramp of piled dirt and planks on the landside. The tower wasn't all that high or wide but was long enough for a horse to be able to take a couple of strides to make the jump into the water.

Most of the townspeople were there. Some had walked; some came in the few cars available at that time; some rode horses or came in wagons pulled by horses or mules. This was a really big event in a country as poor and isolated as ours.

As I mentioned, I was sitting on the hood of my dad's car. My family was lucky enough to have a 1936 Ford two-door sedan. Black, naturally. Ford had not yet discovered paint with color other than black. My father bought the car with some of his share of the money he got from the sale of the family farm, my birthplace. My father put the place up for sale and sold it a few weeks after his father died. He either felt there was no more reason to or did not want to keep it.

I have always regretted the fact that my father sold the farm. To this young boy, it was an entire world. It was one hundred and eighty acres of sand. Not a blade of grass grew on that dry land. The land had not felt rain for over seven years. It had a tree, a functioning windmill, and lots of lizards and snakes. I grew up with a very healthy respect for Diamondback Rattlesnakes and have not forgotten the lessons learned.

Now the waiting was over, horse and rider were led up to the bottom of the ramp at the foot of the low tower. I remember the young lady rider sitting on the horse, which was shaking his head, snorting and stamping in nervousness.

A hat or two was passed to collect whatever offering the scattered audience were willing to part with for the privilege of watching this horse and rider jump into the brownish-red water and swim across the great puddle to the far shore.

Hat passing completed, the horse and rider went up the ramp and paused for effect. The horse stamped a few more times; the rider spurred the horse and slapped the reins on the horse's rump.

The horse took a couple of giant steps and jumped off the ramp, striking the surface of the water with a great splash. The horse did not go under completely and started swimming across the lake with cheers and yells from the crowd scattered around the western shore urging it on.

It wasn't long before the horse was in the shallows near the far edge of the shore; it began climbing out with great heaves of breath and water sluicing off saddle and rider.

After a short rest, the entire act was repeated. Not long after the second successful jump and exit of the horse and rider from the water, people started to drift away home. The show was over.

A few days later, my dad loaded the family into the old Ford and we went again to the rainwater lake. Only this time, no horse would be jumping. Several horses were being used to drag spring-tooth harrows across the lake bottom. The harrows were attached to the horses' harness with long ropes. The horses were led, dragging the harrows.

Two young boys and a girl who witnessed the horse jump a few days before decided to swim their two horses across the lake, riding bareback and with the girl and one boy riding double on one of the horses. All caution ignored, it was so much fun they did it several times until the horse carrying double foundered.

Neither the boy or the girl on that horse could swim well enough to be able to get to shore. They disappeared from sight. The horses finally made it to the shore, the other boy rider safe. He could not see either of his companions, so he swiftly rode to the nearest farmhouse to seek help. Of course, it was too late even before he and his horse exited the water.

People were again standing by, leaning on their cars or sitting on the hoods. Waiting in the hot sun. Observing a far different event from that of a few days before. This time, there was only mumbled conversation if there was any at all. Some people mumbled to themselves over the waste of life.

In the quiet hot afternoon, you could hear the clinking of the harness chain and the soft giddy-up or whoa of the drivers of the horses. These sounds carried softly across the still waters to the waiting people gathered round the west shore. Each time the harrows pulled up empty on the sandy shore, there seemed to be a silent sigh of anguish. This seemed to go on forever.

Not long before sundown, each body was finally hooked and dragged up by a harrow, one shortly after the other. I did not know the names of the drowning victims at that time; nor do I now.

But, I have remembered. A young boy's first observation of death; I have remembered.

Pepper Collins

It happened in an age of both fear and innocence in a town now different; the old town now left far away with the passage of time. World War II was in full bloody bloom. The people of the town were very much aware of the disaster of Pearl Harbor and the continuing slaughter in Europe and the South Pacific. It was a time of unknowns. It was not a time of confidence in the survivability of our nation. If the Pepper Collins crime had happened in a time before or after the war, the people involved in the immediate aftermath might have reached a different conclusion.

His name, near as I can recall, was Pepper Collins...but I never knew him. I just knew of him through my dad. I remember this because it was the second and the latter of two murders that happened in our town when I was growing up. And, strangely enough, both murders were about money. Not a lot of money, though. Both murders were in the town of Muleshoe, Texas.

The first murder of my young remembrance was of an old man named Joshua Blocher, the founder of Progress, a town just west of Muleshoe. His murder netted a total of one nickel, one copper penny and a slightly bent Coca Cola bottle cap. The reason I remember that one so vividly was that I knew Joshua, but barely, as did most every other kid in town. Everyone had seen Joshua walking the streets, tow sack on his back, looking for whatever item he could pick up, put in his sack to later take to his home in Progress. He was only limited in his saving of items by his ability to pick them up and carry them.

Joshua's murder, the arrest of the perpetrators, trial, convictions and double electric chair executions scheduled were well publicized for months;

written up in the town's weekly newspaper. Naturally, it was a subject of thorough discussion over back yard fences and coffee tables for weeks on end. I am certain that to this day, the matter will occasionally be brought to mind even as it happened so many years ago and few are left for remembrance.

Pepper's untimely death was another story. He was the owner of a fairly well known and prosperous café. At least, for that time it was prosperous. So, his worth was more than Joshua's.

The details of the latter situation are not stored away in my memory from any other advantage than that of hearsay; simply what I recall I heard from my father. Pepper's death never received the publicity that Joshua's had. And, as my father passed away a few years ago, I am unable to talk to him further on the subject now that I need and want to know.

In the latter years of my father's life, we did talk of many things. Conversations mostly about our ancestors and the history of our family. Somehow, we never got around to Pepper. So, this somber tale of woe is from the memory of a nine-year-old boy, the approximate age I was when the whole thing happened. Just remember, this is all from memory. It is a tale of justice denied. The death and the unofficial conclusion are true. Of that, my memory is secure.

Pepper was a veteran of World War I. In that day, it is likely where he learned to cook. Pepper was of the Negro race, as it was called at that time. In the Army of then and until recent time, that race designation meant that he would be a cook, mess hall helper or some other similar menial job for the duration of the time spent in the service. It also probably gave him the expertise he needed to create and sustain a café with a reputation for being a very good cook.

Occasionally, several local businessmen would go on a two or three day fishing trip to the nearby Buffalo Lake. Pepper would be hired to go with the men on the trips to function as the cook. The fishermen learned to respect Pepper both as a good cook and as a decent man.

Now, in my own experience and observation, I am sure there was more than just fishing that went on. Nothing of any real significance in this day and time. But, back then, things such as you wanted to do but didn't want your fellow townspeople know that you did it. Poker, maybe some drinking of Four Roses, a popular whisky of the time. Beer, certainly. Things like that;

things fairly innocent now. Serious back then. It all made the fishing trips worthwhile in several different ways.

Pepper was married to a much younger woman. She was mostly in charge of the business end of the café and assisted the various waitresses who worked there from time to time. She had the reputation of being a woman hard to deal with and difficult to be around. She mostly 'bossed' instead of working.

Pepper did things other than cook for the café or fix meals during businessmen's fishing trips. He would come into the café and immediately grab a bottle of his favorite drink, a Royal Crown Cola. He kept his supply separate from the other soda bottles in one corner of the top-loaded double door red Coca Cola icebox. This way he was sure there was always a really cold "RC" (as he called it) bottle waiting for him.

His sudden death was a surprise to all who knew him. He had not complained of feeling 'out of sorts' and really appeared to be in good health. At first, the local doctor could not determine the cause of death, which created a suspicion of foul play. For whatever reason, the doctor decided to take some blood sample and discovered the presence of arsenic in his blood and a residue in the chemical makeup of his fingernails and hair; evidence of fairly long-term consumption: In other words, not a one-time accidental dose of the poison.

This information revealed by the autopsy was presented to the county sheriff. The sheriff started an investigation based on the untimely fact of death and the results of the autopsy. The sheriff found that the Widow Collins had purchased rat poison on at least two different occasions at a local hardware store. Rat poison with the principle ingredient of arsenic.

Further into the investigation, personal interviews were conducted in the hopes that maybe one of Pepper's friends or associates would be able to furnish additional incriminating evidence. None was discovered. The sheriff began to assume that if the Widow Collins had disposed of her husband with her purchases of rat poison, she had covered her tracks really well. He had no additional evidence of foul play. He determined to deliver the problem to the coroner's jury for a hearing and disposition.

The autopsy on Pepper's body revealed his death had been caused by the consumption of arsenic poison. A coroner's jury was drafted after as thorough an investigation as possible by the sheriff had been completed. My father was selected as a member of the coroner's jury for the inquest. All the facts and opinions were presented and discussed at length before the coroner's jury. It did not take long for the jury to reach their verdict. Death resulted from arsenic poison administered by person or persons unknown.

The official verdict was murder. Pepper's death was proved as murder but no one was ever openly accused or indicted for the crime, so it was never reported as anything other than a suspicious death from arsenic poison. Case closed.

My father was really bitter over the verdict. I overheard him talking to my mother about the whole thing. He kept repeating that the jury really believed Pepper's wife had poisoned him to death but without enough evidence to bring charges against her, she had really gotten away with murder.

This presented no particular feeling of tragedy in my young life. In truth, I now suspect I never quite understood. I had never been a remembering witness of death before. It wasn't long before rocks and centipedes and frogs re-occupied my mind and pushed aside any shadowy thoughts of dying and murder.

Now that I am grown and can better analyze situations such as the one I have related, I have come to this conclusion on my own: I speculate that the majority of the members of the corner's jury were not fishermen. That they had never eaten any of Pepper's cooking at a fishing camp. That they certainly had never entered Pepper's café located 'across the tracks' in Darktown, much less eaten there. So they would not be too concerned about the untimely death of a Negro man mostly past his prime.

The really sad thing about that last paragraph is that over all these years, things have not changed a whole lot. Not yet; not now. Maybe not ever.

Coleslaw

For those few of you who are unfamiliar with coleslaw, it is a combination of coarsely ground cabbage, a little salad dressing or milk and a shot or two of vinegar. Tasty, huh?

To most kids—at least those I have known, myself included—to eat this is as bad as having to take a tablespoon of cod-liver oil. In blunt words, that stuff is bad.

Now to supplement the diet of earlier years, there weren't too many different kinds of vitamins. There were 'Doan's Little Liver Pills', Carter's 'whatever' and just your plain old 'One-a-Day'.

That kind of stuff. So, I suppose that's why coleslaw was created. I guess sometimes it was handier than pills and certainly cheaper. There was also the fact that since it tasted almost as bad as cod-liver oil, it really had to be good for you. Mothers like to give kids' stuff that tastes bad. That way it's really good for you.

In the days before good common sense, scurvy and rickets were pretty common. At least, most mothers thought they were. Those were mostly diseases of blue-water sailors, but word got around to most mothers. And, I guess they thought coleslaw was the perfect medicine to prevent both those and whatever other dread ailments there were running around at that time. At least, all the mothers I knew did.

This business of eating over at someone else's house was often preceded with "Your mother's not fixing coleslaw today, is she?" before accepting. Coleslaw was not an acceptable dietary addition to most kids' ideas of things good to eat: Hotdogs, hamburgers, French-fired potatoes, good stuff like that. However, there were many parents—mothers; I should say—who would force their children to sit at the table until the complete meal was consumed. With strategies ranging from "Children all over the world are starving and you won't eat that" to "If you don't eat everything on your plate you'll never see sunshine again."

My own mother subscribed to both positions and was completely backed up by my father. Well, at least he never said anything to the contrary within the range of my hearing. I also noticed (in looking for any escape clause) that he ate his coleslaw without comment or delay.

One time I read in one of those 'supermarket tabloids' where a petrified kid had been found still sitting at the dinner table with an uneaten bowl of what they said was spinach in front of him. I'll bet it was really coleslaw. That kid's mother must have been really serious about what she thought was good diet. That kid was really stubborn, too. So help me, that's what I read.

Threatening a young boy with punishment of 'never seeing sunshine again' in that day and time was akin to today's threat of no T.V. for a month. We are talking really serious stuff. In the case of boys, I mean. I happen to be an authority on the way young boys think. Because I was one once, and I also had a younger brother whom I observed very closely. For some strange reason he seemed to eat his coleslaw without too much complaining. But my brother and I were pretty different. Where I was loud, noisy and quick to complain, he was pretty quiet.

Actually, when you get right down to it, about the only thing we really had in common: Our ears were about the same size. Big. I say, 'had' in common. We don't have that in common anymore. As soon as he got all grown up, he had his ears fixed. So now, in our family, I am the only one left who has ears like my dad's. Mom used to tell me the reason my ears stick out was I used to pull my straw hat down so tight on my head it forced my ears to sick out permanently...I guess she never looked at my father's ears. The reason I pulled my hat down tight was I got tired of chasing it when it was blown off during sandstorms.

Well, back to coleslaw. I was not going to be kept in the house out of the sunlight. Evidence of occasional recurring skin cancer on my forehead proves I somehow managed to be devious enough to spend quite a lot of time outside in the sun, straw hat cocked back on my head. Just ask my skin doctor. He likes me as a patient. He's really a nice guy, but I'm really not all that crazy about going to see him very often. But, in any case, I did not get more than my share of sun by eating coleslaw. Or boiled carrots. I wasn't too crazy about them either. No sir, I will have it known I did not sink to eating my coleslaw.

I tried to be absent on the summertime days I could discover we were going to have coleslaw. I would finagle an invitation to eat somewhere else; have a really serious late baseball practice session at school (that hardly ever worked); or just plain run away. I ran away a lot. Temporarily, that is.

On the meals I was trapped into partaking that offered coleslaw, I finally figured out a way to avoid eating any and still retain my freedom. First, if I could serve it to myself, I wouldn't put very much on my plate. That worked, sometimes. And, sometimes my mother would see through that ploy and say "That's not enough, here…" And I would get about three times what I would have gotten if she had served me in the first place.

Finally, when all else failed, I would sit at the table with a full mouth of coleslaw. As soon as nobody was looking, or if I could take advantage of diverted attention, I would quickly spit the coleslaw in my hand and deftly and discretely stuff it in my overalls pocket. Overalls, the stripped type, had plenty of pockets. So I had plenty of room to smuggle the coleslaw out. Then having satisfied the dietary requirements of that particular meal, I would get outside as quickly as possible and dump the evidence. Usually as far away as possible from mother's normal area of travel.

Now, to this day, I'm pretty sure I got away with that all those years ago. I'll probably find out though, if someone gives this tale to my mother to read.

One thing I did learn when I got a little older and had to leave college for active duty in the Marines. In combat training, I darn near starved… Until I gave up and ate the coleslaw. Like mothers, Marines were really big on coleslaw. Now I hate to admit this here: The stuff really isn't too bad. As long as you try to think you're eating something else. I eat coleslaw now and my wife lets me go out and play in the sunshine. But then, I don't wear overalls anymore. So I have to eat it. All of it.

The Lightning Strike

When I was eight or nine years old I had a scare I have never forgotten. The scare was not for my own safety or well-being, but that of my father.

World War Two was a couple of years old. My family consisting of my father, mother and younger brother lived in the small town of Muleshoe on the northern part of the South Plains of Texas. It was a wonderful town to grow up in; I have many happy remembrances.

My father was just barely too old for the armed services draft program. He was the manager of the electric utility company that served that part of Texas. Due to the wartime situation, all of the crew who worked out of his office location either volunteered for armed service or had been drafted. Even though this was a happy time for most children, it certainly wasn't a happy time for adults.

At any rate, my father had to do everything for his company that needed to be done. He did have a secretary to help with the telephone and do all the bookkeeping and billing and handle the customer accounts. But my father was the line fuse replacer, the meter reader, the do-everything-physical department that needed and had to be done. He has always been the type of person to see that the needed jobs were done. Even to the point of teaching me algebra when I finally arrived in high school and had trouble understanding it.

His work days started long before sunup and ended well after sundown. When it was required he worked on Saturdays and Sundays just as if they were like any other day. And the term 'overtime' concerning work hours had not even been dreamed up yet.

We had a '37 Ford Sedan when the war first started; I remember a few rides in it. But after rationing of gasoline, tires and oil came into effect as a result of the war effort, my father sold the car. But his company furnished him with a work vehicle. It was a '40 Chevrolet coupe that had a short pickup bed to carry tools and work stuff instead of a trunk and inside back seat. He was able to use it for very limited family purposes such as hauling groceries home or going to see a doctor.

The times my father left the house to go somewhere special such as a job trouble call I begged to go with him as all young boys want to go with daddy. And, every once in a while I did get to go. How many times I was allowed to go, I don't remember. But I do remember one particular time.

Just a couple miles west of town a Santa Fe freight train had derailed and dumped several boxcar bulkloads of pinto beans strung out along each side of the right-of-way for a half mile or so. Naturally, the people who came to rubberneck about the accident scraped up all they could that the Santa Fe couldn't salvage and took them home for their own use.

For many years, each spring beans would sprout and grow along the wreck site for a good half-mile. At harvest time, people would come out and pick a lot of the beans for a few meals. At the east end of this volunteer field of beans, an overhead transformer platform was mounted in the center of several power poles. This platform sat on large electrical insulators so it was isolated from the mother earth ground lightning heads for when it strikes objects sitting or growing on the earth. This circuit assembly was also used as a junction center for two or three different circuits supplying a few nearby farms. Each three-phase circuit was fused with replaceable fuse cartridges, something long since improved upon.

One particular evening a very severe lightning and thunderstorm came up. After a few loud rumbles of thunder, our telephone rang with the complaint of lights out. Now, in that day and time, when your lights went out you called the guy directly at home who was responsible for fixing the problem of electric circuit failure. Everybody in town knew everybody else, so there was really no escaping it anyway.

This time when I begged my father to take me, he agreed. The reason for this to this day I have no idea why, he just agreed to take me.

So out to the bean field we went where the trouble was. I recall the wind was blowing, sheets of rain were carried by gusty winds, and lightning was flashing constantly with loud thunder following. A real-life setting for movie drama.

We stopped at the location of the transformer pad. My father directed both the beams of both adjustable spotlights mounted on each side of the windshield to give light up on the platform. Then he got out and put on his climbing hooks, safety belt and heavy insulated lineman's gauntlet gloves. I don't recall him saying anything to me, but he probably told me to stay in the 'pickup' as he called it.

As he climbed up the pole to the transformer platform, he was very visible to me in the lighted area of the spotlights. Right away on getting up there, he started disconnecting and pulling down the fuse brackets. After he had them all disconnected he removed and replaced the used cartridges with the newly replaced fusees and cartridges that he had brought with us. As he started closing in the fuse brackets a bolt of lightning came out of one of the open circuits and flashed over him, arching to ground.

As soon as the bolt flashed, I was blinded by it for several seconds as I had been looking directly up at the area where the flash occurred. I just knew that my father had been hit by the bolt. Finally, when my visibility returned, I could see him pulling the newly blown fuse brackets down to start the replacement cycle all over again. This same situation happened a few more times until the intensity of the storm eased. Finally he was able to finish restoring the fuses for the circuits and came back down to Mother Earth and the safety of the inside of the car with me.

I was still very scared and thankful that I still had a father.

Years were to go by before I was faced with a similar situation in my own employment. By then I knew it really wasn't as dangerous as it looked when it occurred with a person standing on an insulated platform such as the one my father stood on that terrible night. It is still scary, though.

A few years ago, my wife and I were traveling on vacation and drove through the area this occurred all those years ago. I had no trouble locating it; only the overhead transformer platform had been replaced with a small ground level substation.

The pinto beans were still growing as thick as they had most years back then. I hope people still pick them and eat them. It would be a shame for all those beans to go to waste.

The Soft-Shelled Turtle

The summer of my thirteenth year we took our very first family vacation. This was the second summer following the ending of World War II. I have written before of the strict rationing our government had enforced on the civilian population. Things most severely affected were vehicles that used gas, oil, and rubber tires. At this time, a lot of the civilian population in rural areas still used horse and wagon for limited transportation. Among other things rationed were commodities such as sugar and meats. Everything possible had been diverted to the war effort; these restrictions were deemed necessary due to the terrible conditions in the greatest war between the most powerful nations in modern history. The outcome of this war would set the future courses of mankind throughout the world.

Even though a lot of things were in short supply for many months after the end of the war there weren't very many complaints. Probably the people in the cities were most affected by this. The rural communities in the central states were still trying to recover from a severe drought and a world-wide economic depression. A few more things affecting an already meager existence didn't seem to matter. Most people endured their lot in life with the hope that someday things would be better.

Right after the start of the war and the start of rationing, many individuals in the small towns having access to horses either sold whatever type of fuel-consuming vehicle they had or stored in some type of shelter with its wheels up on blocks. Shortly after the start of the rationing program my father sold the family 1937 Ford two-door sedan.

Well, anyhow: Back to the vacation. My father went to the 'Big City' and bought an almost-new Chrysler. The first family car since early in the war. It was really fancy. It even had a car-top 'built-in' luggage rack. By the way we were amazed at the new car when we saw it at home, it could just as well have been a Rolls Royce. After riding around town in old horse-drawn wagons, used up cars and pickups, it was indeed plush. The new car mostly stayed in the garage. We kept it neat, clean and dust-free.

My father had heard how good the fishing was at Possum Kingdom Lake, located some distance from our town and a little west of Ft. Worth-Dallas. We loaded the few possessions we were able to take with us in the luggage rack. Off we went for a week or so of vacation intended to be spent there at the lake with another family my folks had known for years.

Reservations had been made for each family to stay in one of a pair of nice but simple lake-side cabins A plain fourteen-foot rowboat with a pair of oars was furnished with each cabin. The fishing was good; we enjoyed perch and catfish most every meal including breakfast.

The lake water was fairly warm; each evening around sunset my brother and I swam around in it near the boat dock. Mostly before we had enjoyed swimming in ice-cold irrigation pump discharge water ponds.

The few days we were there at the lake passed so rapidly it seemed it was time for our family to leave just after we had arrived. Sadly, we repacked what little gear we had brought in the luggage rack and started west toward home.

Now, all these years later, I think my father realized our sadness on leaving. Trying to ease our feelings he told us of a place on a small creek that was on our way home where we would camp for a night or two. The creek, the South Branch of the Clear Fork of the Brazos River, was not all that far away, just a few hours' travel in our 'new' car.

We stopped and camped at an area about twenty yards or so from the creek. We had no tent. The shelter for our campsite was the high overhead umbrella of the branches of the many huge pecan trees growing randomly around the area, scattered as far as we could see. The girth of the massive trunks of these trees was too great for my brother and me to encircle any one of them with outstretched arms and clasped hands. They were so tall; they seemed to stretch forever up into the sky. The pecans from the trees had fallen to the ground and were scattered all over the area. The nuts were fairly slender about an inch and a half long, and easily cracked by holding a couple in the palm of your hand and squeezing them, one against the other. They were of the 'paper shell' type. We picked up as many as we could find and took them home for later use.

The creek was fairly shallow and warm. It did not appear to be very promising for fishing success, but my brother and I tried. Heck, we would fish anywhere there was water (even shallow muddy rain-water puddles) if we had the chance.

I don't remember catching any fish. We did find some fairly large fresh-water mussels. The only ones I have ever seen. However, I did catch a very unique turtle. It was a freshwater soft-shell turtle colored greyish green. Its body was sort of flat and oblong and its head had a really pointy nose. Now I was familiar with desert terrapin-type box turtles. I was also familiar with the looks of the few green 'pet' turtles I had seen in the five and dime stores. This critter resembled none of them except for the fact it had a shell and four legs. I petitioned my father, with success, to allow me to take it home.

As it turned out, I only kept the turtle a few days; a week or two at the most. My father suggested I take the turtle to a place similar to its natural home; we could take it out to the cooling water lake of the steam-electric generating plant near the town where we lived. My father, having worked many years for the company which owned the plant, had taken my brother and me fishing there quite a few times previously.

As soon as it was convenient, we went out to the plant and released the turtle in the lake. To my disappointment, it swam away without looking back.

I really hated to give that turtle his freedom because he was such an unusual type, but in my heart I knew it was best for him. I would only keep the terrapin box turtles I caught at home a few days, and then I would simply turn them loose in our yard. Usually that was where I found them in the first place.

Occasionally, in the rest of my growing years at home, we would go out to the plant and fish in the cooling water pond. Quite often on these trips, we would see the turtle swimming around. Each time we saw him he would seem to have grown a little larger. Sometimes the men I knew who worked there would let me know they had seen him.

As far as we could tell, he was the only turtle of his kind there. He grew to a little over a foot long. He was probably really lonesome.

After graduating from high school, I left for college. A short time later, the Marine Corps determined they wanted me on active duty more than they wanted me in college. After my service and discharge, I settled in California, working in a steam-electric generation plant much larger than the one I knew of back home where the turtle was.

During the course of work one shift, I rescued a fairly large turtle who had wandered into an oily-water separation pond and was covered with heavy oil. I was reminded of that soft-shelled turtle of so long ago. I took this one home, cleaned him up, and released him in my fenced back yard. I cut my house number on the edge of his shell.

The turtle stayed in the back yard for several years, seemingly content. One day I discovered it was gone. Weeks later, I found that a couple of young brothers had it a few doors away in their own back yard. I did not further pursue the matter.

Years later, my father told me the company he worked for had closed the old plant near my hometown. As the plant's years of service grew long, it had become old-fashioned and very in-efficient. As he was telling me about this, I immediately remembered the turtle I had released in the plant's cooling water pond back in the days of my youth.

A few years ago, I journeyed back to my hometown for a high school class reunion. As I neared the road that led to the old power plant, I thought of the turtle and decided to turn off and drive by the area adjacent to the old cooling water pond.

The power plant was sitting there not too far from the site of the pond. A few of its windows were broken. The yard surrounding the plant that used to be so neat and tidy was now littered with odds and ends of paper and trash blown around by the wind. All those years gone by.

The old cooling water pond was completely dry; growing tumble weeds covered the bottom.

I have read that turtles can live for many years. Some kinds, a hundred years and more.

I hope when the plant closed, someone thought to move my turtle to a more permanent home; maybe the Pecos. That river isn't all that far away.

The Hoe And The Snake

A very old man and a very young boy were walking on a sandy path out behind the house they lived in; walking south toward the windmill that supplied the family's water. The old man stopped when he came upon a rattlesnake laying in the sand just in front of the two of them. The snake was just lying there, soaking up sun.

The old man urged the young boy, barely old enough to understand, to go back to the house and get a hoe for the old man to kill the rattlesnake with. The old man stayed where he was in order to keep an eye on the snake; he didn't want it to crawl off and later become a threat to the young boy or the rest of the family.

The young boy's mother was in the kitchen located at the back of the nearby house and heard the commotion. She went outside and gave the young boy the hoe the old man wanted. The young boy took the hoe to the old man and the snake was quickly killed.

I was that young boy. The old man was my grandfather on my father's side of the family. The house my father built and a few years later, where I was born.

These were among the very first memories I have of my paternal grandfather. This period of time was very shortly before his death. This was the only time I remember seeing him outside of the house.

I remember my grandmother, his wife of many years, lying on a bed in the kitchen. I remember her red hair fanned out on the pillow her head rested upon. Her bed was in the kitchen in order to be near my mother at all times as she was very weak and was not expected to live very many more days.

Now, this remembrance of her red hair may be enhanced by my being told the red hair I inherited was her legacy to me. At this point in time it is of little difference where the memory came from; it is my memory.

Soon after this, she disappeared from the kitchen and the house. The bed was removed from the kitchen.

When my grandfather came home from her funeral he went into his room and to bed. He never again got up from his bed on his own. My father would lift him in his arms and carry him into the bathroom he built due to my grandfather's inability to go to the 'Chic Sales' outside at the back of the house. He also installed a bathtub inside the bathroom for my grandfather's use. My father would carry my grandfather into the bathroom and give him a bath as my grandfather could not do this on his own.

My grandfather retired before I was born. Only retirement back then was a lot different. If you retired, you had to be able to have enough money to support yourself. This was before social security was initiated; nor were there any companies offering retirement fund participation back then. At the time of his retirement, he was the preacher of a congregation of Baptists.

During my grandfather's working life, he was a "circuit riding" Baptist preacher. He covered most of the Panhandle and South Plains of Texas, including some of the nearby parts of eastern New Mexico. Eventually he brought his family to Hockley County in the year 1922. He and his wife lived there until they both passed away in 1939. He and a few other families founded the first Baptist Church in Levelland. He also was instrumental in starting the Fairview Baptist Church.

At the end of his preaching days, the Levelland Baptist Church elders presented him with a small parcel of land, one hundred-eighty acres, near Levelland, Texas. He and my father built a small, simple house on the northeast corner of the land nearest the town limit. That location is now known as Popular and College Avenue. As I wrote earlier, this was the house I was born in.

This house had no electricity at first. Coal oil lanterns supplied light; my mother cooked on a coal oil stove. In the center of the kitchen floor a big pot-bellied stove stood on large flattened tin cans. Coal burned in this stove heated the small house in the wintertime. A cabinet-type ice box sat on the south side of the kitchen back door kept food cold.

My father went to work as a lineman for the company that later became Southwestern Public Service Company. He worked for that company for over forty–six years. Shortly after his employment began, he was awarded the 'fringe' benefit of free household electricity. He wired the house he had built for electricity so that he could take advantage of this benefit. It turned out to be a blessing for my grandmother. Her middle son, on a visit, brought her a present of a small black Westinghouse Electric oscillating air fan. The moving air from this fan cooled her some in her last summer. Years later, I acquired that fan; it still functions. It is among my most cherished possessions. Gradually, my father wired the house to the extent that incandescent lights were able to be used in the house. The cabinet ice-box was replaced with an electric refrigerator. My mother still cooked on the coal-oil stove.

The next clear memory I have of my grandfather is of seeing him in his coffin placed on sawhorses in the living room. I wasn't supposed to see what was going on inside the room. I was able to see inside of the room as I was standing near the living room door one time when it was opened. An adult opened it in order to go down the hall to the kitchen. I saw that there were several old men sitting in chairs grouped around the coffin, and talking in hushed tones.

The death of my grandfather changed my family's life considerably. My father put all of my grandfather's possessions into the storm cellar located a short way outside the back of the house and caved the storm cellar in, covering everything up. For years afterward, my father hardly ever spoke of my grandfather. He buried all except his own grief.

After a short time, my father sold the farm and we moved for a brief time to the big city to the east. After a few months' training, his company transferred him to another small town similar to Levelland where I was born. In this town I started school and attended classes through several years.

Some years ago, my wife and I traveled from our home in the west to the town of my birth. My father, now up in years and himself retired and living in Colorado, asked me if I would stop at the gravesite of his parents and take a picture of their headstone. This I did. At this time, I observed there was enough space for the rest of the family to be placed there.

I grew up singing *"Farther Along."* This hymn is in my earliest memories. Sometime in my pre-teen years, my mother heard me singing this song. She asked me if I remembered learning it. When I replied "No," she told me my grandfather sang it to me as he rocked me most evenings near the pot-bellied stove just before bedtime.

I am certain that the rattlesnake I saw my grandfather kill wasn't the first that he had ever killed. But, more than that, I am also certain it was his last.

Fence Posts And Iceboxes

In the early settlement days of the Llano Estacado in the state of Texas, cedar fence posts and iceboxes played an important part. The fence posts allowed the farmers to protect their land from the roving cattle. The iceboxes allowed milk, eggs and such to be stored and kept fresh for the family diet. Both posts and ice for the iceboxes had to be "imported." Both were brought in by railway to support the settlement of great areas of the southwest by the farmers or "squatters" as some were called by some ranchers. For even in the early stages of the incursion of the rails over the land the railway investors knew that the return on their investments lay mostly on the goods the farmers would both use and produce, and not the occasional shipment of beef cattle to market.

The iceboxes were small cabinets about waist high, made mostly of wood; the nicer ones were varnished with brass fastenings and the interior lined with copper. The cheaper ones had iron fastenings, painted exteriors and were lined with galvanized tin. The ice was regularly furnished by a deliveryman in fifty or one hundred pound blocks. Regularly, that is, assuming you didn't live too far away from town. The frequency of his visits depended on the time of year, naturally more often during the warmer months. The ice cost, as I seem to recall, about five cents for 100 pounds. As the ice melted, the water drained into a hidden pan underneath the cabinet, which had to be emptied regularly, or it would run over onto the floor.

The cedar fence posts were about six feet long, three to four inches thick, mostly straight, and covered with their natural stringy bark. The posts were about four feet above ground and strung with four or five strands of barbed wire. The bark not only protected the wood from bugs and weather, it made a really pungent smoke when slightly shredded, rolled in paper and used as a substitute for tobacco as most youngsters did, myself included.

When I was very young, we had an icebox in the farm house I was born in, and most of our farm had cedar fence posts. Most every family was living under the same conditions as we were. Most people still used horses for their transportation and plow pulling…only no one had plowed much lately, as there had been no rain for several years. It was so dry, even weeds couldn't grow.

Years later, when I was in my early teens, my father told me a story that occurred a few years before I was born. Folks were then living much under the conditions I have described. My father has never told me very much about those early years. Some of those years were painful unto the day of his death for him to talk about. But all he told me I believe to be the honest truth. When he told me the sun was going to come up, the sun came up. When he told me the sun was going to set, it set. When he told me I was going to get a licking, I got a licking. So, you see I never had any reason to doubt his word.

Now for the story: Two families lived on adjacent parcels of farmland; both were fenced with cedar fence posts with the aforementioned barbed wire strung on the posts. The two neighbor men, Tull and Wayman, (aliases) met one day, both on horseback at their common fence line. Being neighbors and fair friends, they stopped to talk for a while, mostly about the weather. When it was going to rain, and how much. That's not a guess on my part having been around farmers and ranchers all my life. When either of the two get together, the first sentences spoke concern the weather. Guaranteed. Next comes the family news. In this case, that's where the trouble all started.

Tull commented on Wayman's wife, something not too complimentary, I reckon. Anyhow, Wayman replied with "Tull's wife was about as attractive as a crooked cedar fence post with the bark all peeling off."

Needless to say, Tull did not take kindly to Wayman's remark concerning his wife's beauty; over the years Tull had a few doubts himself, and nobody likes to be reminded of an unpleasant truth. So, in order to save face, Tull pulled his saddle rifle, normally used for coyotes, and shot Wayman. I guess you could say he "blew him out of the saddle" because Wayman fell off his horse on the far side and landed in the dry sand. Seeing that Wayman didn't appear to even try to get up, Tull put "done" to the affair in his mind and rode off.

Later that night after supper had been over a while, Tull heard a car sort of belch and cough, stopping in front of his place. Tull, knowing the only car around was a Model T Ford that belonged to the county for the sheriff's use, went to the open front door to see what was up. Naturally the sheriff asked Tull to step out for a talk. By this time, Tull had pretty well figured out why the visit, but he didn't say anything much as he stepped out and off the front porch.

The sheriff was never known to beat around any bushes. So he told Tull even though Wayman was a newcomer and not particularly well liked; it would be best if he, Tull, packed up and left the country even if just for a while. Or else, he might find himself on the short end of a rope under the gin pole of the local stable barn. Needless to say, as soon as Sheriff Cox left, Tull went into the house, packed his tote bag, kissed his wife and two kids good-bye. He then went out to the barn, saddled his bay horse and rode away.

A few weeks later Tull wound up working on a ranch near Lusk, Wyoming. After a few more weeks had passed, he decided he would use a phony name and write his sister in Slaton, Texas. He wrote to ask her to tell his wife where he was and for her to go to Slaton and wait for another letter; he would send her the directions on where she and the two kids could meet him. It was several weeks later before he received a reply; it was from his sister, and not at all what he expected. His sister had delayed her reply as long as she could, because half the news was bad and half good. The bad part was that Tull's wife and kids had ran off to Wichita Falls…with the iceman. The good half was that the farmer Wayman wasn't mad at him anymore for trying to kill him. He still did miss his left ear occasionally; mostly when he looked in the mirror to shave or comb his hair. But, as said, Wayman was willing to forget how he lost his ear.

Eventually it rained. It had been almost ten years between decent rains back then. On the "Staked Plains" in the state of Texas, the sand sprouted grass, the farmers plowed and planted, and grew some pretty fair cotton for the few more years remaining for dry land farming. Tull came back to his farm bringing a new wife and child, paid the taxes up on the land and started farming again. Now, my father told me as far as he knew, Tull never had to shoot anybody after that. I guess his new wife must have been prettier than a crooked cedar fence post with the bark all peeling off…or maybe his reputation for his shooting ability and short temper was better known.

PART 2

The Top Of The Hill

Quilt Of Many Dresses

Before I write about the quilt, you should know something about the lady who quilted it. Her name was Mary Ola Conatser. She was my grandmother, my mother's mother. She was the head and heart of the family. You might, in one way or another, identify with something within this story in your own family.

My grandfather, Charley J. Conatser, his wife and six children moved to Hockley County from Ralls somewhere around 1924. He was a farmer there in Ralls and continued farming for years here in Levelland. The family helped start the Austin Street Church of Christ in those early hard years.

My grandmother had a very strong personality. This, over the years, resulted in her having the most influence in family matters than any other individual of the large clan. I knew long before it was her time to go to her heavenly reward that the extremely close cohesion of our family was a direct result of her concern for the family's situation. This earlier opinion came back into my mind as I and five other grandsons bore her coffin through the church doors to the waiting hearse.

Very soon after she died, the family inadvertently began a gradual separation and isolation that was pretty complete in a very short span of months; less than a year. The individual members each went their own way and turned their backs on the other family members. No disagreements, no problem. Just no more glue.

Most of the family members I have seen little or none of in the last almost forty years. That is a sad statement to make. However, what is truly sad on my part, I really don't seem to care all that much. No more glue.

My grandfather and grandmother started off life just about as poor as most everyone else was during the era they were all born into and grew up in. The years of their time together, they both lived very full and satisfying lives. They raised three boys and two girls into responsible adulthood; one male child, Edwin Earl, died of diabetic complications at the age of ten in the winter of the year 1932.

Right after the Second World War, my grandfather stopped active farming and became a commodities dealer. He was very successful in buying and selling cotton and some pinto beans. This success in the world of business enabled him to purchase two parcels of good farmland. Each consisted of one section (640 acres) with mineral rights included. Both these farms were leased to good hardworking families. A few years later oil was discovered and a half dozen wells were developed on the parcels.

No longer poor, but still careful with money, he decided to purchase a couple of rent houses and build a couple more. One extravagance he did succumb to was to initiate routine purchases of two new two-door Ford sedans just about every other year. Both black. One for her, one for him. As far as any of us knew at the time, he never even asked our grandmother if she wanted a car or even what kind or color. But, she did use each of her cars in their turn. Some.

My grandfather died at the age of eighty-three in 1969. I was unable to attend the funeral; I was living in California and work prevented my traveling to Texas at that time. I have been told that shortly after his funeral, our grandmother stopped in at the local Buick dealership and traded both black Fords for a new tan 4-door Buick. A day or so later, a dealer representative came out to the house and picked up the other Ford car.

She enjoyed a few more new Buick sedans (none black) in the following six years until the summer of 1975 when we six male grandchildren carried her out of the Austin Street Church to the hearse. She died twelve days short of her eighty-seventh birthday.

Her funeral was 'standing room only'. People were even standing should-to-shoulder in the vestibule. A path was opened for us pallbearers as we walked down the aisle and exited the church carrying her in her coffin.

In the early lean years of their life together, my grandmother made most of her family's clothes as well as her own from necessity as did most other women of that era did. However, she kept this practice of making her own dresses as time went by and the years grew in number. As she retired each of her worn dresses, she cut swatches out of each and kept them. As years went by, the dress swatches accumulated and eventually she had enough to make a quilt. Most of the women back then would make quilts and give them to their children or grandchildren. Maybe even a quilt or two for an old close friend. However, this one quilt Grandmother made from swatches of her dresses she kept as her own. For memories' sake, I guess. For whatever reason, she kept this one quilt. My mother acquired the quilt when my grandmother's personal property was divided among her children a few weeks after her funeral.

A few years after my grandmother's funeral, my wife and I took a trip to my parents' home in Colorado for a two-week visit. Near the end of our visit, my mother mentioned the quilt and told me the story of its creation. I recalled having heard of the quilt years before. She went on, telling me she really didn't know what she should do with it. Lately, she has been trying to find homes for her old family pictures and other keepsakes. She asked if I would like to have the quilt. I told her I certainly would. On our return home, the quilt came with us.

A few years ago, I took the quilt out of its case. I spread it out on the divan and admired it. The quilt had a smell of new cotton. It was obvious to me it had never been used.

I stood over the quilt and admired it. I started counting patterns. I counted thirty-one different patterns of cloth, held together by thousands of neat tiny stitches. At the rate of retiring two or three dresses each year—a high figure—it would appear the saving for the quilt spanned near to fifteen years.

Grandmother, I thank you for the quilt even in the round-about-way I received it. When I use it, I will think of you and the swatches, needles, thread, love, and hours it took to create. All those tiny stitches. It will keep me and mine warm during cold winter nights. Now, right here in Levelland. Where the quilt and I belong. Where we both started out. Thank, you, Grandmother.

Remembering Frank

Quite often when I see a bird flare in early morning flight or a fish break water capturing a flying creature on a still evening, I think of my old friend Frank. He has been away scouting fairer meadows for seventeen years come this fall.

Frank was an Irishman by heritage. He was a man with Integrity; he believed in a day's work for a day's pay. Frank tended to overlook most people's shortcomings; seeing only their good qualities.

We met one cold winter morning on dayshift at a power plant where we were employed. He worked in the mechanical maintenance department; I was assigned to the operations section.

At first, it seemed we were certain to be only tolerant of each other.

This occasion when I first met Frank was sort of stormy. He was using high pressure water to wash the ferric oxide from the interior of two mud drums on a boiler we had taken out of service for scheduled overhaul. The water and loosened sludge was cascading down through the deck grating that framed each boiler deck elevation level walkway. This falling water was contaminating the uncovered barrels of chemical used for boiler water treatment.

I was a recent transferee into the operations department from the substation construction section and was not thoroughly aware of everything that was to occur that first day of boiler overhaul. I should have realized exactly what was to take place and had the boiler water chemical barrels covered with plastic. This would have prevented contamination of the chemicals by the dirty water splashing down from upstairs during the use of the high pressure wash water. All I thought of doing when I discovered water falling down into the chemical storage area was to yell upstairs for whomever to stop spraying water around.

Pretty soon, having heard my yells, Frank came down to the area where I was. As soon as he saw what had happened, he started chewing me out for being derelict in my duties.

I (being young, dumb, and redheaded) did not take kindly to Frank's chastisement of me. At the time, I figured it was solely his fault. Later, I came to realize it was some of both our fault. He should have checked that morning before he started spraying water around; I should have checked the area myself on starting my shift.

Well, as time went by we stayed out of each other's way. This was fairly easy for me as I was a shift worker; Frank normally worked straight days except for overhaul periods.

One dayshift morning I was walking around the boiler area and piping, looking for leaks or any other problem. I came upon Frank working alone. He was trying to lift some very heavy galvanized steel deck grating without too much success. He needed to get it out of his way so he could repack a small leaking steam valve on an instrument sensing supply line. Without saying anything, I grabbed hold of the grating and helped lift and move it out of the way. When we had finished, Frank looked at me, grinned, and said his thanks. From that day on we became very close friends.

When I would be working dayshift and have my routine work completed, I would look up Frank and he would give me instruction on the repair job he was doing at that time. Later on, as days and time passed by, he would hand me his tools and watch me make the needed repairs.

On time off, we started fishing together on the nearby riverbank.

He invited me to go inland bird hunting one season. These activities became habits and continued for years.

One day Frank asked me if I would like to join a fishing and hunting club he belonged to. As I sort of looked doubtful about the situation and thinking about the expense, Frank continued talking to me about joining. He knew I was trying to raise a family and didn't have a whole lot of extra money, he pointed out that the initiation fee and the monthly dues were very reasonable and that he would pay the first year's dues for me. Then, if I liked the club, I could pay him back. If I didn't like the club, I could just quit and I would be out no expense.

Well, as it turned out, I had to pay him back the first year's dues. I stayed a member of the club for years, even after I had moved to Wyoming.

Frank was almost fifteen years older than me. He and his wife never had any children. Probably because of this, Frank became more than just a good friend. He and I became very close. When my family was torn apart by divorce, he quietly helped to keep me on a sensible new path. By the time I finally remarried, he became a part of our family. He had retired from his job of thirty five years, and was able to spend more time with me, as I was still working shift with time off in the middle of the week.

I remember well the last time we were together. I had resigned my job in California in order to take a higher-paying job in Wyoming that was also a promotion.

My wife Nancy and I had a "clean out the refrigerator-freezer" dinner; Frank and a few other close friends were there. It was at that dinner my wife found I was really telling the truth about once having to teach my German Shorthair dog to swim (The Dog Who Couldn't Paddle). Nancy told Frank the story, thinking it would bring a good laugh all the way around the dinner table. Frank informed her he had done the same.

After we had moved to Wyoming Frank and I would exchange occasional letters and share an occasional telephone call.

He hunted every year on a ranch in Colorado for deer and elk. The ranch belonged to Frank's distant kin; he had hunted there each season for many years. After we moved to Wyoming, he had planned on his next trip to come up north and visit us on his way back home. In the fall of 1980, we received a post card from him saying he was in Colorado hunting and would see us on the way home. As it turned out, it never happened.

That was the last communication I had from Frank. No more telephone calls, no letters. I did not realize this until the end of that year.

On New Year's Day, 1981, I was talking to a friend of mine in California on the telephone. He had called to tell me that Frank had a heart attack on that last hunting trip to Hayden; that he had not survived it. His hunting party went looking for him in the evening as he had not returned to camp. They found him, sitting at the base of a fir tree, his rifle across his lap. He had apparently sat down to look out over the whole beautiful valley of the ranch stretched out in front of him. Knowing Frank as I did, if he had a choice in the location and timing of his death, he would have had it exactly as it had happened.

All these years later, I have finally completed this long overdue tribute to my dear old friend. I had started it several years ago. For some reason I stopped working on it. I guess it was that I really didn't feel that I knew the whole story. That is, until last night.

Last night I had decided to clean out my filing cabinet; to throw away the junk and outdated material.

To my surprise, in my letters' file, I found the last communication Frank had sent to us. From the date on the postmark, I realized he had written and sent it a day or two before he died. Somehow I had neglected to answer it; the card had lain hidden in the bottom of the file where I had placed it years before. It had survived the space of almost seventeen years of time and three household moves.

The postcard begins:

> *My dearest friends: I'm so close yet so far. I'll write you a letter when I get home & explain everything. I blew it on elk but tomorrow deer season opens, no problem there. Guess you gave me up but have faith good friends never part I assure you. We love you both very much. Got lots of news when I write. I came by bus here to the ranch; as I have for 17 yrs. If I get a chance here I'll phone, might be collect tho, ok? My love, (s)Frank.*

Frank, my dear old friend. I hope every day is spring for you with a gentle warm breeze at your back. I hope the path you walk as you hunt rises to meet your feet. I hope the birds rise and flare for you as you crest the hill. I hope your new dog can swim.

Harry Noonan's Golf Clubs

Poor Harry. I had not thought of him in years until a few days ago, God rest his soul. In fact, I guess I sort of pushed him back in a corner of my mind not too long after I left home. It wasn't that I didn't like him. On the contrary. I liked Harry pretty well. It was just that he was one of my father's friends and a lot older than me, so we didn't exactly travel in the same circles, as the saying goes.

Bringing Harry out of my mind's corner was sort of a freak twist of fate. I was sitting in my favorite chair in my favorite room watching the evening television news in my favorite house. I usually do not pay too much attention to the sports portion of news programs. Maybe I'll watch the coverage if it's Super Bowl time or the World Series.

This night, however, for whatever reason or other, I was sort of idling through the sports commentary when a picture of an American pro golfer filled the screen. He was attempting to sink a put on a green at a golf course located somewhere in the British Isles. He had started falling over on his face just after the stroke of his putter sent the ball toward the cup. Somehow he lost his grip on the putter, and it went sailing off toward the cup sort of following the path of the ball. Just as the ball rimmed the far side of the cup, the putter came to earth, stuck the ball and sent it sailing away. The golfer finished his fall, almost flat on his face. Everyone visibly present practically collapsed laughing. Even the unfortunate puttee as soon as he was able to sit up.

As I mentioned, I was sitting, so I just laughed wholeheartedly. And, these days, there isn't a heck of a lot on the news to laugh at. The next thing on the screen was a commercial, so I 'muted' it out, still thinking about what I had just seen. All of a sudden, Harry Noonan was standing there, right in front of me. He was looking away in the direction of the ball he had just hit off the tee on a sand-green golf course near Denver City, Texas. In time, somewhere around 1952.

Harry was, for several years, the manager of the Chamber of commerce in my home town. By blood, he was an Irishman, fair skinned and almost but not quite, red-headed. And, blessed with some freckles. I'm not sure that you could call his temperament Irish, but he had plenty. Normally, Harry was a very gentle person, very friendly and well liked by all who know him. But he did have a temper. Especially when it came to his inability to master the game of golf.

There are some people in this old world who should never be allowed to get near a set of golf clubs, much less use them. Harry Noonan was one of these.

The Scotsman who invented the game of golf should have seen to it when he passed out the clubs and balls that Harry was busy shoveling the stables or some other well served activity.

Somewhere, somehow, someway Harry discovered golf. He bought a fine set of clubs. He bought good balls. A very nice two-wheeled cart held his expensive leather golf bag containing the clubs, balls, tees and a hand towel to make certain his hands were clean and dry for perfect grip on the leather handle of the clubs. For that era, Harry was as well outfitted as any other avid golfer; better than most. A really good set of signature clubs that, at that time, cost in the neighborhood of four hundred dollars. Naturally, Harry had the best clubs he could afford. Signature clubs of another albeit famous Texan: Ben Hogan.

During most of the years I knew Harry, I worked in a local pharmacy. The old fashioned kind, a combination drug store and soda fountain. I was both janitor and part-time soda jerk. I knew Harry pretty well (or so I thought) seeing him almost daily, usually serving him coffee with the other gentlemen who frequented the store each morning at coffee time. As I mentioned, I thought I knew him well. But that was before I saw him on a golf course for the first time. Occasionally when I wasn't working at the drugstore, I would accompany my father and a few other gentlemen to the golf course where I would caddy for my father.

Right after the Second World War, golf became pretty popular in the small towns around my part of the country. At that time, golf courses were pretty scarce and pretty crowded. The few Sundays my dad invited me to go with them, I would caddy for him and he would pay me a quarter-dollar for the privilege. I went as often as I was asked and able to go. I could not go on weekdays after school as I worked evenings and Saturdays at the drugstore. When I could, I really enjoyed going. However, I never became a golf addict. It was too rich for my financial situation then and now.

The first time I went that Harry was one of the group of four was a beautiful early spring morning. I can remember seeing each breath I exhaled. As we arrived at the golf course the sun had just started its morning climb in a crystal blue sky.

After two or three uneventful holes had been played by, Harry was up at the next tee. This next I remember well due to the disastrous result of Harry's drive. I had not seen this previously as I had never been along when Harry made the trip. Harry hit a terrible slice. It went across the gravel road that bordered that side of the fairway rough. Harry stated his displeasure with his drive in language a sailor could learn from. Even now, most boys at the age I was then have a remarkable four letter word vocabulary. Harry used words I defined only years later. Then he swung his driver around again and let it go; successfully aimed at the nearest tree. The flying club hit the tree so perfectly and so hard it actually bent the club in the shafts' middle.

I stood there, totally amazed and sort of embarrassed for Harry. Not at the language; at the result of the violent swing of the golf club.

Kids lose their tempers and sometimes try to flatten each other's nose in mutual rage. But grown-ups never express their loss of temper in such a violent fashion as I had just witnessed. Well, almost never.

One trip I accompanied the golfing foursome (including Harry) to a community course near Lamesa. It had a fairly shallow lake in the fairway on the approach to the green. The center of the lake was somewhat narrow and a wooden footbridge allowed access to the remaining yards of the approach to the green.

You guessed it. Harry teed up his ball and promptly hit it just about in the center left of the lake. His 'club shot' was even better. The club landed exactly on top of the ball resting in the mud on the shallow lake's bottom. Reason I knew the lake was shallow? One of the members of the group waded in and rescued Harry's club. But not the ball. I guess it disappeared in the mud.

Over those few years, I spent quite a few Sundays on the golf course with Harry as a member of the foursome. I saw him destroy a club almost every time.

I am sure you have guessed by now that Harry was not a good golfer. In fact, you could say he was a really lousy golfer. Off the course, he was a perfectly normal rational, sober and well liked Irish member of society in our town.

Harry, where ever you are now, I hope there are no golf courses. Or else, that maybe you finally learned to play without feeling the need to lose your temper. Or if all else has failed, maybe the course you are now playing on doesn't have any trees. Or lakes.

The Slow Burn

In my observation over the years it has become apparent to me that, concerning redheaded people, there are two kinds. One kind of redhead has the ability to flare up in instant anger when pushed. This type of redhead, the least common, is also known as having extremely short fuses.

They have the ability to get mad at the drop of a hat over…what may seem to other people…any matter of little consequence. But, after the initial explosion, they cool off fairly quickly. Then there is my kind with a much different temperament. The slow-burn type. It takes us…the slow burn type…forever to get mad. When us slow-burn people finally get mad, people had better stay out of earshot and clod-throwing distance. Of course, both kinds of redheads have freckles. Some, more than others. That's the way you can tell if the redhair is real or not. Freckles. The more the freckles, the realer the redhead.

There is a distinct advantage in being an instant anger redhead. After some people discover you are an instant anger type, they mostly leave you alone. But…when some people discover you are a slow burn type, they like to see just how far they can push you before you finally light up like a Roman Candle.

Burt, (an alias) a boy I went to school with, was one of those temper pusher people types. Only, to his poor judgment and bad luck, he always pushed me too far and was not able to gain any safe distance before the light-up occurred.

This pushing of me seemed to start when we were in the seventh grade. During daily school recess we boys would play tackle football on the bare dirt playground. Every day, most of us wore t-shirts and Levis. That was back when Levis cost about three dollars each, were made of heavy duck cloth and lasted practically forever.

The dirt playground was due to economics. All West Texas schools were poor and did not have the money back then for irrigated grass playgrounds. This made no difference to us; we had never known or played on anything else.

Burt and I were about the smallest boys in the class and about the same size. I guess we each weighed about seventy-five pounds dressed for a Texas Norther and dripping wet.

One day at recess we were opposite each other on the scrimmage line. He told he was going to clean my plow. Waiting for the center to snap the ball gave my slow burn just enough time to get going. When Burt charged with his right arm cocked, I ducked and whopped him just in front of his left ear. He immediately put both hands over his face and started howling. A couple of boys took a look at him and suddenly started running, dragging him to the school building. Play resumed half-heartedly. Soon the two boys came back without Burt; they told us the coach had taken Burt to the doctor; that I had knocked his eye out of its socket.

Right about now, I am soaking wet with sweat. I didn't really believe them, but then I could not know for sure. I had never heard of anything so impossible; getting your eyeball knocked out.

After a while, trouble came for me with the arrival of a student aide with the message I was to report to the coaches' office.

On arrival, I found Burt sitting and sniffling with his left eye bandaged up. The coach was sitting also, but he was slapping a wooden paddle into the palm of his hand. He told us that Burt and I were going to trade lickings as punishment for fighting. I don't remember now who was the recipient of the first paddle stroke; but we traded ten very gentle swats. The disgusted coach then took the paddle and gave each of us ten very substantial whacks and then threw us both out of his office. Burt and I were too busy crying to exchange any conversation; we simply went to the next class.

Things were quiet between Burt and me for the rest of that school year. However, at the start of the next school year, Burt informed me he was going to get even one of these days. Day after day went by; nothing happened except he would occasionally remind me of his promise. Me? I learned to bite my fingernails in anticipation.

The fateful day finally came. I realized this as soon as I left the school grounds on the way home. Burt was behind me; he lived in the other direction from the school grounds. Finally he caught up to me, taunting me and trying to knock my books out from under my right arm. Finally I slow burned enough to turn around and hit him half dozen times so fast he didn't have time to react except to cover his nose with his hands. It had started bleeding. He turned round and left. I continued on my way home, sniffling as I went. Burt had not laid a hand on me.

This exact same situation occurred once every school year through our high school years until we became seniors. Burt would push, we would fight, we would part. Him with either a bloody nose or back eye. Me? He never once laid a hand on me. Each time I sniffled the rest of the way home.

During the summer before our senior year, I heard that Burt and his family moved away. I did not believe it; it seemed too good to be true. They had lived on a farm during the time of our years of school we spent together. I knew where it was but I wasn't going to go out there to check and find out if the rumor of the family moving was true. When it was time for school year registration, Burt did not show up to register. I was elated beyond all normal reason.

Over the years, I gradually forgot about Burt. The close-contact people I met over the years recognized the fact that I was a redhead and of unknown temperament and nobody seemed to want to test me. I never felt neglected in the least.

Forty years later, our graduating class had a customary five-year celebration and reunion. This included attendance at the Friday night homecoming football game. Sitting there in our class' designated area of the bleachers, I realized Burt was sitting just down and over from me in the next row. He now appeared to be quite a bit bigger than I.

At half-time intermission we met and shook hands down near the hotdog stand. As we stood in the line progressing to the stand, we talked for a few minutes about our separate lives. Finally Burt asked did I remember he and I used to have a fist fight every year? I told him I did; that I'd always regretted it. I could never come up with a good reason why we did it. Burt laughed and opined it must have been because he and I were the smallest in our class of sixteen boys.

After a meaningful pause, Burt looked at me and grinned, "If we had never fought, we probably could have been the best of friends."

What did I say? Nothing. Absolutely nothing. I just grinned.

The Golden Key

It was a hot summer, the one between our junior and senior high school years. Charles and I worked full-time at the new drive-in movie named the Eagle after our school mascot. Our town was small, but the drive-in movie craze was going full tilt, so it was usually well attended. This was, of course, before the magic of television had hit the small towns of South Plains, Texas.

During the daytime, we would get the shipping cans of films from the delivery point at the indoor theater in town, take them out to the drive-in, patch in the advertising trailers, the news reel, and the comedy. After we finished that chore, we would clean the lot of paper and whatever leavings there were from the night before; clean the restrooms and snack bar, then restock the goodies for the snack bar. After that, our time was our own until showtime. Of course, on the days we had a repeat showing, we had no film patching to do, which gave us more free time. This small amount of extra free time is what eventually got one of us into a very embarrassing situation.

Charles's financial circumstances were not as fortunate as mine. I had an old crate of a car that I dearly loved. However, it looked like its better days would have been in the junkyard. Charles had managed to buy a red Cushman motor scooter in pretty fair shape. He could cover many more miles (and did) on his scooter than I could in my car even though gasoline was only nineteen cents a gallon at that time. This minor fact of the cheap price of gasoline also contributed to the very embarrassing situation one of us got himself into.

Referring now to the title of this narrative, "The Golden Key," a dentist had, at long last, moved into town. Heretofore, the town had a tooth doctor that visited only on Wednesdays. Well, it could have been on Thursdays; I really don't remember. The important thing was the town finally had its own permanent, full-time dentist. Actually, we younguns didn't really care— except for Charles. He came to really care, and this situation contributed to the embarrassing situation. The dentist brought with him a wife who was the spitting image of the movie star Susan Hayward. And, I mean SPITTING IMAGE in real capital letters. Since both Charles and I worked in the "film industry" we had very accurate knowledge as to what Susan Hayward looked like even though our vision of her was mostly in black and white film clips. And this lady was a perfect double for Miss Hayward.

But the really magic thing about the dentist's wife was not only that she was beautiful in face and observable physique. Her name was Key, and to advertise this fact of her name, she wore a small golden key on a delicate chain around her neck. This key was in the exact same shape of the old-fashioned skeleton keys in use in most houses at that time, only this neck-chain key was about an inch long.

Key was a lady about town. The couple had no children, so she was often seen driving around in a very stylish new black Buick: the hardtop model with red leather upholstery. I forget the model name, but I am sure it was the top-of-the-line. I can still see her in that car, driving around town. She was beautiful, so was the car. Now I realize she dressed for the car, but in my younger years I didn't realize people had such wiles. I guess maybe all of us young, soon-to-be hot-blooded boys fell in love with her. I know I did. But none so desperately as Charles.

Things progressed to the point that Charles would follow Key around town when he happened to discover her out and about. For all I know, he might have staked out her house in his free time, waiting for her to come out and drive off so he could follow her. At any rate, it was soon obvious to most of the townspeople that wherever Key went, Charles was to be seen following her and at not too great a distance. That is, it was obvious to those people who were observant enough to notice things like that. It really was not a laughing matter, though I guess most observers smiled at the sight and remembered their own similar in-the-springtime-of-life actions. Probably

Key knew of Charles's passion of following her. I do not see how she could not have known.

The embarrassing situation occurred one hot afternoon. At this point in time, I cannot remember exactly how it came about, but Charles and I left the indoor theater, him on his scooter and me following in my car. He was taking the scooter home, I was to follow, and then he and I were going out to the drive-in theater located a couple miles south of town. All of a sudden he veered from the usual route he took home. Pretty soon, I saw why. He had seen the object of his unrequited love in her car and had immediately taken off after her in discrete desperate pursuit. I followed, somewhat unhappily.

After a short journey, she came to the only traffic light in town, which changed to red as she approached it. Now, I don't know whether the sun was in Charles's eyes (we were all facing west into the lowering afternoon sun) or whether he failed to realize she had stopped. For whatever cause he ran into her back bumper. Now that was bad enough, but the embarrassing situation immediately got more embarrassing. Charles parted company with the motor scooter and sort of slid over and across the top of the black Buick and came to rest on the hood of the car, looking directly into Key's eyes. Me, I had slowed to a stop, safely.

There is no way I can imagine myself recovering from an incident of this sort short of committing suicide. Key leaned out her open window and asked Charles if he was all right or something similar. I was too far away to hear. At any rate, whatever conversation occurred came to a mutually satisfying conclusion, for Charles got off the hood of the black Buick and walked toward the scooter while Key drove on. The scooter did not appear to be hurt much; Charles restarted it, sat down on the seat, and continued on his way. I looked over to the nearby gasoline service station and to my horror saw several people standing there having—I guess—seen the whole thing. They were just standing there, looking.

Knowing Charles as well as I did, I never, ever, said anything to him about the embarrassing incident, nor did he ever mention it. I never mentioned it to anyone even years later. Not until now.

Another thing I know for sure: he never, ever followed the Golden Key again, and I know now he will never read this.

I never laughed over the incident. Not once. Not even now.

Addendum (November 4, 2014, Levelland, Texas):

Just the other day, I called my friend William, who still lives in my old hometown with his wife of almost forty-five years. I do this quite often to catch up-to-date news of our classmates. William gave me the news I hungered for; he told me that Charles had died earlier in the year from the effects caused by cancer of the spine. William hesitated as he told me this; he knew that during our younger years, Charles and I were very close. We continued and talked some about how we hated to hear of the death of another of our classmates. So far, six of our family—and we are family—have come to the end of their journey. Too many, far too soon.

William knew at this point in time that over the years I had written many short stories mostly about events that occurred growing up. He had read most of them. Just before we ended the telephone conversation, I told him some of the story I would soon write, "The Golden Key." The Golden Key that shines no more.

The Black Plume Of Smoke

Most of the time I try to write about happy or funny things I remember from my younger years. Many people tend to store tragic or bad things in the darkness of their minds, stuffed in a corner. Rarely ever to be examined in full memory again. In that respect, I am no different. I do not like to remember the tragic things that have happened in my life either to me or those closest to me.

Once in a while, odd things happen that trigger a recollection and I recall an event from this dark corner. One such thing happened to me recently bringing a very sad memory back to the light of day. I am thankful that at the time that I was only a bystander; that it was not a personal happening to me or my family in my own early years.

It was early spring; a beautiful time of year in the country of my youth. The school year was beginning to wind down. We were freshmen; back then the first year of high school. It was early in the morning and we were all attending the first class of the day when we heard the town's fire siren wailing over the trees and housetops.

In a town of about fifteen hundred people, the sound of the fire siren is of concern to everyone, even to the smallest child. The town being so small, there was really no place you could be, either indoors or out and not hear the dreaded mournful ominous wail of the alarm.

Most all of the people able to respond to the location of the trouble would get there in any manner they could: By car, bike, or walking. The people who responded all those years ago were not there to see a tragedy, they were there to help in any way they could. Even to the point of placing themselves in harm's way. For back in that day and time, one family's tragedy was every families' that lived in the town.

And, when the good things happened: Everyone celebrated. Every knowing individual in the town took everything personal; be it bad or good.

That's why, when we heard the fire siren, we all abandoned class to get outside to scan the horizon for smoke, so that we might know which direction and how far the fire was; sometimes we might even be able to tell if it was a building or brush fire.

You could see the black smoke for this fire rising for a mile, it seemed, straight up in the cool, clear early spring air.

This time we could tell what it was. My friend Gene and I were standing there on the western edge of the school grounds, looking north at the column of smoke rising high into the clear blue spring sky. The smoke was as black as any you ever saw. Both of us knew instantly what it was; Gene's house. There were no other buildings in that direction for many miles. His house was at the end of that stretch of road, one mile away. Right at the end of the paved section, where the road made a hard turn to the west; where the pavement ended and the road changed to fairly smooth gravel going on for miles.

Gene looked at me, his brown eyes appearing huge and scared. I'm sure my look at him in return was scared also. We both knew his mother was alone out there with two-maybe three small children.

Gene's father was a drunk and seldom home. Gene's father was not an alcoholic—he was a drunk. He went out of his way to stay drunk. In that one thing he was really successful. Seldom ever did anyone see him sober. On the rare occasion when he was sober, he was mean. He would beat his wife for whiskey money. Or take whatever meager amount of money away from any of his children who had been able to find an occasional odd job.

The family's major source of income was from the mother's well-known ability as a seamstress. Usually her sewing or ironing was paid for with groceries or by paying a bill that was owed. Most people in town paid for the family's work efforts in ways other than cash if possible.

There were thirteen individuals in this family; Eleven of them children, living in that one room tarpaper covered shack at the end of the paved part of that road. I had seen the inside once. The beds were bunk made of two-by-fours nailed into the wall studs, two bunks high on each wall that had room. There was a table in the center of the room with benches around it instead of chairs. As I recall, all these years later, that was the extent of the furnishings for the house.

There was no electricity for the house even though the power lines bordered the road in front. The family could not have afforded to pay the monthly bill. A coal-oil stove was used both for cooking and heat; coal oil lanterns gave light. The bathroom was a wooden Chic Sales outhouse some ways out behind the house.

Regardless of what impression you might have formed of the situation, all Gene's school age brothers and sisters appeared each day scrubbed so clean their skin glowed. Their clothes were not the best in fashion, but they were clean, patched and no buttons were missing. The buttons might not all match, but they were there.

Gene's mother also required regular church attendance of all the children, every single one of them, every church meeting. Those children obeyed their mother without hesitation or question.

The family morale was high in spite of these terrible situations.

Gene took off on a run, heading toward the fire. I followed, he in the lead, both of us running as fast as we ever had. About a half-mile down the road, the fire truck passed us, siren screaming. Then, car after car. Nobody stopped for Gene or me; we just kept on running.

By the time we got there the house was gone. There was nothing left but the charred coal-oil stove sitting crookedly on the ground in the ashes with a few embers still glowing. Gene's mother and young sibling were standing by the fire truck. All of them were crying. Maybe Gene was crying too. I couldn't look at him because I remember I was crying. I could not believe how fast the house had burned.

There is an old saying that goes something like this: "There is little bad that happens that does not bring some good." Well, in this case it was certainly true. The town owned a small house that was usually occupied by a city employee and family. At the time of this tragedy, this house happened to be vacant. So the town fathers moved the family in. Everyone in town donated clothes, furniture or whatever they could to the destitute family. In several ways, the family actually was better off than before. They no longer had to walk to town; they were in it. It also helped the mother with the picking up and delivery of the sewing and ironing she did for the various townspeople.

The town fathers told the drunken father to sober up or they would run him out of town. Today this would be just about as illegal a threat as you could dream up. But back then it only seemed fair and right.

So the old man stayed sober for a couple of weeks. Then, one last time, he 'fell off his wagon' and got all boozed up, beat his wife and in trying to leave, somehow drove a borrowed jalopy into the front porch. The next day, the old man was gone. I never saw him after that; neither did anyone else, at least to tell about it. And, nobody seemed to tell.

A few good peaceful years later, Gene graduated from high school, enlisted in and made a career in the Air Force, earning promotion to captain. His older brother graduated from a seminary college and became a Methodist minister. I have no idea what happened to the rest of the younger children. I am sure in my heart they all did well.

After Gene went into the Air Force he gave financial assistance to his mother and younger siblings still at home. This helped his mother to re-open an abandoned dry-cleaning establishment. She also continued to do clothing alterations and sewing until her death a few years later. She lived and dealt with life as best she could, a decent Christian woman. It is rare today to find a family strive so hard to be self-sufficient. Back then it was obvious to us: The mother was the driving force. But the children were willing to be driven.

A few years ago I heard from a former classmate and mutual friend, Ted. He had found that Gene completed his career in the Air Force, and had become a charter pilot, working in various parts of the country. Ted had learned that Gene was going to be near Houston for a few days flying charter. Ted called the charter's airport office to try arrange to see him but was unable to make contact.

As far as I know, Gene has never returned to our home town for a visit after our high school graduation or attended any of our five-year class reunions. I guess maybe in these later times, Gene might feel sort of embarrassed about the miserable living conditions of his younger years. Thinking about it, if that truly is the reason he hasn't returned, I guess maybe I might feel that same way too.

Sometimes, when I allow myself, I can recall clearly from the darkness of my mind that tall black plume of smoke rising forever in that early morning Texas sky.

Why Wait Forty Years

I have often written that growing up in a small town had very distinct advantages. However, I don't recall having written of any disadvantages, at least not to amount to much. Don't get me wrong, though. None of the kids, me included, every really considered ourselves dis-advantaged. Or picked on. Or mistreated. Or poor: Which everyone was.

Well, not really poor. In today's vernacular, we were materialistically disadvantaged. Funny thing was, at the time we didn't know we were disadvantaged. If we had known, we wouldn't have even cared. We were too busy trying to:

1. Get the most fun out of our lives as they were;
2. Learn at school;
3. Work at odd jobs wherever and whenever so we could have a few nickels to help accomplish the much more important first priority.

Now, I knew of our superintendent of schools, Ross Buckner, long before I knew him as a person. I guess he knew who I was, right enough, as I was a student in one of the schools he was the superintendent of. He and my father were really good friends. Mr. Buckner also attended the same church I did. Now, according to these facts, anyone could see I had two strikes against me before even coming to bat. Not just in general, but for any particular area, direction or subject the two strikes would be useful for either of those two guys giving them a head start. Like wild card jokers in a hand of cards. Use as needed when required. You could say those two strikes (renewable when called for), hung over my head for the entire length of my school career.

As far as I know, those two strikes were used only once. But that once caused me more grief than the use of the strikes would have for any other of a possible hundred dozen infractions. Not that I was a really bad boy. I was just really active. Afterwards I never hated anybody for it. I just figured I had gotten away with practically murder long enough. Longer than I expected to, considering everything in a very practical manner.

No matter. I knew those two strikes were there. I just never figured the third strike would ever come up. Me being smarter than Mr. Buckner and Dad put together.

I had been smoking pretty regularly from the young and tender age of twelve. Most of us kids could buy cigarettes at a small store across the street from the high school. The owner of the store, Bill, was disabled and catered mostly to the school kids as far as the stuff he kept in stock. I suppose the adults in town knew we could buy tobacco products there. At that time, it was only an unwritten law that young people should not be able to buy cigarettes or some of several forms of chewing tobacco in the State of Texas.

Most of the boys chewed or smoked. Anything similar to advertising gimmicks such as Joe Camel had nothing to do that. It was simply a matter of wanting to do things grown people did. Just pretending and wanting to be grown up.

By the time I was a junior in high school, I tried to convince myself that I had a pretty good tobacco habit. I had even occasionally chewed Day's Work or sweet Beechnut.

My father had lost his sense of smell several years before I really began using tobacco fairly regularly. Due to his lack of sense of smell, I figured I had an advantage in getting away with messing around with tobacco.

Sometimes at school, several of our classmates would gather beneath the fire escape stairs located at the end of the second story auditorium and have a smoke or two.

When it was time for rehearsal of our Senior Class play in the spring of 1953, these sneaked smoking sessions under the auditorium fire escape stairs became fairly frequent. On one of those days in particular, Superintendent Buckner opened the upstairs auditorium exit door to the fire escape, stuck his head out and looked through the stair landing grating down at us for a very long minute.

Now at this late date, I realize one of the teachers had seen us and reported to him where we were and what we were doing. He said nothing to us. Just took that very long look down. After he turned back into the auditorium and closed the door, we went back to enjoying our cigarettes. A few more drags we quickly and conveniently assumed he had not realized what we were all doing down there. We then forgot the entire matter.

During that senior school year a fellow classmate and I worked weekend evenings south of town at the fairly new drive-in-movie theater. The drive-in was open weekends only in late spring and early fall; during the school summer recess it was open every night. It was a fun job. One night, one of us would run the two big new Monarch carbon-pencil arc movie projectors; the other would patrol the grounds during the show. We not only were able to see a lot of the movies, we could hassle our peers walking around and shining a flashlight at the neckers. Ha.

About that time, my folks decided to build a bigger house than the one we had lived in for several years. Here I was, getting old enough to leave home and they want a bigger house. They sold our old home and we moved into a rented house downtown while the new house was being built.

This rent house was only one long block from the in-town theater which was headquarters for the drive-in. Most of the time, I used the pickup furnished by the theaters' owner for transportation out to the drive-in and back, a few miles south of town. When I was not using the truck it was kept parked there at the downtown indoor theater.

One night after my partner and I closed the drive-in, I was having a cigarette during the long walk home after having left the pickup at the in-town theater. I put the cigarette out about a hundred yards from the rent house. I accidentally made a real obvious streak of sparks as I threw the butt down on the street pavement in order to step on it as I walked. As soon as I had reached the sidewalk in front of the house and started walking up toward the door, I was surprised to see my father sitting on the front porch in a rocking chair. Waiting for me. He asked how long I had been smoking. I lied and told him not very long.

He told me to sit down on the porch. He went inside and came back shortly with a bottle; he explained he had gotten a weak solution of silver nitrate at the drug store where I had previously worked for several years. He told me to take a swig, gargle it and spit it out. As I obeyed his order, he continued: "If you smoke after the gargle of the dilute silver nitrate liquid, it will make the tobacco residue in your mouth taste so bad it will make you sick to your stomach." And, he would see to it that I was going to gargle the solution each morning and afternoon. Hooray.

You know, it was several years before I realized that I had gotten that third strike that day long ago for smoking under the steel fire escape stairs behind the school auditorium. And that Ross Buckner had given it by finking on me to my father about catching me smoking. As I mentioned earlier: When caught and having to face the music, we didn't have hard feelings about it. We figured we pretty much deserved what we got.

Well, after quite a few attempts to smoke the silver nitrate solution began to lose effectiveness. It did take me several weeks, but I was finally able to smoke without gagging. Even then, however, it still did taste pretty bad.

Somewhere along in those years, Ross loaned my father a book called *Maverick Town, The Story of Old Tascosa* which was a history of the famous XIT ranch, the largest active single-owner ranch in the world at that time. The original ranch occupied most of the ten counties of the Panhandle of Texas.

My paternal grandfather had been a 'circuit riding' Baptist preacher. When my father was very young, his family had traveled extensively over the land of the XIT by covered wagon in the performance of his father's calling.

After my father had finished reading the book, I managed to get my hands on it and read it. The book fascinated me; it still does.

Years later, on a visit back to my old hometown, I was standing on the large front porch of the church having a cigarette while talking to my old school superintendent, Ross Buckner. It was a beautiful spring day; a Sunday morning. I mentioned the book and how much I had enjoyed reading it. I laughingly suggested to him that I would appreciate it if he would will me the book in forty years or so. Very seriously, he told me he would do just that.

A few years later, Ross retired and moved near Paris, Texas. Shortly after he moved, I received the book in the mail with his new return address on the package. Inside the flyleaf of the book, Ross had penned an inscription ending: "Why wait forty years?"

I still have the book. It is one of my most treasured possessions.

I finally quit smoking. In 1994. Just a month or so more than forty years later.

Another Fish Story

Actually, this isn't a true fish story. That is, it's not really about fish, but it is a fisherman's tale. But, unlike most fishermen's tales, this one happens to be true. All of it happened back in 1960 or so. Some years ago.

I was out of the Marine Corps by three or four years, working at a regular job and continuing to raise a family. Sometimes baby food and baby shoes took all the extra money. So anything extra you could come up with in the way of not needing but wanting seldom came to pass.

In my case, anything extra was anything that had anything to do with fishing. I bought my supplies in bulk, most of it from Herter's, a mail order house back in Minnesota. This firm, I am told, has long been a victim of progress. I would buy raw fishing materials from them, tying my own leaders, making snelled hooks, casting sinkers. The entire ball of wax. And, only able to fish from the bank.

Somehow I amassed enough money to buy a second-hand Sears "Elgin" five-horse outboard boat motor. I think the advertised price was thirty-five dollars. As I recall I paid twenty-five. And, years later I sold it for fifty dollars. It was a really good motor. It plowed through a lot of water for me. For several years: all in rented boats. I guess you could say I sure 'nuff got my money's worth out of it.

But to get down to the real nitty-gritty: One year, my younger brother came out with my mom and dad on one of their regular yearly trips. If I recall correctly, it was during Easter vacation because my brother brought his schoolbooks in order to study some as he was still in college. He took his getting an education seriously. Finished with a PhD in the field of geology.

My brother was and is, much like me. A dedicated fisherman. The type of fisherman who would work all night grave-yard shifts, then go fishing and nap when the fish weren't biting.

I had the boat motor. All it took to be able to go fishing was the cost of an all-day boat rental which was two dollars at the time if I recall correctly, and change for bait.

Away we went to the boat harbor near where I lived. They had fourteen-foot rowboats for rent; a pair of oars and one anchor with rope were provided. If you wanted life vests or floatation cushions, you furnished you own. Those years, the Coast Guard was strictly 'blue water', the game wardens looked for current and valid fishing license and nothing else, and the sheriffs were busy chasing bank robbers. The state had not yet thought of taxing the small guys with boat registration. During those years, in a boat, you were on your own. Big Brother ignored you. The "Good Ole Days".

As we were loading our gear into the boat I remarked to the harbor master that the anchor rope looked rotten. Actually, that was being generous. The darn thing was in really bad shape. The harbor master came over to the boat and looked at the rope. I was informed that the rope was "Plenty dependable; just like all the others."

Well, the "Just like all the others" part looked to me like all the others' ropes were in pretty good shape compared to the rope in the boat we were given. But young and dumb, and in a hurry before the big ones got away, we accepted the boat as it was, started the motor and away we went.

We had a grand time. I don't remember whether we were landing a lot of fish, but we were sure enough going through the bait we had. We were fishing in a part of the river that was subject to the change of tides and all of a sudden it changed; started going out from flood. After a while, it became pretty swift. The resultant strain on the anchor rope was too much; all of sudden the boat jerked and we started going out with the tide. As I had originally feared but chose to ignore, the anchor rope was really rotten and had taken matters upon its own to prove me right.

Now, we had invested our money for an outstanding time fishing with a whole day of boat use, and all of a sudden we had no anchor to prevent the boat from showing just what the bottom side of the big Golden Gate Bridge looked like as we sailed out to the Faralons.

I had seen the bottom of that big bridge once before on a great big gray-painted ship. The only real impression I had about that was it sure was good to be back. I did not notice at the time whether the bottom side of the bridge need painting or not; nor did I care.

After some discussion, my brother and I decided if we went back to the harbor to get another anchor, we probably would have to pay for it. We really weren't carrying much extra cash, either, even totaled up between the two of us. At best, that would take care of the rest of the day for our fishing.

Into the shore we went. We picked out a really big sort of flat rock. One that we could lift; flat enough and heavy enough to hold the boat against the current of the tide. Equipment problem satisfied, we went back to fishing.

Late in the afternoon, my brother hooked onto something really big and heavy. We finally decided it was a sunken log. However, in order to not lose his leader, gear and line, my brother started playing with the whole thing. He gently started sawing the rod up and down, taking in the freed line as it slacked as best he could.

Lo and behold, he finally got his sunken log up for viewing. It turned out to be a really hard, stiff five-eighths diameter manila line. He had hooked it somewhere in its middle. Working together, we pulled the entire line in. One end had a shackle on it, the other had a sixteen-inch Danforth anchor. It did not, in the wildest imagination of any sober person, resemble the anchor we had lost. Tossing the big rock overboard, we attached the shackle to the bow hook, set the Danforth anchor, tied the line off and resumed fishing.

At the end of the day and our return to the harbor, the harbor master came out to greet us. Maybe we were the only people fishing out of his harbor that day and possibly he was glad to see us return safely. Or could be he wanted to see our catch. More likely he wanted to be there to berate us on our admitting we had lost the anchor to drive the replacement price up. More likely.

My brother and I said not a word to him other than "Howdy" as we tied the boat up. We unloaded our gear as he came over to the boat. He didn't volunteer a whole lot of talk as I recall. I do remember him standing there, quietly watching us as we unloaded.

We finished unloading our gear, placing it on the dock. I went to get the station wagon and backed it up as close as I could to the dock. After we had completed the loading of the gear into the car, we stood there, observing the harbor master. Apparently he had spotted the 'new' anchor. He was just standing there, smoking a cigarette and looking at the anchor.

The two of us got into the station wagon, started the engine and drove off. As we left, we could see the harbor master was still standing there. Looking at that Danforth anchor. Ha.

As I mentioned earlier, a few years have gone by. I have never told anyone of this. Until now, that is. My brother or I would sometimes mention it in a conversation between the two of us, but that was the extent of it.

Think about it. When you get right down to the nitty-gritty, who the heck would believe another fish story? Like this one?

Joltin' Joe

When you are a young boy, you have heroes. At least one. The younger you are, the stronger your feeling for your favorite is. Now, being very much male, I cannot write anything of young females' heroes. I'm sure they each must have them, but at the present time I cannot imagine what type or even what for. Now, that statement ought to raise a few neckhairs.

Getting back to heroes: My biggest and best was not by any means an unusual choice for a boy. Joe DiMaggio. A far second was Bob Feller. Both of these gentlemen lived their lives, professional and personal, with honor and dignity. They were head and shoulders above almost all of today's professional ball players in their high standards of performance and personal morals.

Now I'm not saying today's crop of pros are no good. They just are not as good as yesterdays'. Today's players do not play ball for the love of it. With them, it is a business. For instance, consider Willie Mays and Willie McCovey. Their era seemed to me to mark the last of the 'white-hats'. That is, until this past year. The year of the homerun contest by two outstanding men. Maybe "white-hats" will be in vogue again.

I have never met any great baseball player. For that matter, I have never met any really famous people. I had the opportunity to meet the famous Harry Truman when I was in the Marines. But that's not the same thing. He didn't play baseball, and he wasn't my hero. Back at that time, he wasn't much of anybody's hero. How times have changed! Now Harry is one of the 'white-hats'.

Back to Joltin' Joe. One day I came close to meeting him. Real close. It was summer, 1958. Still makes me mad; I came so close and that was that. Never got that close again, and back then I figured that lightin' would probably strike both of us at the same time before I ever had another chance.

At the time this story transpired, I was living in Pittsburg and was a very young shift-working employee for a plant just on the other side of Antioch. The operations crews working on the same shift used to ride together whenever possible to save money and car miles. We would take turns driving; the driver of the day would pick the others up whenever practical.

Usually there was plenty of conversation on the way to work, as the riding crew was accumulated one person at a time: Tales of the things that happened at home during the past time off; joking and kidding around. When you work for a time with the same crew members you eventually develop a kinship for each other unique unto itself.

On this one day, it was my turn to drive; to collect the riders one at a time. We had recently had acquired a new rider, a newcomer on our crew. This day he was last on the pickup route. He had recently married Vince DiMaggio's daughter. Vince was one of Joe's two brothers; only at that time I did not connect all the dots. All these years later as I write this, I cannot remember our new rider's name. But it is of little significance. We did our dayshift, and it was time to go home. Vince's son-in-law was the first on the route to be let out at home. As we pulled up to the Vince DiMaggio house where he was living, he said, "Aw shucks, Uncle Joe has left."

I responded with "Uncle Joe who? DiMaggio?" instantly realizing that the 'Uncle Joe' he was talking about had to be THE Joe. Joltin' Joe, that is.

His reply was in the affirmative. I said to him in a very caustic tone, "You mean to sit there and tell us that Joe DiMaggio was in your father-in-law's home all this weekend and you didn't say anything? Get outta my car!" He meekly got out and I drove off as if in a huff.

Now, I really wasn't mad. But I wanted the new kid on the block to think so. Then maybe next time we would all know when Joe came back to visit his kin. I really wanted to meet Joltin' Joe.

That was the closest I ever got to my hero. Earlier that morning, I had been within the width of a front lawn.

As I remember, Joe married Marilyn Monroe sometime around 1954. Most of Joe's fans feared for him. They felt that Joe had married out of his league; that he had entered the fast world of Hollywood as well equipped for the fast life as the proverbial "babe in the woods" would have been.

The marriage became stormy for both. Marilyn wanted to continue making films and living the fast life; Joe wanted her home as his mother had been. About 1957 their marriage ended. However, they did continue to see each other occasionally for a few more years. After the divorce, she came to regard him as her best friend. And he was. He was the most decent man she had ever known. She came to know that also; to call and ask him for advice.

When Marilyn died, Joe made the arrangements for her funeral. Invitation only.

A picture taken of Joe at Marilyn's funeral was published in Norman Mailer's book "Marilyn." A picture of a man hurting beyond hurt. Joe never remarried.

For many years, actually from the date of Marilyn's death, someone secretly had roses placed regularly on her grave in Westwood. Red roses. People have believed- wanted to believe- it was Joe who had this done.

Years have passed. It is early morning, December 11, 1998, and I am wintering in an R/V park north of Phoenix in Arizona. I am watching NBC's Today Show on the television in our travel-trailer. It is reported that my hero was in a hospital in Florida. While undergoing surgery for the removal of some of the cancer in his lungs he had suffered a heart attack and was on life support. My heart was heavy.

Then, a few days later, Joe recovered and was sent to his home to continue his recuperation. It ended by mentioning that Joe was eighty-four years of age. I was not too encouraged by this report; it never stated whether he was coherent or even able to walk.

A few weeks later, the NBC released an urgent bulletin. Typed on the usual white background across the bottom of the TV screen during regular programs came the statement that Joe had, in fact, died at his home in Florida.

It turned out Joe was sitting in his home watching that program with his personal secretary when the announcement appeared. His secretary reported later that Joe was not only still alive; he was really upset by the erroneous report.

Then on the 8th of March 1999, I was watching the NBC evening news. It was again announced that Joe had died. Only this time it was true. My hero; the World's hero, was gone from this life.

For all the years I continued to work in that area, I was never able to meet Joe. I did know his brothers, Vince and Dom. But never Joe.

Joe, I hope someone puts roses on your grave. Red Roses. Until the end of time.

Buck And The Bloodhound

First off, I want to describe the town of this story. Most people have heard of the expression, "one-horse town." Well, this town was a "one-dog town." One Bloodhound dog, that is. To my recollection, there had never been an honest-to-Pete bloodhound in my hometown. For one thing, nobody ever needed one. If anyone ever did anything devious or wrong, the dust had hardly settled before it was a topic of conversation across backyard barbwire fences. That is, a topic after the sun came up, assuming the deed was done under the cover of moonless night.

Then along came Buck...actually, Buck had lived in town for years. But now he was the Town Constable: A very responsible position. His job was to corner and incarcerate the occasional local drunk. He also was responsible to run down and capture the young highschool drag racers showing their stuff in front of all the girls along the three block-long main street most Saturday nights. Of course, the few times he was able to capture the speeders, he usually just chewed them out: "The next time I catch you guys doing this..."

To sort of protect the innocent and the guilty, I will use only first names in the telling of this story. A story that happened a long time ago in the town of Seagraves on the South Plains of the State of Texas. Of course, the people of the town of the middle fifties will recognize the details and know the perpetrators of this really stupid incident of so long ago. One of the main characters went on to become a fairly respected member of a nearby community of many thousand people, the town's Chief Postmaster, USPS, I think. The other, lessor guilty of the two...I have no idea what happened to him or where he is at the present time. He just sort of vanished into the sunset, you might say.

In the town's heyday, all of the store buildings on the previously mentioned three block-long main street were occupied and enjoying a modest measure of success. The main street of the town was actually named Main. Street corner signs read so. The reason being that back when the town had hitching rails along the dirt street all the early stores fronted on, it was simply called main street. Everybody was too busy chasing steers and dodging fast trotting horses to much care what the main street was called. Just the 'main' street. Nobody hardly noticed, but one day the name finally stuck and was now forever capitalized whenever anyone talked about the "Main" street of town. First thing you know the street got paved. All three blocks of it.

Stopped by the grocery store on the west end of it. Grimes' Grocery, the sign over and across the front entrance said. Now just a vacant lot, these years later. This grocery store is at the heart of this story and, as I just mentioned, was located at the end of the now paved Main Street. There were three or four other such stores around the town at that time, but Grimes' was the largest and fairly well established. The end of the street split at that point, the left as you faced the store changed direction slightly to continue on due west. The right part changed to the north, both streets continuing past the grocery store with its fairly large parking lot in the front.

The store had been in existence for years; the owner was a well-respected member of the community. Over those years, many young people worked part time in the store as was the practice for all of the stores of most any type in the town at that time. In future years, most of those stores would disappear and the town almost die. The complexion of Main Street now is sadly different with empty stores and display windows frosted over on the inside with Bon Ami.

Don, the star of our story, worked part time for a while there in the store. As a result of this employment, he was fairly knowledgeable of the layout of the store and the habits of Joe, the owner-manager. One night Don and a companion named Freeman, another shining example of youth in motion, were walking around town. They were either out of cigarettes and broke or just plain greedy. Greedy gets a lot of people in trouble, and people in small towns are not excepted. Anyhow, the two of them decided to take advantage of Don's knowledge concerning the layout of the grocery store and somehow get inside in order to obtain some cartons of 'free' cigarettes.

The two went around to the rear door and unscrewed the back porch light; somehow got the door open (it normally may not have even been locked) and went inside. They helped themselves to a few cartons of cigarettes. About this time, owner Joe was coming home from the nearby town of Seminole, located a few miles to the south. Doesn't make much difference why he had been to Seminole, he just had. As he passed his grocery store on the way home, he noticed the back porch light was off. He apparently decided to stop and replace the bulb; he drove up to the door, stopped his car and got out. He observed the light bulb had been unscrewed so he screwed it back in and the bulb came on. Suspicious now, he went on inside the store.

The two apprentice thieves had heard him drive up and even though not knowing who it was, quickly hid in the store's restroom located next to the backdoor. Joe came on inside and made a quick inspection tour of the store. While he was walking around, the two boys decided to hotfoot it out of the back door and quickly did so, making their "getaway." Shortly after the exit from the store, the two boys separated, each walking to his own home. From Joe's next move, I suspect he noticed something unusual. He made a telephone call to enlist the aid of Buck and the Bloodhound.

On arrival, the Bloodhound worked magic as soon as he was released and made to understand what was to be done. That dog worked magic. The two men followed the hound right to each of the culprit's front doors, one at a time. However, nothing more was done that night. Next morning, bright and early Joe, Buck and the Bloodhound went to school and enlisted the aid of the high school principle, Gerald Shelly. The two boys were called into Shelly's school office and confronted with their deed of the night before. Both wound up being placed on probation and served their time without further misdeed. These two guys wound up being kind of famous. After all, how many kids have you heard of that were tracked from the location of their crime of theft to their own homes by a bloodhound?

Especially in a "one-dog town."

The Big Send-Off

Many years ago, in the small town of Seagraves on the South Plains of Texas, an incident occurred that was as near to a disaster as you could have without really being a disaster. The whole world blew up; all you could see in front was a huge sheet of fire that completely obscured everything in sight: Top-to-bottom, side-to-side.

The night before we had celebrated our high school graduation. All twenty-eight of us. Early the next morning we had met at the high school and loaded up a loaner school bus to start our final class trip to Colorado Springs, Colorado. We had scrimped, saved and worked for four years to continue what had been, at the time, an annual affair the previous senior classes had enjoyed for several years before us.

The night of our graduation, we gathered in the upstairs library across the hall from the auditorium. We were all pretty quiet. We were standing around in our black caps and gowns. Thinking of the steps we would take tonight; steps that would put us out in the real world on our own. All of us had been fairly independent for years; most of us had worked at various jobs around the town, starting at a fairly early age. The kids on the farms: They had worked longest of all, almost from the time they had learned to walk. Things were really different then. The whole world was different. But the major differences were in the small country towns and villages. Young people had responsibility forced on them at very early ages. None of us seemed to mind or even know any difference. It all was just a fact of life. You worked. Period. But all of a sudden it seemed any choice you had was now gone. The party was all over. Period. Tomorrow was for real.

So this was our first venture into our new world. We were all especially happy and light-hearted. Maybe we sensed a reprieve of a couple of weeks before we shouldered our newly-won responsibilities. At any rate, we were all loaded on the bus and headed out of town to the north. We had one stop to make; we were to pick up a husband and wife who were additional adult trip sponsors. We were supposed to meet them at the gasoline service station on the edge of town they owned and operated. Just as we neared the station we could hear the town's fire siren wailing; it filled the quiet early morning air with its request for the town's volunteer firemen to assemble and conquer whatever emergency had occurred.

Two of our adult male sponsors were volunteer firemen. One was on the bus, the other we were to meet at the service station. As soon as we stopped at the station, we all got off the bus to try to find out what was going on. Rarely did disasters of any significance happen in our small town. Fires mostly consisted of storage shed, grass and weed, or sometimes overheated cooking grease. Most of us were more upset by the trip's delay than any thing else. After all, the lot the station was situated on bordered the city limits; we were almost out of town. Once out of town, the whole thing was the responsibility of the people left behind.

A small, clean burning jet of flame shooting straight up in the air was visible to us over the treetops to the south of us. We could now hear car engines starting and racing, ending the quietness of the morning. One of us borrowed a station employee's car, a fairly new Ford Victoria, chartreuse colored body and black vinyl top. All of us boys, it seemed, crowded into the car and we took off in the direction of the visible jet of flame.

All these years later, I really don't remember how many of us boys were able to get in the car. I suspect all of us that were on the bus for the trip, and anyone else that might have been hanging around the station that early morning. I know this for a fact: There were no spare laps in that car. I was too small to be a lap; I was sitting on someone else's in the front seat of the car. That car was so full of boys that if it were possible for a car to have bowed legs, that car would have had bowed legs. Why the tires didn't blow I had no idea.

As we neared the location of the fire, we all became aware of just exactly what was on fire at exactly the same instant. And we realized we were in pretty deep for a bunch of kids. Whoever was driving stopped the car right in the middle of the highway. The fire happened to be located inside the butane storage yard. Where somewhere around 40,000 gallons of butane was stored to supply most of the farmers in that section of the county.

This was before people decided that the stuff (later propane) should be stored well outside of town. And the Butane yard was right in the middle of the Cities Service, Texaco and Magnolia wholesale gasoline storage yards. Most of the gasoline storage tanks were above ground back in those years.

There we were right in the middle of all that stuff. Somebody in the car said "Holy ----!" and the whole world blew up. I remember seeing the saucer-shaped end of one of the large butane tanks rolling across the street in front of us. It continued rolling over the railroad tracks, finally stopping and dropping down. I heard no sound. But it must have been terrific. The flame was everywhere- a solid sheet. I could feel the heat of the flame on my face right through the windshield. Boys started to get out of the car; someone hollered to "stay put," reverse gear was somehow accomplished and the car was driven very quickly backwards out of what the driver considered harm's way. Finally the car was turned around and we headed directly back from where we came, each of us thinking it was all over. By the time we had driven the mile or so back to the gas station, the remaining tanks had exploded, one at a time, and no more fire was visible. We were stunned to the point of silence over what had happened. We just knew our long-awaited trip was all over. I think, at the time, we figured there would be nothing left of the town by the time this disaster was ended.

It became so quiet, the lack of sound hurt our ears. Actually, our hearing was probably dulled by the series of concussion we had all been exposed to due to our close proximity to the explosions.

Finally, our two volunteer firemen-sponsors returned. Every person who had been in the vicinity of the fire and subsequent explosions was safe. Two of the men did have bad sunburns; One on his face, the other through his shirt on his back. The butane yard was no more, but all else was ok. We were told to get back on the bus; very quickly it was driven across the city limit line. We were out of town and on our way to Colorado, to a place some of us had never been.

We were and are, those of us who are left, the Seagraves High Class of '53. As the years passed, our class members have, for the most part, kept in very close contact. Maintaining contact hasn't been all that hard. After all, there were only twenty-eight of us to begin with; less now these years later. And, one thing for sure. No other class, before or since, received the sendoff we did. No sir! None before, and none since.

Makin' Texas Chili

Most people at some time or other have eaten something represented as Texas chili, either home cooked or in some greasy-spoon type road-house restaurant. And, I reckon reading about someone cooking up a pot of chili doesn't really sound fascinating. But…the REAL Texas Chili you can easily tell by the fact in taking a single spoon full, chewing and swallowing, and the wait of a few seconds to see if your tongue starts to swell and your throat closes up…ooopps, that was Texas Chili you very soon surmise as you reach for the water or whatever other quenching liquid you happen to have handy.

The chili powder…now that is really where this story begins. The chili powder. That is also where real chili begins. The fact of that particular powder that happened to be used in the making of this genuine Texas Chili was simply a co-incidence. The odds of it ever happening again are really pretty much like next to never.

One day some months ago in a weak moment, I decided I wanted to once again taste the definite authoritative delicacy of Texas Chili. However, I did not have the recipe for the genuine article and in thinking about the situation; I realized there was no way I could remember how to make it. So, thinking the matter over, I decided to try to get the Texas Chili recipe from a former schoolmate, an almost girlfriend back then and still a very good friend and dignified lady. With this in mind, I contacted my old friend by E-Mail who graciously responded to my request.

My wife is from California, and due to her sheltered childhood, had never even heard of Texas Chili, much less tasted it. She willingly agreed to put a pot together as I had gone to the trouble to get the recipe for it.

The next step in this process was to go to the grocery store and obtain the necessary ingredients for the...well, you really can't call it a delicacy, even though I already have in writing of it. There ain't nothing at all delicate about Texas Chili. I am not certain exactly what you call it except Texas Chili. The shopping done, you go home and at the first opportunity you start the over two-day process of the Chili. Step one is to begin the overnight process to re-hydrate the pinto beans. Now, that is just about all the Texas Chili recipe detail I am going to reveal. Us Texans really don't want too many people cooking around making Texas Chili. You know, too many cooks spoil the broth...er, Texas Chili, that is.

My brother was on his way for a Christmas visit to our home. A visit delayed by around forty years or so. I had, for those past years, visited him and my parents twice a year. For that reason, neither he nor I found the need for him to drive the long distance to visit me. However, none of these get-togethers had occurred during any holiday season. But the need for my normal twice-yearly visits had changed with the almost simultaneous death of our parents the year before. Now we are trading visits. We had agreed to my wife and I spending Thanksgiving with him in Golden and he would journey up to Douglas for Christmas. We also agreed to visit the other any time the occasion came up. Now, it was the Christmas season and my brother's turn, and he was on his way.

My wife wanted to please him during his visit and impress him with her culinary ability by serving him real Texas Chili. For much of the last years of our mother's life she had not been able to even smell Texas Chili or go to the trouble to prepare it, so my brother had been growing older in a very deprived fashion.

It was nearing supper time when my brother arrived. After the arrival welcome and unpacking were over, and he and I were catching up on each other's recent activities in front of the fireplace pellet stove in the downstairs den while my wife continued the chili preparation.

Before too much time had passed, I heard my wife call for my assistance in a somewhat desperate manner. I go upstairs and into the kitchen as she had requested. She asked me to look into the huge pot that held the maturing chili. There were several small black objects floating around in the liquid that strongly resembled small beetles. Maybe seventy-five or a hundred of these small objects.

Calmly, I requested and received a white paper towel and a teaspoon. Using the spoon, I captured a few of the black spots and deposited them onto the white paper towel. Taking the samples back downstairs into my office, I examined the very small spots with a very powerful magnifying glass. Sure enough, they were perfect…very small, very cooked beetles.

We gathered all the remaining portions of the chili preparation purchases, the receipt from the grocery store together in a sack and taking the partially cooked pot of chili, and my wife and I headed to the store for a quick consultation.

On entering the store, we were very discreet; we asked to see the night manager who promptly appeared. We explained the problem to her and asked if she would like to see the result. She quickly declined to come out to the parking lot to see the evidence in the pot we had left in the car. She asked if we would like for the store to replace the ingredients to which we quietly agreed. My wife selected the replacements and we left the store.

That night we had a hastily prepared substitute supper while the new pinto beans were tenderizing in a pot of fresh tepid water.

The following evening, the entire scene was mostly a repeat of the night before. My brother and I were downstairs in the den; my wife was upstairs in the kitchen continuing the preparation of the new pot of Texas Chili. Suddenly I heard my wife's again desperate summons. I went upstairs and observed the now familiar small black objects floating in the liquid in the top of the newly created pot of chili. As before, I took some of the small black objects placed on a towel down into my office and examined the objects with the magnifying glass. Again my suspicions were reaffirmed; I called my brother into the office where he confirmed my earlier opinion. Small black beetles.

Back to the laboratory—I mean, kitchen—and some questions for the cook. I suggested that she should recount each step in the process. As she did this, all of a sudden my brother and I could see by the expression on her face that an idea occurred to her. She held up the small can of chili powder and said in an amazed voice that her suspicions were impossible; it could never happen that way. She offered the can of chili powder for our inspection. I dumped some of the powder out on another clean white paper towel sheet and sure enough, there were the offending little black beetles. Feets up. Probably had been that way for some time as the container was around twenty years old.

After a tense moment or two of discussion, we decided that the beetles, having matured for years in the container, would probably add to the quality of the taste of the Texas Chili. I scooped as many of the little critters out of the pot as I could. We sat down at the dinner table and had an excellent supper of the unintentionally modified recipe of chili and wheat crackers. It had been years since our taste buds had been so treated and it was worth the wait, critters and all.

One thing kind of bothers me about this whole episode. I never did notify the grocery store about the discovery of the true source of the tiny petrified critters...but the next time we were in the store we bought a new can of chili powder. Same brand. No bugs. I checked as soon as we got home.

The Onion Incident

When my brother and I were young and living at home, our father took us on an occasional camping trip to some good fishing spot. No hunting excursions, though. I don't know why we never went on any hunting trips unless it had to do with the higher expense of having to buy rifles over fishing rods. During those early years, the only armament we had in the family was a .410 single-barrel shotgun. Each of us did have a fishing rod with the appropriate gear and tackle box.

It was not the most affluent of times for our family, nor was it for others. World War II had just ended, and our part of Texas was still in a bad way economically. Some of the leftover of the depression of the thirties.

All three of us had wonderful family times back then. Now my brother and I are orphans with the passing of both of our parents and those times are long gone. All these years later I look back and realize exactly how precious those early times were. With the passing of years, those camping trips the three of us made together sort of went by the wayside.

But...let's go back in time to the last few years of our father's time. A few years ago, I was able to find employment and relocate to Wyoming, a land I had grown to love. My father, my brother and I were able to resume taking camping trips together.

But things had changed. Instead of fishing, we now had the money to afford hunting gear and the locating and bagging of deer was now the purpose of the trips. Another change was that quite often there would be other people along on these trips. Sometimes close friends of my brother would be made welcome. Or, in some situations, an occasional business partner. This one particular trip there were two other men, John and William, both business partners of my brother.

At the time of this story, I was living in Green River, Wyoming. I made the trip from Green River down to Craig, Colorado, to meet the four of them at a sporting goods store there on the main street. I bought my out-of-state hunting license there; the others bought odds and ends. Soon we were all supplied and left for some government BLM land thirty miles or so south of Craig.

My brother's two business partners were traveling in John's new Chevy Blazer which he had bought earlier that day. I had looked carefully at it when we were in the sporting goods store's parking lot. It was a really nice rig; leather upholstery and all the other bells and whistles.

On arrival at the hunting area, we picked our campsites and started setting things up. I observed my brother determinedly looking over and over among the various things packed in the back of his truck. It wasn't long before my brother threw his hands up and told me that he had inadvertently left the poles and stakes for the large crew tent back in the garage at home in Golden. So, Dad, my brother and I decided we three would all go back to Craig, a nearby town, to buy poles there rather than take the four-hour trip back to Golden and the garage.

Back in Craig at the same sporting goods store we had patronized earlier, we found tent poles were not sold as separate items. At that point, my brother decided he wanted a newer and different tent anyhow, so he bought a new and larger wall-type tent.

Now at full dark and back out at the hunting grounds, we discovered that the other two had eaten and sacked out for the night in their new tent. By the light of the campfire and flashlight, the three of us managed to get the new wall tent up, all gear stowed inside, supper cooked and eaten and in bed before midnight. Brother set the alarm for the darkest hour before dawn.

Early the next morning after breakfast in the dark, we split into two groups: John and William in the first group, my brother, Dad, and me in the other. We all beat brush and hiked all over the mountain we were camped on. Lots of deer sign but none of it very recent. Late in the afternoon, dark, heavy looking clouds appeared on the western horizon and seemed to be gathering and headed right for us. We decided to head back for camp just in case those clouds meant business. Being out in the middle of nowhere in a high mountain snowstorm is not the best place to be, even for a bunch of fairly capable and suitably outfitted woodsmen.

Thanks to my brother, we were well outfitted. Each of the three of us always had our own topo maps for this area provided by my brother. We also had our own personal compasses, canteens, hunting knifes, a box of cartridges each, a small-pack raincoat and water-proof matches. All except the canteen and knife stowed in what is now known as a "fanny pack." In actuality, they were WW II US Army surplus gas mask packs. Ideal for what we used them for.

As we approached camp, we could see by the two glowing gas lanterns that we were not the only ones who decided to call it a day. By the time we arrived, darkness was full and we could see the wind-driven snowflakes in the light of the lanterns.

Now, recalling the following events that happened the rest of that evening: If I had not been there, I would not have believed it. If someone had told me it happened, I would not have believed it. But, I was there. I saw. I believed. I think…

John and William had started preparing their own supper of liver and onions. Personally, I do not care for liver and onions for supper, lunch, breakfast or any other what-ever- you-want-to-call-it meal. Simpler put, I don't like liver and onions.

Now the snow had really gotten down to business and was being flung around by about a hard wind blowing up the mountain slope from the west. After each had a couple of good shots of Early Times, John and his buddy decided they were going to cook their supper on a Coleman gas stove inside the back of John's new Chevy Blazer to get out of the snow and wind.

At first, we did not notice what the two of them were preparing to do. We were trying to arrange a sort of shelter for the firepit so we would be able to cook our own supper. It wasn't very long before I decided we needed some help. I asked John to please move the Blazer to the upwind side of the fire to create wind deflection; he quickly complied. This made our situation a little more comfortable with the new partial shelter.

Pretty soon the party inside the Blazer began to get a little noisy. I guess we started noticing the inside activities when they rolled down each of the front side windows a little for ventilation. Now we could really smell the odor of the onions carried by the ventilating wind. In fact, it smelled like all they were cooking was a lot of onions. That's all you could smell. No liver. Just onions.

Pretty soon the surrounding outside air got kind of teary for us. And the laughter inside the Blazer got louder. It wasn't too long after supper that the three of us decided that the sleeping bags inside the tent warmed by the catalytic heater were much preferable to the steadily worsening colder weather. So we went into the tent to discover that it smelled really strongly of onions.

Earlier, we had left the front entrance flap partially open and the small rear plastic screened 'window' flap up to help air out the newness of the tent. We now discovered this was a big mistake. This had allowed the aroma of the supper cooking in the Blazer to waft through our tent. And, most fabric, such as sleeping bags and extra clothing readily absorb various odors, desirable or not.

Well, by the time our hunt period was over, all of us really smelled like onions. Really stale onions. We did not bag a single deer. I suppose they could smell the onions. Raw onions, they might have ignored that odor, but the odor of cooked onion probably made them suspicious. If there were any deer there to smell it, that is. We returned home to well-desired hot showers with soap.

The poor Blazer? Well, I'll just bet you a dollar that it still smells like onions. That is, if it still exists. All of these twenty-five years later.

Nope. If someone had told me of a tale like this, I would have never believed it. Nobody, but nobody would do that to a brand new vehicle. But, I believe. I was there.

The Night The Golden Gate Bridge Fell Down

You can guess the title is not true. But it seemed it was at the time. At least, a lot of people thought so who were not too familiar with that part of the country. But as it turned out, it was not the Golden Gate Bridge that suffered damage. Part of the double-decked Oakland-Bay Bridge had collapsed in on itself on the Oakland side of the Yerba Buena Island, many miles east of the Golden Gate. Many people were killed that afternoon right at evening commute. But many more would have been killed had it not been for the World Series starting just at that time at Candlestick Park in South San Francisco.

Most area employers had given their employees the afternoon off as it was to be a one-of-a-kind World Series. The San Francisco Giants were playing the Oakland Athletics and game one was just then in the process of starting. So at that particular time, commute traffic was light; most everyone had already traveled to where ever they were going.

My wife and I had left our home in Oroville, California on a vacation trip shortly after the first of October in 1989. We were on the way to visit my brother, mother and father in Golden, Colorado. That was the main purpose of the trip; they were both getting along in years and I felt the need to visit them as often as possible. We had been there with them in the late spring; for the last few years we had tried to visit them at least once a year.

We also combined other activities on each of the trips as I didn't want the expense of the trip to be solely for my benefit of visiting my kin. I wanted my wife to see some things she had never seen before as well as try to visit mutual friends during each trip.

This particular trip we had traveled directly east on I-80 and had stopped in Green River, Wyoming for several days visiting old friends. We had lived in Green River for a few years in the early '80s and had developed a very close relationship with this one couple a few years older than we were: Rose and Ed.

Earlier in the time we had lived in Green River, my wife, Nancy, had met Rose at the hospital in Rock Springs. Rose was a longtime volunteer for the 'Pink Lady' group at the hospital, and Nancy also volunteered as a 'Pink Lady' for a time.

About the same time, I met Ed out at the Jim Bridger Power Plant where both he and I worked. He was a welder for the construction company that was constructing Unit No. 4, the last unit to be built at that time for that plant. A short time after these separate and co-incidental meetings, Nancy invited Rose and her husband for dinner at our house. You can imagine the mutual laughter between Ed and I when he showed up as we both knew each other due to our own separate activities.

After we moved back to California, we kept close contact with Rose and Ed. We had become very close fast friends.

Rose and Ed lived just north of Expedition Island, the general area where John Wesley Powel and his group of pioneers made their start, rafting down the Green River and all the way to the Colorado River and on through the Grand Canyon back in the late nineteenth century. There was room for us to park our R/V trailer on their property just off the street; we had done this several times over the years when we would travel to Green River for a visit with our two old friends.

This one time we again decided to go to Jerry's Steakhouse near the truck stop between Green River and Rock Springs. The four of us had eaten there several times. Usually during each visit we would take the two out for dinner just as a gesture of appreciation for their hospitality. But it was sometimes a futile gesture as Ed would always try to pay for the meal.

We decided to go early as the first game of the World Series was going to commence that night. A really historic game. The Oakland Athletics were the American League Champions; the San Francisco Giants were the National League Champs. Both Bay Area teams and highly competitive.

This series had all the potential of being a really memorable contest. All four of us wanted to watch the game on television. Nancy and I were still living at Oroville in California at that time; both of us had been living in California many years excluding the few in the early '80s that we were there in Green River. So we intended to go early to eat and get back in time for the series opening pitch.

We had the usual good dinner and great conversation. When everyone was about finished, I excused myself on the pretense to go to the restroom, when in truth I was going to get the meal ticket from the waitress and pay early, both to save time and also to avoid Ed's offer of payment.

I went into the bar area to the cash register on the end of the counter. I noticed everyone in the bar including the cocktail waitress huddled at the far end of the bar with all attention and eyes glued to the small overhead television. I couldn't see what was going on but I assumed the first game of the World Series had started early. I waited a few moments and finally picked up an ashtray off the counter and set it down sharply enough to draw attention to the fact I was standing there.

The cocktail waitress abruptly turned and upon seeing me, she started quickly down the backbar aisle to where I was. As soon as she got fairly close, I asked her, "What's the matter; did the series start early?" She quickly replied: "They had a big earthquake in San Francisco and the Golden Gate Bridge fell down!" I gave her my credit card and meal ticket and walked down to where I could observe the reporting on the television. It was not quite dusk on the West Coast and I could see the bridge they were showing on the TV was not the Golden Gate but the Oakland-San Francisco Bay Bridge. They were alternately showing a broken part of the bridge and a fire in the North Beach area of San Francisco.

When the waitress brought my charge receipt to me at the end of the bar, I explained to her and the people gathered round the TV that it wasn't the Golden Gate Bridge but the Oakland-Bay Bridge that was damaged. It was a section of the connecting bridge between Oakland and San Francisco called the San Francisco-Oakland Bay Bridge. The collapsed section was actually located between the Yerba Buena Island and Oakland. That small island was located near the center of the San Francisco Bay and the approximated mid-point of the bay bridge rested on it. The fire was located in the north part of downtown San Francisco called the North Beach Area.

I then went back into the restaurant section to gather the three up and told them what had happened; the bill was paid and "Let's get home and turn on the TV."

Later that evening, we tried to contact Nancy's two boys and my one son by telephone. All three families lived in the general area of the quake. There was no way that we could connect. However, I was able to get through to my work location and learned that the earthquake had been really bad but the most severe damages were localized in several areas and that the entire Bay Area was not decimated as we first feared.

I was informed of the general areas of severe damage and with that information, we could determine that our families were more than likely safe; our and their homes undamaged. This, of course, was strictly informed opinion and nothing else. But it was obvious that major communication centers were out of service and probably would be for several days. We reached the realization that any contact with our families was several days off.

Early the next morning, we again attempted telephone contact with the California Bay Area and again had no success. At that point, we loaded up the trailer and left for the Denver area and my folk's home. We decided that if we determined it necessary, we would leave there and travel home over U.S. 50 to avoid possible damage in the I-80 area in California.

As it turned out, shortly after we arrived in Colorado, we were able to establish contact with all our families and found that they all indeed were safe.

Nancy and I were and are thankful to God for the safe keeping of our sons and their families.

The Dog That Couldn't Paddle

For some reason or other, I grew up thinking all dogs could swim. As a matter of fact, I thought almost every animal of nature knew how to swim. Excluding people. They have to be taught how to swim. With some people, after some minor demonstration or observation, they pick it up right away. Other people, it's really a big deal, learning how to swim. A few never try, and another few never learn.

I grew up in Texas. I grew up where there wasn't a whole lot of water laying around just waiting to be swum in. About the biggest thing within twenty-five miles or so was an irrigation pond fed by a deep-well pump with outlet ditches conveying the water to the plants growing in the fields. We used the ponds for baths, swimming, and keeping watermelons cold. If we were really lucky, there might be a six-pack or two of Lone Star. The water was really cold. Kept the six-packs or watermelon just right. It also kept your teeth chattering.

All of us who had dogs were joined by them for a swim. Dogs like to get cooled off, too, just like people. Then there is always the dog that never grows up and plays in every puddle he can find just like a young human boy. Those dogs, for whatever reason, are not fond of water mixed with soap for baths. Just get a bar of soap, let them see it, and they disappear until chowtime.

The dog I have now is much the same. She loves to play in the water. Any water, clean or dirty. However, she will submit to a bath with the most reluctance you could possibly imagine. She figures it out pretty quick as I am assembling the stuff for her bath: Water hose, drying rags, soap and a stool for me to sit on. She will disappear into the depths of the backyard. If the backyard wasn't fenced, she would probably go visit a neighbor or two. When I finally locate her, she gives me a look like "Oh, are you looking for me?" When it's finally over, she is so happy you would think I had just given her a fresh cow leg bone, right from the butcher.

Let's get back to dogs that can't swim; what I am supposed to be writing about.

I had not been able to have a dog of my own for many years. The only one I previously had was given to me when I was about five years old. I had no other after that, for reasons not complicated. Having a dog was not practical for the places we lived. That's what my father told me. We had no fenced back yard suitable for occupancy by a dog.

Years later, making my own way in the world, I decided I wanted a dog. I now owned a house sitting on a large fenced lot and this was suitable for a dog. I read this ad in the paper offering a 3-month old male German Shorthair "free to a good home." So I called, got the address, went out and looked at the dog. He seemingly fell in love with me on the spot. At least, that's what he wanted me to believe. I figure he was just lonesome.

He was tied to a big oak tree in the back yard. No grass, but plenty of shade. I told the old gent who owned the dog I had a big fenced backyard of a half-acre, and I would like to take the dog. As he untied the rope he told me the dog's name was "Duke." He handed the rope to me and wished me well with my new dog.

Duke and I walked over to my pickup. I opened the passenger side and Duke jumped in. I went around to the driver's side, got in, and Duke crawled into my lap. Believe me, it is not easy, driving home with a seventy pound (or so) dog sitting in your lap. With a steering-wheel mount gear-shift lever, that is.

Duke made a very good family dog. He even proved to be an excellent watchdog. Many times he prevented the garbage collector from stealing the garbage can, especially if I forgot to tie him up the night before garbage day.

He was a natural born thief. But he was smarter than most thieves. He would sneak home with his booty and bury it in the back yard. Once I found a leather strap sticking out of one of Duke's graves. It proved to be attached to a purse. The purse had a lot of stuff in it. You know, the usual stuff; money, credit cards, driver's license. When I took the purse back home to a close neighbor, her son answered the door. I just told him I found it in the yard. Later on, a fur coat was a different problem. I traced the owner of it through a summer storage furrier tag sewn in the lining.

A few months after Duke joined my household, he and I were up north camping for a few days on Cache Creek. We were lying in the sun on a small beach area, relaxing after a hard hot day of rock hunting.

For whatever reason, I picked up a small flat rock and skipped it across the wide area of the creek where we were soaking sun. Duke really watched the rock. He acted as if he wanted to go in after it. I picked another small, flat rock, tossed it in the creek, and told Duke "Fetch!." In Duke jumped…and promptly disappeared. The fact of his submergence did not at first register. I was watching Duke's progress by the trail of bubbles rising to the water's surface. The bubbles stopped going away from me and started coming back toward shore. That's when it really hit home. Suddenly, Duke burst out of the water and dropped a rock at my feet. It wasn't the rock I had thrown, but it was a rock. Naturally, I told him what a good dog he was.

Even holding the evidence in my hand and not quite believing, I let him rest and catch his breath. After a few minutes, I selected another rock and skipped it across the water. This time I didn't have to say anything. He was in the water before I could speak. As soon as he disappeared, I went to the water's edge, leaned down and stuck my head in the water. It was really clear. I could see Duke, trying to walk on the bottom, yet not quite touching in his progress. He finally was able to get down on the bottom, grab a rock with his teeth, and turn toward shore. I t dawned on me…he couldn't swim. At least, not on the top of the water like all retrievers should be able to do. The word 'courage' was invented for that dog. He couldn't swim, but he would try to walk on the creek's bottom… just for me.

A few weeks later, an acquaintance of mine made fun of both Duke and me about my hobby of rock hunting. I told him that Duke really was a better rock hound than I; he could find rocks underwater. Naturally, this statement of mine was met with absolute disbelief. So I proceeded to get an empty five gallon bucket from the barn.

I filled the bucket with water and selected a rock from the flower bed border just off the patio deck where we were sitting. I called Duke, showed him the rock, and dropped it in the bucket. Duke immediately thrust his head in the water. We could hear his teeth grinding on the rock; the one

I had selected was a little too big for his easy grip. I was about to call the whole thing off land yank him out of the bucket when his head suddenly came out of the bucket, slinging water in all directions. He was proudly holding the rock in his teeth.

The acquaintance looked at Duke. "I don't believe it!"

I said, "Here, I'll get him to do it again!"

My friend said "No! This one time was enough!"

I was glad that one time was enough. Thinking it over, I made up my mind to not ever play that game with him again. That dog was so dedicated to me that he would have drowned rather than not return that rock to me. He couldn't help the fact that he could not swim. And his total loyalty to me was all too obvious.

About a year later, I was staying for several weeks in a cabin down at Anderson Reservoir, east of Morgan Hill. I was there to recuperate from a knee operation; restoring muscle strength by doing a lot of swimming. Duke very badly wanted to swim with me. He would stay on shore, running back and forth, barking. I decided I should try to teach him how to swim. I taught him. He raked my chest with his claws so badly I was scabbed and sore for weeks. I owed him that; teaching him how to swim. I owed him at least that much.

Years later, after Duke had gone where all good dogs go, I married, and told my wife of this story. She didn't say so, but I could tell she really didn't believe me.

One evening we had some friends over for dinner. One of them, Frank, a long-time friend of mine, happened to see a picture of old Duke. He made the remark to my wife he used to have a shorthair that looked very much like Duke. My wife quickly told Frank that I had discovered that Duke couldn't swim and that I had eventually taught him.

Frank laughed, and told her that he had done the same with his shorthair; the dog couldn't swim and he had taught it. I was standing nearby, listening. My wife turned and looked at me. She stood there, just looking at me. In total silence. I didn't see the need to say anything. I just looked back at her. In total silence.

Ed Cantrell: Justice's Tragedy

A lot of people believe that Ed Cantrell, formerly of Sweetwater County, Wyoming, had gotten away with committing a contract of murder. I am inclined to think that is the case.

I met Cantrell a couple of years after the not guilty verdict of his trial for murder. At the time, I did not realize who this person was I was dealing with until a few hours after the meeting was over. The result of that incident did not alter my feelings concerning the matter. In retrospect, it actually affirmed my original opinion and feelings concerning the trial verdict.

Years later, there was a report on the entire incident published by Arts & Entertainment Television company. That A & E Television program presentation tended to enforce this feeling of mine. The program rehashed the original incident and, as I recall, fairly accurately.

I will relate the story as best I remember it. My part happened several years after the original incident. My wife and I moved to Green River, Wyoming, in the late fall of 1979. Rock Springs is situated fifteen miles east of the town of Green River. The trial and subsequent publicity was mostly over and done with by the time we had moved to the great state of Wyoming.

On a summer evening in 1978, Ed Cantrell killed Michael Rosa, a fellow Rock Springs Police officer who was sitting in the back seat of a department undercover sedan in the front parking lot of the now defunct Silver Dollar Saloon. The saloon was located near the Interstate 80 overpass and Elk Street intersection in Rock Springs. According to news accounts at the time, Ed was sitting in the front passenger seat. He turned just enough to his left in order to draw his gun and extend his arm enough to shoot the victim. The victim had a glass of wine he had taken from the saloon positioned on the seat between his legs. One other off-duty officer was present, sitting in the driver's seat of the car.

Cantrell was consequently brought to trial and used the defense that he could see in the victim's eyes he was about to draw and shoot him (Ed Cantrell). Bear in mind that it was night and in a dimly lit parking lot. I know that the parking lot was not well lit; I had driven by that lot many times at night on my way to work preceding the demise of the saloon. But I guess Cantrell's night vision was so good that he could discern the cruel glint in the victim's eyes. That claim even beats that of the "Twinky" defense used in Dan White's San Francisco murder trail when he shot Mayor Moscone and Councilman Harvey Milk in the San Francisco city-county hall a few years prior.

At any rate, Cantrell was found not guilty but as a result did lose his job as a Rock Springs police officer. However, he managed to get an appointment from the Wyoming Cattlemen's association as a range detective, a job he held for a few years. Payback? Maybe.

Later news releases stated that the victim officer was to testify the very next day on weeks of undercover work before a special grand jury concerning vice, corruption and narcotics sales and usage. A very few hours after Officer Rosa's death, officials assigned to supervise the corruption case Rosa had been assigned to went to Rosa's house to collect his papers and notes concerning his investigation and reports. Previously, Officer Rosa's wife had been taken by car to the hospital on the report that he had been involved in an accident. Apparently as soon as she was absent from the family home, the house was broken into and all Rosa's papers had been removed. Officer Rosa's investigative papers on those matters were never found. That investigation was necessarily but reluctantly concluded without any charges being filed on anyone who had been under suspicion.

For me, it all started innocently enough in the summer of 1982. I was working at the Jim Bridger Power Plant located in Southwestern Wyoming about thirty-five miles east of Rock Springs. The plant was situated about nine miles north of Interstate 80 on a paved two-lane open range road. My crew was working graveyard and due on the site by 10:00 p.m.

At that time, all the plant crews were on eight-hour shifts; the crew supervisors were on 12-hour shifts. This extended work period for the supervisors was an experiment by upper management to demonstrate the pluses and minuses of such a work period as the union had been considering that length of shift for the plant labor force. Twelve-hour shifts did mean less workdays resulting in less total travel time and expense. But it also meant a minimum 14-hour day in good weather including travel time. It was confusing at the time for the three plant shift supervisors having to schedule work for two overlapping shift crews.

This one night in particular we were having problems with the coal delivery into the plant fuel system. I received a message on my portable radio that I was needed at the plant main entry gate. As soon as the problem situation was somewhat resolved, I got in my service truck and drove to the gate security office. On arrival, I was informed by the security captain that one of the younger employees on my crew, Greg, had hit and killed a steer on the unfenced open-range plant road. I could see Greg through the half-glass wall in an adjacent office, trying to fill out the required accident report form. He was near tears as his new candy-apple red Chevy Love pickup had sustained a fair amount of cosmetic damage.

I entered the office and observed Greg had a small bump on his forehead. I patted him on the shoulder and suggested he wait and complete the form later. He agreed it would probably be better to fill out the form when he had an opportunity to "settle down." So, we both got in my truck and drove out to my office. After a few hours had passed with the shift activities, I had pretty well forgotten the incident.

A couple of nights later, I received another radio message from the security captain that I was needed at the main gate security office. Again, I was pressed for time due to the shift activities, but I headed for the main gate as soon as I was able. On arrival I went directly into the captain's office. The captain informed me a range detective and a deputy sheriff were in an adjacent room who wanted to talk to me about the butchering and theft of the vehicle-slaughtered beef of a few nights previous. The security captain and I went into the room where the two men were waiting; both standing by choice. Without any introduction from them on their part, the security captain introduced me as the supervisor of the employee involved in the accident.

The shorter of the two, a sort of seedy looking individual told me he was the local range detective and was here to arrest the guy who killed, butchered and stole the meat of the steer.

At this time I was not in the best of moods having being called away from my duties for an insignificant matter of no concern to me or my responsibilities. I tersely pointed out to this range detective he obviously did not have the authority to arrest anyone, as he did not have the deputy sheriff badge on his chest. Continuing, I mentioned this was private property and not his open range. I also pointed out to him that the employee could not have butchered the beef since I had driven him to his duty station almost immediately after the accident. Consequently, after the conclusion of his regular shift, he had been held over an additional half-shift. I also pointed out that the swing shift crew had learned of the accident on their way home. Anyone of them could have stopped and butchered the beef- for whatever the meat was worth after sustaining physical damages as a result of the accident.

This range detective insisted he was going on the plant site to arrest the so-called-perpetrator. Repeating my earlier statements, I told him he had no authority to go onto the plant property. He had no right to enter without my permission and I was not going to give it. I also informed him I had more important things to do other than stand there and discuss the situation with him.

As I started to turn to leave, the detective's eyes turned to a real icy blue. I considered he was about to lose his cool so I didn't waste any time on exiting the security office and getting back into my service truck and return to my duties.

Around 7:00 a.m. as I was leaving the plant for home the security captain met me at the gate; he had been watching for me. I stopped and lowered the passenger side window with the push-button in response to his approaching that side of the truck. He then asked me if I knew who the range detective was. I replied that I did not. He then asked me if I knew of Ed Cantrell, the police officer who had shot the other police officer in Rock Springs a couple of years previous. Yes, I responded, I remembered reading of it; was this guy the infamous Ed Cantrell? "None other," he said. I then told the Captain I had not only read much about it but I had several conversations with concerned and informed people who were very unhappy about the result of the trail. I mentioned that at the time of the incident, Cantrell was renting a house from a good friend of mine. After this conversation, I went on home. But I did not forget the incident or conversation.

I made it a point at the first opportunity later on to tell Greg of the meeting concerning his accident. I stressed he should sort of lay low and not be too conspicuous in his day-to-day off site activities for a while. Also if he was arrested, to immediately call me as I could verify the times of the two pertinent incidents of the nights in question by the station logs. Neither of us ever heard any more about the situation.

I do admit I was a little nervous for some weeks after that meeting with the deputy sheriff and Ed Cantrell. However, I gradually finally and completely forgot the whole thing.

Then a few years later, in California, I bought a San Francisco Chronicle paper that had a report on the front page concerning a Chronicle reporter's interview of Cantrell. As I now remember, it fairly well glorified the infamous Range Detective Ed Cantrell. Picture on the front page, still sporting a handlebar mustache and wearing a big silver Stetson. I both laughed and shook my head at the ridiculous article.

Sometime later, my wife and I had moved to California. One evening I happened to see an Arts and Entertainment Television channel advertisement that "City Confidential" intended to offer a feature about Rock Springs and the Cantrell incident. As it happened, I missed the program, so I e-mailed the A & E parent company, ordered and received the VCR tape of the program.

In a later viewing of the tape, Mr. Cantrell looked much worse for wear than when I had run into him all those years ago. During the program interview concerning the shooting of the policeman, his ice blue eyes were as hard as I remember. He was still sporting his (now graying) handlebar mustache and wearing a silver Stetson.

He was and is just plain scary. I guess maybe during his trial he gave such hard ice blue eye looks to the jury who found him "not guilty."

Marvin

This is not a happy revelation. I enjoy writing of happy things and happy times. But, for some reason, I have the need to relate this tale about Marvin. It is the truth, so far as I know and can recollect. Marvin is his true first name. I will not reveal his last. He had no blood kin that I am aware of, but that is not the reason I am not going to disclose his full name. Perhaps you will understand if you continue to read on.

Working shift work with a crew in a power plant you experience all kinds of stressful situations. Working in a power plant is sort of like working in engine compartments on board a ship. After a time, you learn to depend on each other for your own safety and the operation of your own private world: Your ship. You begin to believe you know your partners as well as you do your own family. In the passage of time, they sort of become a second family. Quite often, you spend a lot of your free time together on your days off.

Marvin never knew his natural mother or father. His first memories occurred in a Catholic Church orphans' home. After a while, he was in and out of several foster parent homes. In most of these he did not receive the proper care and love every child needs and deserves. In fact, he related to me he was often mistreated. One day, he showed me a few ribbon scars he had between his shoulder blades on his back. Scars from a coat hanger used as a wire whip.

Marvin and I worked together for years. I was one job grade ahead of him, so he worked mostly under my direction. We got along well; he knew his job and did it with a good attitude and with proper results. He was fairly small, and like some small guys, he had a pretty large ego and was pretty cocky in his mannerisms. He didn't seem to realize the fact of his physical size.

Now, I am about average height. But, I can understand why a shorter person might have a big ego. It was alright by me, Marvin having this large ego. I sort of envy guys who are a little on the tall side; for instance, my brother. Before he got old, my brother was six foot six inches. Being older now, he has shrunk some. But he is still taller than me. I have always blamed the fact of my lack of loftiness on the possibility that my starting smoking (I stopped just a few years ago) at a very early age limited my growth in the upward direction.

Working together on cold, lonely night shifts sometimes you confide in each other about home life, growing years, hopes and dreams. Marvin's dream was to become a pro bowler. We bowled together on occasion. He was good at it: He had several 300 games to his credit. My wife was usually there with us on these bowling nights. My best score was my very first game: 128. For me, it never got any better. I eventually quit trying, and sold the ball, shoes and satchel I had bought for the sport with such great expectations.

Marvin met a beautiful young single girl fairly close to his own age and height one night at the bowling alley. I'm going to call her Joleen for the purposes of this story. It seemed to be love at first sight for the two of them.

Joleen worked as a clerk in one of the county offices; a regular weekday job. It wasn't long before they were spending all the time together Marvin's irregular work hours would allow. As Marvin and I worked together a lot of the time, that meant the four of us started spending quite a bit of time together, my wife included. Quite often one or both was over at our house.

Just prior to one long change weekend, Marvin and Joleen told us of their plans to be married. My wife and I had planned to fly to Colorado on that particular weekend and visit my folks in the small city of Golden, near Denver. Marvin said he and Joleen wanted us to go to Reno with them that same weekend and witness their marriage. After the ceremony, they would take us to the airport for the Denver flight.

After some discussion, the plan was agreed to and all reservations were made. The four of us would leave for Reno the next day, Thursday, as soon as Marvin and I got off shift. My wife and Joleen would take off work on that Friday.

Things went as planned. We witnessed their marriage; they took us to the airport where we made the Denver flight as scheduled.

After a few weeks had passed, I received a promotion and transfer to another plant. Marvin and I were no longer working together, but I managed to keep the same shift rotation I had previously worked; the four of us were able to continue common activities.

After a few weeks had passed, my wife informed me we needed to have a conference. When she approaches me like this, I pay attention. I know that it concerns something that really is bothering her. We sat aside a time.

The discussion, as it turned out, concerned Marvin and Joleen. My wife had observed some very dark bruises on Joleen's chest and upper arms when they were changing clothes together prior to one of our nights out on the town. Bruises on areas of her body that were normally covered by clothing. My wife continued, talking in a quiet deliberate manner. Some of the bruises were very dark as if recently acquired, others faded as if older. I did not know what to say.

My wife reminded me that Joleen had quit her job a few weeks after they had married. She then told me that Marvin had required Joleen to plan her day as if she were working shift work with him; to do housework and shopping as best she could when he was working. To sleep only with him when he slept, regardless whether it be day or night. She was to give him all of her time when he was not working. This way, he knew exactly where she was and what she was doing. He would call her randomly when he was on the graveyard shift to make sure she was home and awake.

I repeat, I did not know what to say. When we were all together, everything seemed to be just fine. Just as it had appeared to me before they married.

I was raised to never lift your hand in anger toward any woman. To place them above your own well being; to protect them when required. To cherish them. Especially your wife. I could not believe Marvin was mistreating Joleen. So, I stuck my head in the sand over the whole affair.

Shortly after this conference my wife and I had, I received a job offer in Wyoming at a substantial increase in pay and a promise of regular weekday hours. I accepted, putting all other matters on a 'back burner'. In other words, I purposely ignored a problem I could not even comprehend the facts concerning or the solution of: Marvin physically beating Joleen.

For a going away present, the two of them gave us a large framed print of a cabin in the wilderness, accompanied by a "Best Wishes" card. Inside the card they had written: With Love. Friends Always. Marv and Joleen.

Years went by. After a few holiday greeting cards and the exchange of some brief letters, communication between the four of us finally dwindled to nothing. The way things happen sometimes when miles and time separate. Eventually my wife and I moved back to California. I started a new job, the same type of occupation, but with a different organization.

One of my new fellow employees, as it turned out, had worked for the same company in the same plant as Marvin, and knew him. One vacation time, this co-worker and mutual friend went back to his hometown where the plant was for a visit.

After his return and a few days later at the first opportunity I had to talk with him, I asked him about so-and-so and this-and-that. He responded to all my queries in detail, some of which were humorous and we laughed over those together. Finally, I asked him if he had seen Marvin.

He paused, his mood instantly changing. He looked very seriously at me and informed me that Marvin was dead. That Joleen had stabbed him in the chest with a butcher knife in the kitchen of their home; that he had died. Immediately afterward, she had called the police. They responded; after a short time, an ambulance took Marvin away. The police had been called to the home so many times before due to Marvin's violent abuse of her they didn't even consider any legal action. She was never arrested or even charged.

Sometimes, when memories take me back to those years now passed so long ago, I do regret not having the courage or knowledge to have responded to the problem. Maybe I could have stopped it, somehow.

I don't feel sorry for Marvin. It is too bad he died. It's too bad when anyone dies before their natural time. It is fortunate they had no children.

As I mentioned, I do not feel sorry for Marvin. Any man that raises his hand in anger at his wife doesn't deserve any better. Nor do I fault Joleen for Marvin's death. For her, I do have compassion. Knowing her as I did, she will never be able to forgive herself.

I have put the wilderness cabin print and card away. Maybe Someday I'll hang it up again. With the card. Friends Always.

Different Targets

Just to set the record straight so everybody knows what's what, I'll give you some pertinent information. Concerning pistols, my buddy Steve is a really good shot. When Daniel Boone became a ghost and no longer had the ability to pick up, aim and shoot a rifle, the Great Marksman in the Sky decided to think about getting a replacement and along came Steve. So the great and terrible responsibility of the Daniel Boone Syndrome just got dumped on him more or less by default: He just happened to have been there at the right...or wrong time. Whichever. Concerning pistols, that is. Rifles...well, that was something else.

Now this wasn't all bad. 'Cause Steve enjoyed messing around with his hands and stuff like that. Him being an educated man and having to make a living working with his head instead of traipsing around the country living off the land like his predecessor did, he really needed to have some of the opposite end of the scale, so to speak.

So Steve, for reasons unbeknownst to himself, desired and acquired an arsenal that puts Sam Colt's to shame. If such a caliber existed, Steve got one: Pistol, rifle or musket. This was just meant to be. Then he proceeded to fill out the inventory by finding and obtaining the reloading equipment needed for each and every single caliber including a supply of lead, zinc and bullet molds.

Now as time went by, Steve became proficient in figuring the best type and charge of powder, shape and weight of bullet that would hit the desired spot on the target when propelled from one of his many propellers. Eventually, he and I became acquainted through mutual friends. We discovered we had the hobbies of reloading, target shooting and hunting in common.

Now I sure am not a Daniel Boone. Or Buffalo Bill Cody. But, being USMC trained, I am not exactly a sorry shot, either. I can, on occasion, hit the target in the desired and proper place using my rifle. But I can't outshoot Sure Shot Steve using pistols. But then, I don't try. I, having seen him in action, right away decided I was going to enjoy his company on bullet-throwing outings and such, but I was never going to challenge him or be a threat to his invincibility. Nossir.

People who are really good and have a great talent at certain specific things sometimes are a little temperamental. Take golfers, just forstance. When they are standing on a tee box and preening for a drive, nearstanders better not move, shuffle their feet, cough or point out that the clubhouse is on fire. They just better stand there, totally silent until the down stroke swing and follow through is completed, the ball has stopped right where it was intended, and the wooden tee is recovered and pocketed. Daniel Boone type people are much the same way. Plus the fact, they can swing a club-type weapon the same way a golfer can. At any chosen target within range.

Anyway, one day Steve and I were target shooting at a public pistol and rifle range on the 200 yard target line. If I remember correctly, Steve was shooting a .17 caliber varmint rifle; I was using my full military .30-06 caliber 1903-A3 Springfield. At target check break, we walked up to the target line and started stapling new targets to the heavy cardboard backing on top of the first target. Actually, I had hit my target so few times it was hardly used. But, by putting up a new target, I gave the appearance of needing a clean sheet, so to speak.

As soon as Steve finished stapling his new target, he started to attach a small-varmint silhouette on each corner of the four foot square target. About then a guy wandered up to staple a target just to my right. He observed the small targets Steve was stapling to each corner. Suddenly the newcomer very decisively told Steve he shouldn't do that; it was out of the normal target area and the bullets would destroy the cardboard backing sheet. Furthermore, the cardboard was expensive and the caretaker-club running the range was responsible for the replacement cost of each cardboard sheet. Steve made no reply, he simply removed the small target sheets he had stapled up.

When we had finished our target replacement work, we turned and walked back to the firing line. The target area of the range was determined empty of people and safe for shooting, the commence firing order was given. After a few slow, carefully aimed, well placed shots fired by Steve and me, the same guy who had chastised Steve earlier at the target line walked up to our bench rest area lugging two fairly large scraps of limp cardboard. He began suggesting that Steve should go up to the target area at the next cease- fire and hang the cardboard scraps. Then Steve could staple the smaller varmint targets onto the scrap cardboard just anywhere he pleased. He kept haranguing Steve about other people unnecessarily damaging the expensive heavy cardboard target backing sheets by not using the cardboard as it was intended to be used.

Writing of people thoughtlessly and carelessly haranguing armed individuals: When I was deer hunting years ago in Colorado near Craig, one of our party shot a buck that managed to get off huntable BLM land onto fenced supposedly private farmland before it was still. As luck would have it, naturally, a farmer saw the whole scenario. And, being the good-natured fellow most Colorado farmers who have leased BLM land, fenced and illegally locked the fenceline gates as if the land were their own, the unarmed farmer greeted the armed hunter with a "get the hell off my land."

Same smart thing here. A guy is sighting in on a paper target with a loaded rifle when a 'rocket scientist' sort of fellow walks up and starts harassing a guy of unknown temper standards. I guess that's sort of like trying to play Russian Roulette with someone else holding the gun.

Finally, on seeing the fairly frosty look Steve was giving him, he asked, "Am I bothering you?" Instead of shooting him, Steve very quietly answered, "Yes."

Mr. Rocket Scientist quickly retrieved the two pieces of flimsy cardboard he had leaned against the bench rest Steve was using, and turning, walked quickly and quietly away. Quietly, until he considered he was a safe distance away. On approaching a group he appeared to be with or at least was familiar with, he started complaining about some people not being at all friendly. I looked over at Steve who was again concentrating on his target. I wasn't about to draw his attention away from the target back to Mr. Rocket Scientist.

Steve had previously acquired an old original .45-70 Government issue rifle and civilian RCBS Company loading dyes. One of the very few American-made rifles he lacked prior possession. It was beautiful. Looked new.

He loaded up a few rounds and we headed for the range to try out the new toy.

At the range, I was assigned target 10, Steve target 9. Target 11, to my left, was being used by a guy shooting a Remington carbine chambered .243 Winchester. To Steve's right was a guy shooting a copy of the NATO issue chambered .223 Remington on target 8.

After we were set up at the bench rests and the 'commence firing' order had been given, he offered me the first shot with the new possession. Naturally, I took it. Surprisingly enough, the rifle did not kick much harder than my full military Springfield, the rifle I had brought that day.

When I had shot a half dozen or so rounds with my Springfield and Steve had fired only two or three, he commented that he could not find the point of impact on his target. He asked me if I would step back to the twin-barreled spotting scope set on a permanent mount just to the rear of the firing line to observe his target as he resumed shooting. I did as he asked and observed absolutely nothing. He fired a couple more with the same result. Nothing visible. Over and over we did this. Same result.

Cease fire came, and we all opened breeches and headed for the targets. On arriving, Steve is looking dumbfounded at his totally unused paper. Looking at my target, I could see the thumb-sized hole in the four-ring on mine made by Steve's .45-70 rifle I had used that one time. There were also several smaller holes fairly well patterned in the 8 ring from my own .30-06 rifle.

The guy on target 8 using the .223, arrived at his target a little after we had. Examining his target, he commented: "Wow, look at the really big holes on my target!" Steve looked at that fellow's target. I could see his shoulder's sag, realizing those were his bullet holes on the wrong target. He sad nothing to the other fellow still standing there scratching his head wondering how his little bullets made such big holes. This I am never going to let Steve live down.

On another excursion to the same public range, instead of using small paper varmint silhouette targets, Steve hung up three or four golf balls, each hanging by a two-foot piece of monofilament fishing line attached by a single staple. After the 'commence firing' order was given, Steve proceeded to totally destroy those Spaulding II golf balls, each in turn. This at twenty-five yards. With a .45 Cal semi-auto pistol. He invited me to try. I politely declined, stating I had no grudge against golf balls as my father was an avid golfer and I could not, in good conscience, shoot at golf balls, much less be able to hit one. A mental block, you might say. Excellent excuse.

Back at home, a few weeks later, Chuck, a fellow target shooter and I had plans to meet at a local pistol range early one Spring Saturday. We had made the date several days earlier. Then Sure Shot Steve called and asked if he and his wife could come up that same Saturday for a visit and also to get in a little target practice. So I notified Chuck that Steve had called and asked if he could come up on that same weekend that he and I had target practice planned; that Steve would like to go to the range with us. Chuck quickly ok'd Steve's accompanying us. Now, not thinking of the previous golf ball feat, I suggested Steve wasn't all that good a shot and we should sort of make allowances. I personally figured that with the three of us simultaneously shooting at paper targets no one of us would pay much attention to the other, so Steve's probable shooting superiority shouldn't be too obvious. This way no one would be embarrassed. Still, not thinking of golf balls. No big deal.

On the fateful day of the practice, Steve and I met Chuck at the pistol range and after introductions; we set up to start our target practice on a thirty-five yard range. We shot at paper targets for a few rounds; occasionally stopping and going up to change target sheets. Then at one new target time, Steve carried three or four golf balls, each with a foot-long string of monofilament fishing line attached by a staple. He hung the balls on the top target mounting wire, each about a foot apart. As we walked back to the firing line, Chuck, having notice Steve's change of target choice, sort of looked sideways at him. Sure, now, (I know he was thinking) we're going to hit one of those little old round golf balls. Maybe up close with a baseball bat. Ha.

I guess the last straw was when Steve knocked one of the balls up the hill on his first shot, and as the ball started rolling back, he bounced it back up the hill with another easily placed shot. Chuck just put his stuff all away, tipped his hat to us and left. Steve finished off the rest of the balls.

Steve, calling timeout, went back up to the target line with another half-dozen stringed golf balls and hung them. Really proud of my own ability, I also put my stuff up. But, I didn't leave, I just sat and watched Steve get even with the rest of the golf balls.

At this point in time, when Steve and his better half come up to visit, I will specify no golf balls. And no pistols. Range is closed.

Days Of Golden Sunshine

A few years back I had made up my mind I was not ever going to have a hunting dog or rather, a dog of any kind of my personal own again. The last dog I had I lost to old age long before I was ready for her to be old. She was, I think, about the best hunting dog I had ever owned.

Normally, a bird hunter doesn't have all that many dogs. He finds a good one and they hunt together as long as health and life allows. So maybe four or five good hunting dogs is the usual for most people, figuring a hunting lifetime of twelve years per dog.

Bird hunters really become attached to their dogs. And the hunting dogs really become attached to their masters. Don't misunderstand me, most bird dogs are truly fine family dogs. But they answer to only one master when the chips are down; when the shotgun is slipped from its cover. The hunter is master.

Bird dogs, ninety-nine out of a hundred, are just about the most gentle dogs God ever created. They reserve the most of their love for their fellow hunter, their master. The bond between hunter and dog is like that of no other human-animal combination. I'm not sure which it is: whether the dog begins, over time, to think like its master or whether the master begins to think like the dog. Or maybe, simpler, they learn to read each other's minds. Only another bird hunter can understand what I've tried to explain.

The day of my downfall and lost resolution came by surprise. One day at work a fellow employee on days off came in to pick up his paycheck. And, he brought Sam with him. Sam was an English Setter and, at the time, two years old. He was wonderful. That night, after shift on the way home, I thought about my last hunter, Lady Bridgett Rhett III.

A few days later, I was still thinking about hunting dogs. What a pleasure they were to be around; how their intelligence sometimes amazes you both at home and in the field. And the affection they show no other animal is capable of.

Without having really made up my mind, I mentioned my thinking to my wife. She was not too encouraging. I guess she was thinking about the loss of Bridgett. That hurt was not mine alone. At this point, she didn't really say much about it, one way or another.

Now that I had voiced aloud my intentions and admitted them to my own inner self, I started thinking very seriously about getting a new pup. The more I thought about it, the more reasonable the whole idea became. I finally decided to look for a Golden Retriever. That breed of dog has very good all-around characteristics: Sturdy, enduring, loving, obedient and intelligent, adapted to cold or hot weather, and most important for a hunter: Calm and determined.

A few days later in our local paper I found an ad stating "Golden Retriever puppies for sale" and made note of the telephone number. I called and made an appointment for the next day. On arriving, I was asked into the living room to wait for the pups to be let in. I sat down in an open space on the carpeted floor, waiting for the pups to arrive.

As soon as the puppies came in, they all bunched around me sniffing and being generally nosy the way pups are. All except for one. It simply crawled into my lap and squirmed around, making a nest for itself, and lay down. As I picked it up to check out the plumbing, I said to it, "If you are a little lady, you are mine." It was a female. Holding the pup under one arm, I stood. I paid the owner and received the AKA paper applications. With me carrying my new puppy, I walked out the door of her old home to take to her new one.

When we got into my pickup and I sat down, she crawled into my lap. She stayed there all the way home.

Her first night in her new home was a disaster. I was working the night shift, and my wife was sick with bronchitis. She wouldn't let the pup on the carpet in the house, so out in the garage the dog went.

Now my wife is really softhearted. After hearing the poor lonesome critter crying for company for a few minutes, she let the pup in the kitchen and closed the hall door, penning the pup in the kitchen. She soon discovered that didn't work, the pup still cried. Finally, she gave up and, as sick as she was, the two of them spent the night on a couple of blankets on the floor in the kitchen.

The next morning when I got home my wife told me, in no uncertain terms, I was to take the pup with me to work that night, and each night until I finished working the night shift. Period. So the next three nights or so, the pup spent the night in the cab of the pickup parked at work.

My poor pickup survived the occupation of the pup, and the pup survived the remaining graveyard shifts. Every time I came close to the truck, I could see the pup standing in the seat with her front feet on the seatback, looking out the rear window…I suppose, looking for me. Occasionally, as my shift duties would allow, I would stop and let the pup out to piddle or whatever. And, give and get a little love.

On the first of my days off at the end of the shift, I decided it was time to give the puppy a name. Her face seemed to glow and her eyes shine with pleasure every time I appeared into her view. After some discussion, my wife and I decided the name would have to be Sunshine. After all, her coat was the color of golden sunshine and shiny all by itself. Matched the beginning of her personality. And, she was a female. I decided on the name "Lady Golden Sunshine," quickly filled out the AKA registration papers and mailed them in.

Sunshine lived up to her name. The appearance of any familiar person brought a sunshiny smile to her face, a glow into her eyes and nonstop tail action. Later, as she grew and matured, the additional development of the many parts of her personality amazed me. She was one very sensitive, intelligent animal. I have raised my hand in anger for discipline only once, and I knew better when I did it. My tone of voice alone can bring her to tears. I mean, actual tears. On the other hand, I can also make her grin. Really big. With dancing eyes.

However, her training of me began right away. She let me know she expected to be near me at all times possible, she expected me to talk to her; she expected many touchings and caresses. She also let me know right away if I told her what I wanted her to do, she would do as I asked whether she agreed or not. Of course, as long as she understood. As I mentioned, she will cry easily when scolded. Raising of voice was not at all necessary. Unless she happened to be investigating something out of my line of sight, then it was permissible for me to call her in an extremely loud voice at early morning mealtime.

Normally she is awake before me and has quietly readied herself for her morning vitamins and breakfast. As I open the door, she is sitting up, greeting me with a smile and polishing the clean garage floor with her tail.

As far as becoming housebroken...it happened. I was never sure how it happened, but it happened. She did it all herself. I had a terrible time training children. They could have taken lessons from her, believe me. To this date she has never made a mistake. Even on very frequent long trip confinement. She simply waits until I decide it's sandbox time. And, I do that as often as I think she needs to go for her comfort. This is sometimes wasted effort. At each stop, she enjoys smelling everything everywhere as most hunters do, even if the stop is otherwise unproductive.

When she was about four months old, my wife and I needed to make a quick journey to Colorado. Sunshine had not yet been exposed to any lengthy travel, so we decided to board her as there were no accommodations at the other end. A friend of mine I worked with, Chuck, had a beautiful boarding/training facility in the hills not too far from our home. I decided to leave her with him for the duration of the trip, as I knew he loved and loves most dogs more than people.

Chuck agreed to board her so we arranged to meet to transfer Sunshine to him just as he started his way home from work after his graveyard shift. This transfer location would save me the several miles time and travel to his home and kennel facility. His questioning of me concerning her needs included whether she was prone to be carsick. I told him I had taken her quite a few places in an auto and pickup with no problem whatsoever.

So, on the morning of the transfer, I got up and fed Sunshine her morning ration, and then we got in the truck to go to the work meeting place. Chuck arrived shortly. I gave him Sunshine and told her goodbye. He drove off with her head in his lap; before he had gone more than a mile she promptly threw her breakfast up in his lap. He told me this on my return a couple weeks later. Even that much later, he still was a little unhappy about it. However, he did allow us to continue to board her there with him from time to time until I decided I wanted her with us on trips.

Sometimes on a winter evening as Sunshine and I sat by the fire, me watching a program on the television, I would reach for some dried almonds I kept on a table by the side of my favorite chair. Now, Sunshine is the same as all dogs. If she could really talk and you were to ask her, she would tell you she is constantly on a starvation diet. However due to her inability to express herself vocally, her eyes let you know exactly what she wants you to know and understand.

One evening, I decided to give her one almond just to see if she really liked it. Big mistake. She loved it. After that evening, I would give her exactly five almonds, one at a time, counting out loud as I gave her each. After my wife observed this ritual a few times, she asked me why I was counting. I told her I was counting each out so that Sunshine would learn when she had all her ration. My wife gently teased me that I really probably thought I was teaching her how to count; that I should only give her four and she was sure Sunshine would not know the difference.

The next evening as I started the ritual with my wife watching, I only counted out four almonds and gave Sunshine one at a time, counting out as usual, only stopping at four. Sunshine sat there, looking at me, eyeballing me and partially wagging her tail, looking like she wanted to jump in my lap. In other words, we were not through with the almonds. I took another from the jar, spoke the word five, and gave her the fifth almond. She promptly chewed the five nuts and lay down, completely satisfied. I looked at my wife who was sitting there, shaking her head in obvious amazement.

My father really liked Sunshine. Of course, all people who care for dogs admire the Golden Retriever breed. One day on a visit, he and I were sitting talking. I told him of the almond incident and my wife's amazement at Sunshine's intelligence. He didn't really believe me. So, Sunshine and I demonstrated to him. Same thing. She let me know that four nuts were not enough. After I gave her the fifth, she was again content, ate the five nuts and lay back down by my side. He then admitted that Sunshine was a pretty smart dog. Personally, I think it was a great part of her desire and willingness to please me and the following praise she gains that enabled her to both learn and appear to be very intelligent. I think this is probably the way with most domesticated animals, especially dogs.

Early in our association, Sunshine began to show a peculiar form of possessiveness. As I drove up to the front of the house on my return from work, I would open the garage door in order to go in the house through the kitchen door. When my wife would hear the noise of the garage door opener, she would go out the kitchen door to greet me. Sunshine, having identified the sound of my truck engine, would also meet me just outside the garage. As my wife and I would hug and kiss, Sunshine would "nose" her way very positively between us, so that Nancy and I would have to make room for her. This became a normal thing, and continued until shortly after I retired. I suppose Sunshine thought that now she had me around all the time, she didn't need to protect her right of ownership.

I mentioned she learned to identify the sound of my truck engine. She also learned to identify the sound of both the truck and car of our good friends, Millie and Ed. This couple would frequently journey to Oroville from their home in Clear Lake and visit us. When Sunshine had her first (and only) litter, we had given Ed one of her largest pups. As Cid, Ed's pup, became full grown, Sunshine would look forward to their visit. I assume that is why she learned to identify both of their vehicles. Even after Cid's untimely death from leukemia, she still would meet them on the driveway or give them a greeting bark or two through the closed garage door as they drove up. It was a long time, though, before she quit expecting Cid to romp out of the vehicle to greet her.

In the evenings when Sunshine is allowed in the house, summer or winter, she will lay on her special pad, napping in front of the fireplace. Since I have retired, I have encouraged this as a form of togetherness, especially in the wet weather when I am unable to spend much time outside with her. Each evening, around 8:00 pm, I will mute the television volume and whisper "Cookie?" Sunshine will immediately be completely wide awake from a very sound sleep, look around for and pick up any toy she might have brought in with her, and start for the kitchen's garage door. Visitors in our home who witness this evening ritual shake their heads in amazement. I follow her into the garage. She will go around the car to the rag barrel where I keep a sack of dog biscuits inside it. I will select two; she will immediately sit down on her bed and try to "nose" the biscuits out of my hand. After two or three attempts at this, a normal thing for us, I give her the biscuits and leave her for the night.

Back to Sunshine going on trips. When she first became old enough to begin to realize we were making preparations for a journey, she also began to understand sometimes she might be left behind. At first I was unaware that she was beginning to understand what was taking place. But, later after we decided it would be a regular thing to take her, I began to realize as she observed us she was very unsure as to whether she would be included in the trip my wife and I were busy making preparations for. She began to go to the backyard garage door and lie down directly in the passageway with her back toward me and my busy doings. After seeing this two or three times and thinking the situation over, I began to be very obvious about the initial preparations and to make sure she knew what I was doing and that it was her odds and ends I was packing: Her brush and comb, her medicine, biscuits, daily food rations and dishes. Now, upon observing me doing all of that, it seems she is hardly able to wait until I finally lower the truck bed tailgate and invite her to get in.

Time has gone by; Sunshine is now just over eleven years of age. I was never able to take Sunshine bird hunting; of this I have severe regret. I wrote earlier of packing Sunshine's "medicine" in preparation for trips. Even though, after examination of her x-rays, the vets at the University of Missouri gave her pelvic and hip development a clean bill of health prior to breeding, she has developed a form of hip dysplasia. We now give her a half tablet of Cortuba once daily. As long as we give her plenty of exercise with the medication, she still gets around pretty well. For now. I have no idea how many more days of Golden Sunshine there will be. But, I am grateful for every single day.

Letter To Charlie

July 8, 2010
Dear Charlie:

Well...I guess enough time has gone by at this point...I can't justify any longer to myself not writing this. It is well overdue for both our sakes.

I should have written this letter years back when you first asked me to do it. I procrastinated as nobody likes to think of mental problems like Alzheimer's happening. But I was talking to Pete the other day down at the Santa Fe Jr. Railroad Café and he was telling me no more hunting trips for him; we were going to have to do it by ourselves. His wife's mental condition had deteriorated to the point he felt he could no longer leave her for more than a couple hours. He was sure that was going to change pretty quickly as things with her seem to be happening more rapidly as each day passes. So I decided if I am gonna do this, I better get it done. While *I still can.*

Looking back now, it really was a long time ago. It has to have been at least fifty years ago since it all began. Maybe a little more. Back in the days of our youth. Could we have really been that young? Certainly long enough for me to not be able to remember some of the best parts. I will really be on my guard as I write this.

I remember you were single then, but if I recall correctly, you were trying to make up your mind whether to ask Ann to marry you. You weren't too long out of the Navy and on coming back home, you had moved back in with your folks. You started to work at the plant in the operations department where I was already employed, and you and I wound up working the same shift together. I was supposed to be breaking you in on the various responsibilities of the job.

Your mother had given you her pink Ford Thunderbird…the model with the portholes in the hard-top…You were driving it around like it was black or some other male-acceptable color.

I was married, and had just bought a house on Mildred Avenue using the G.I.Bill with the no-down payment feature. I wasn't too long out of the Marines and didn't have much money to spend on extra personal things like bait and fishing gear even though we lived almost right on the river.

I had been fishing the waters of the confluence of the Sacrament and San Joaquin Rivers the year or so with almost no success just before you and I met. It wasn't too long after our first meeting that things changed. Boy, did they change.

You remember at work one early sunny spring afternoon we were both out at the plant cooling water intake, checking the water differential across the inlet trash racks. Making sure there was little or no unseen underwater debris collected on the screening racks.

As I recall, the tide must have been full ebb, and we both saw these monster striped bass eating small marine and plant life that collected and grew in the mud on the top of the square water intake tunnels. The size of these many large fish feeding there astounded the two of us. The only problem was this fish-feeding activity all taking place inside a fenced-off rectangular area of pretty fair dimensions. This feeding area seemed too far for us to be able to cast to it fishing from the bank. And there was no way we could get a boat where we needed it to be able to capture these monsters on hook and line. We spent all next week trying to figure out how to accomplish this from the outside of the fenced piling area.

One of our next days off, we decided to go ahead and try fishing off the shore inside the fenced-off area. So we went to Tony's Bait shop for bait. Tony had no fresh or frozen sardines, the favorite striper bait. The sardine netting season was yet to open for the year. All that Tony had was frozen anchovies. We bought a few pounds of them.

Now at the fishing site the cast to the feeding area was, as we figured, beyond our ability. We did spend the whole of the day there, catching only small stripers which we had to return to the river as they were all below the minimum keeper size of sixteen inches.

Finally, we decided the only thing we could do was to scrape enough money together to rent a boat at the old San Joaquin Boat Harbor and tie it up to the upstream side of the fence piling during outgoing tide. I had a six horse Elgin boat motor we could use to get the boat back and forth to the harbor so we were in business. And we were really in business.

We caught plenty fish that first day with the boat snugged up against the pilings. But all we brought home was a bunch of broken leaders with no hooks left. The big guys would take the bait, we would set the hook, and the fish would head for the nearest piling to wrap the line around and around the piling posts in order to break the line. Smart fish. It wasn't long, that first day, before we mostly ran out of bait and hooks. I think we ran of bait first, though. But we did prove to ourselves we could catch fish, really big fish.

I am sure you remember the next trip. We determined the only way we could bring any of these fish home was to get inside of the piling area. You suggested we use the small green two-man rubber raft of yours you use for support when you went scuba diving in the ocean. Then, at low tide, we could ease our way inside the piling area using the raft and probably be able to play the hooked fish keeping them away from the piling posts.

On our next days off, we loaded the blown-up raft and our gear into the back of your brand-new white Ford pickup. We went to Panfili's bait shop and asked for ten pounds of sardines. All we could get were frozen sardines as it was not only out of season for sardine, it was out of season for strippers. It was legal to fish for the strippers alright, it was just out of season for them to be in our area. Wrong time of year. The late spring run was still weeks off. The guy at the bait shop openly laughed at us. We just grinned and bore it because we weren't all that sure ourselves.

We 'killed' them. After a few first losses, we got the hang of it and were catching so many, we were putting them back in the water. That was back in the days before catch-and-release was legal, too. Only it had been such a long dry haul for both of us in the fishing department, we plumb forgot that catch-and-release was illegal in the excitement of our success.

You remember, we even gave a ten-pounder to each of our two fishless buddies fishing on the bank that first day. We felt sort of guilty, us catching all those fish with them watching us. Especially as they were catching none.

Bait gone, we took the six large ones we had kept a limit of three each home and cleaned them. Stuck them in my freezer and in our enthusiasm, went back for more bait. This time, the guy at Panfili's accused us of lying to him when we told him we had such great success with the first batch of bait. In spite of his attitude, and as he had the only game in town, we bought him out. Twelve pounds, all he had left, at twenty-five cents per frozen pound.

Later that day, when we had run out of bait again, we decided to take our second limit apiece to the bait shop to show the guy we weren't the usual type of fisherman. That the big ones really didn't get away. He was so astounded he took a picture or two of us in front of the bait shop holding a stringer of those huge bass. He gave us each a Polaroid that day, and had one published in the Delta Fishing Guide, remember? I still have mine, somewhere. But lately I have looked all over and not yet found where I hid it.

One of the many times we went fishing there, I remember you hooked this striper that was bigger than the raft. Only, it was just barely hooked through the tough skin on its lower jaw. You had pretty well played him till he was plumb tired out and he was lying there by the side of the raft, looking at us. He was the biggest darn fish I had ever seen that was still able to swim. You told me to grab it with both arms and pull him into the raft. And, I told you there wasn't room for the three of us. Anyway, I tried, and knocked him off the hook. I thought for a minute or two you were going to make me follow him into the water.

Then one day, not too long after that, you were getting a haircut in the old barber shop in downtown Pittsburg. You told me a day or so later the barbers and clients there that day were talking about the two nuts that had been seen several times in a small green rubber raft running around the river in all kinds of weather. That it must have been a couple of dumb kids that didn't know how dangerous that part of the river could be. However, they admitted the two guys were catching big stripers when there weren't supposed to be any big stripers around.

Well, no matter. Our bacon got saved. Our boss found out it was us fishing there inside the pilings. You remember, he didn't have a whole lot of sense of humor. Told us if he caught us fishing inside there again, even if it was on our days off, he was going to fire us. That we were pushing our luck...every time we took the raft inside the piling area.

You know, Charlie…I have always wondered. If I had of been able to get aholt of that big bass of yours…I'll bet he would have broken the all-time record for striped bass. The United States all-time record.

Well, that's it, Charlie. As best as I remember. Like I said, and as you know, it was a whole long time ago. I hope I got it mostly right. I'm also glad the statute of limitations has run out on this even though that one taking of the two limits in one day was the only time we ever did that.

As I mentioned above: As best as I can remember. We were sure 'nuff young…and maybe a little stupid, too. But them sure wuz golden days, weren't they? We really had the world by the tail…

Your old buddy,
Eric.

The Johnny Jones Affair

One day, around 1950, Johnny Jones arrived in the town of Seagraves, Texas. Just like that. He did not come in the dead of night; but a brass band didn't welcome his arrival. It was just that all of a sudden there he was in town. After some little time had passed, it was as if he had always been there.

He took a room in the old stately Simpson Hotel. And, I guess he stayed there off and on until the day he died.

In younger, more innocent days, most small towns had their strange, unique individuals. Sometimes they were a packrat type of hermit, walking the streets of town day after day with no clear purpose in mind, and having a tote sack sung over their shoulder. And living in a shack just outside of town. Nobody knew much about them; where they came from or what they did. They, all of a sudden, were there and seemed to have been there all along and you were just now noticing them.

Johnny Jones sort of fit that description. One day, he was just there. But he didn't carry a tote sack or pick up small objects of junk and leave it lying here and there on the ground around his shack. On the contrary, he was very neat and well dressed. He always wore ironed and starched long-sleeved shirts and pants, both gray in color and of the semi-dressy type. As I have mentioned after a while he just seemed to have always been there. People accepted him just as if he had always been around town.

It became obvious after a while that he loved kids. And kids took a very strong liking to him. No one knew if he ever had any children of his own or even if he had ever been married. Not many people knew much about

Johnny. He kept a whole lot to himself, and didn't volunteer much of his past life. He just sort of adopted all the kids in the town. And, they all took to him it seemed right away.

On the south end of town there was a fair-sized triangular shaped vacant lot. It fronted on the Seagraves-Seminole highway. It was really too far out of the main part of town to be of much use at that time. But Johnny had visions of it being of plenty use to him. It would appear that he had looked around town to see what he could do to make life more interesting for the young people of town. So he bought the vacant lot and in time built a first-class roller skating rink.

He also threw in a one-lane bowling alley on the south side of the building. For some reason or other he never quite finished the alley. It never had a pin-setter, manual or automatic. Maybe he ran out of money. Or changed his mind, maybe some other really good reason. What there was of the bowling alley was added after the rest of the place was mostly finished, like maybe it was an afterthought.

Needless to say, the roller rink was the best thing that happened in the town for the kids since the swimming pool was rebuilt. The whole thing from the very beginning was constantly on the mind of the entire town and the topic of conversation at coffee time in all of the drug stores and cafes, such as they were. And coffee time conversation was a big thing back then.

After all, this was before television and folks were mostly tired of plain old radio. Everyone held their breath waiting for the completion of the building of the rink. The way it seemed, back then, was that Johnny wasn't in all that big a hurry to finish and open the roller rink. I guess maybe he never figured to get rich from it because he never did. And I guess he figured stringing out the duration of the wait was worth more than arriving at the end of the wait.

Finally the rink was finished. He opened it up without much of a fanfare. At least, not one that he organized.

What I mean is, there was no brass band. But I figure everyone in the whole town was there. Few of the teenagers at that time had cars. A lot of them had bicycles; the rest hitched rides to places or walked. Back then it was alright to pick up hitch-hikers; if the people doing the hitching and the people doing the picking up all knew each other, then it wasn't really hitchhiking, was it?

Anyway, cars were parked all over the place. The vacant spaces all around the rink was filled up with cars and bicycles; people had to park their cars across the highway. I reckon you could say the opening of the rink was a big success. And I don't think that many people were ever there at one time again. Not even for birthday parties and such.

Sometimes Johnny would find out about a circus or two going broke, or by some other way of advertisement, and he would buy a few caged wild animals. He would keep them on the north side of the rink in sort of a sheltered area. All the kids in town would go out to see the animals. One time he had a baboon with a very nasty disposition. The baboon would blow spit at people who came within range. Johnny had an African lion for a short while.

He wound up keeping a brown bear for years, even after the rink closed. All this was for the young people's benefit. That was Johnny. That was the way he was.

Years went by. Television cut the rink's attendance considerably. The two movie houses, the Wallace and the Pix closed. The Wallace closed first, but that was mostly due to the opening of the drive-in theater south of town. It was about as popular with the kids as the roller rink had been. You could not only hold your girl at the drive-in, you could kiss her with practically no one the wiser or even care.

The drive-in closed after the Wallace, a while later the Pix closed. Then the roller rink finally closed its doors. It sat there empty and unused for years. As I mentioned before, I don't figure Johnny ever thought he was going to get rich from the roller rink, and he didn't.

The whole thing was sort of like Larry McMurtry's book, "THE LAST PICTURE SHOW." Everything just sort of folded up, one thing after the other. The businesses and stores on Main Street closed one after the other. Pretty soon the store buildings on the street were mostly deserted. Store windows were frosted over with Bon Ami.

Johnny kept on living some at the Simpson Hotel. Quite often he would stay out at his rink in the very modest living quarters there. However, that was pretty lonesome, and Johnny liked people. Especially young people.

Life in our small town pretty much went on as before he arrived. Television became a big thing. Prosperity occurred with enough influence that allowed many more young people to either drive Momma and Poppa's car…or have one of their own of some sort or other.

One warm summer bright moonlit night, Johnny decided to take a walk, down past the sad empty roller rink. The rink that once had many kids going round and round on its oak floor; in time to the recorded organ music. For many, a really happy place in a really happy time. For some reason, Johnny wound up walking south on the ties between the railroad track rails that were laid just east of the highway that fronted the rink.

At the same time, also for whatever reason, a carload of kids had let most of the air out of the tires on their car, and mounted the car on the railroad track. There wasn't much danger in them meeting a train, and the low air pressure helped the tires sort of grip the rails.

When the west carbon black plant was open, the train came and went each day at noon. But since the plant had closed train traffic was very rare. So the kids went north speeding on the empty rails, headlights off, silver rails shining in the moonlight. They met Johnny Jones. He didn't figure on them, they didn't figure on him.

Johnny was hit and knocked off the tracks by some of the very young people he so loved and served all those many years. As the car headlights were off as they traveled, I doubt if they knew they had hit Johnny.

He managed to walk back into town to the open Gulf Station. The owner helped pick the stickers out of Johnny and his clothes. The both sort of laughed about the whole thing as Johnny's dignity was hurt worse than he was physically.

Not long after that, Johnny died of a heart attack. It was just before Christmas. December 17, 1966. A sad day for all who knew him. A sad day for the town.

No kin claimed Johnny; he is buried in a lonely grave in the community cemetery just north outside of town.

He really wasn't very old. About fifty-eight years. Today, most of us who still remember him are older than he was on the day he died.

A few years later, the empty roller skating rink building burned to the ground.

The lot now stands vacant again. Every sunset it looks empty and lonesome with the silent echo of organ music. Maybe it is waiting for another Johnny Jones to come by in the full circle of time.

For The Love Of Cid

I know that I am going to cry as I write this. I know this, as surely as I know the sun will rise over the eastern range of mountains this next morning, whether I am aware of it or not.

Cid was my friend. His owner, Ed, was my friend. I had known Cid since the early morning he was born. I had known Ed for many more years than that. They both have since crossed the rainbow bridge, Cid leading the way as he most always did.

I wasn't Cid's only friend besides his master. Cid had many friends. Most everyone who met him became his friend. Few people, if any, disliked him. And, if he ever disliked someone, he never let it show.

Cid died Tuesday, June 18, 1996 as a result of leukemia. Ed died a few years later in 2004. I miss them both.

Cid (El Cid del Oro, the registered name Ed gave him) was a Golden Retriever of noble ancestry. Both parents had impressive blood lines. He was one of a litter of twelve of which nine survived the trauma of birth. He had five brothers and three sisters, born of April 2, 1990.

I helped Cid's mother, Lady Golden Sunshine X, deliver her litter that early morning. So I can truthfully say I knew him from the very first.

Cid was a most unusual animal. All animals are unique unto themselves. But some have outstanding distinguishing characteristics that shine above all else. Cid was, to this day, one of the most unique I have ever known.

As the litter matured, Cid seemed to be the quietest and deliberately the slowest of the crew. One of his brothers, later named Flash, was a real flash. Flash was everywhere at once, seeing all that went on. For instance, after they were all weaned to a feed bowl, Flash would runaround chewing on all the other pups' tails as they tried to eat. Cid? Well, he would lie in a corner, watching the whole thing. Consequently, both Cid and Flash became the skinniest two pups of the litter.

Flash was the next to the last to get a home. Cid was the last. I am sure they weren't chosen earlier because both were so skinny. Suddenly Cid found himself alone with just his mother. Now he decided as there was nothing much left to watch at mealtime, he might as well eat his meals. Very soon he grew to a proportion I could not believe. I don't remember for sure, but I think he weighed around thirty pounds by the time he was fourteen weeks old. Not fat. Just big. Either of his front paws was as big as my hand and I have big hands. The rest of Cid was in proper proportion. Later, when he was fully grown, he weighed just over one hundred-twenty pounds. Very little, if any, of this was fat.

Cid's personality of detailed observation before acting reminded me of one of the two closest friends I have ever had. So, one of these two friends, Ed, lived not far from me. The next time Ed came over, I went outside and located Cid. I picked him up and carried him into the garage where Ed was and, holding Cid out at arm's length, I told Ed to hold the pup. Ed took Cid in his arms, and Cid cuddled right up into the crook of Ed's neck and tried to lick Ed's ears. I knew I had made the right choice.

I told Ed the pup was his. He tried to pay me for him; I told him no way. The pup was a special gift from me to him.

The two were a perfect match. They soon grew to love the other and became inseparable. Ed was a retired fire chief, and had plenty of time to give to his dog. They went everywhere together.

Ed had a habit of walking a mile from his home to the U.S. Post Office each day to collect his mail. Certainly Cid became a companion on this jaunt. One time after Ed got the mail from his box, he decided to walk a few blocks farther to buy something at the hardware store. After a few yards, Cid started to limp favoring his right front leg. Ed stopped and closely examined the foot and leg to try to determine what the matter was. He found nothing. Ed started off again, leash in hand, and the two walked a few more yards. Shortly Cid started limping again. Ed stopped and again examined Cid and found nothing as before.

Ed stood there thinking: He should get Cid home. As Cid was too heavy for Ed to carry, especially the mile back home, he needed to get Cid to walk before the limping problem got worse. So, Ed turned and started home. After a few yards and Cid understood they were going home, the limp completely disappeared.

Later on that day, Ed called me and related the tale of the morning mailbox trip incident. Laughing, I apologized to Ed for "Giving him a dog that was smarter than he was." Ed did not laugh so I am not sure about what he thought concerning my remark. But, Ed was forewarned.

One afternoon Ed's wife, Millie, was downtown shopping. During her travels, she passed a pet shop that had some pups in the store display window. One of them caught her eye; she decided Cid needed a younger brother. So she brought home J.D., the initials stood for 'Just Dog'. Cid and J.D. became exactly like brothers. Only J.D. was mostly wire-haired terrier, and fully grown wasn't much bigger that a good sized cat. But, he was solid. He weighed an easy thirty-five pounds and seemed to have all the body characteristics of a rock.

J.D. was pretty smart. He would tease Cid until Cid would take no more. J.D. would scurry off with Cid chasing him. J.D. would make it into the bedroom ahead of Cid and get under the bed where there was not room for Cid to be able to reach him. By the time J.D. would come out from under the bed, Cid would have forgotten the whole incident. Or maybe he just forgave his little brother.

Quite often Ed and Millie would go to a privately owned public campground over on the coast near Ft. Bragg, taking both dogs with them. Occasionally Nancy and I would join them; we would also take Cid's mother, our Sunshine, with us.

On one of those trips, Ed and I were walking on the wide sandy beach just off the campground. Ed had Cid on a leash which he dropped to give the dog freedom to run and splash in the shallow, and on that particular day, gentle surf.

For whatever reason, J.D. was also free to run. He took off after Cid, trying to grab the end of the trailing leash with his teeth as he had often done before. Finally he succeeded in catching the leash with his teeth. J.D. immediately applied all four brakes, skidding in the beach sand. Skidding in the sand, that is, until Cid reached the surf. All of a sudden, J.D. was no longer skidding in the sand, he was water skiing, and in surf over his head. He held on for dear life, a rooster-tail or sea water trailing him as he went. Finally, Cid ran out of surf, and veering away from a cliff that ended the path of travel slowing Cid down, J. D. was able to let go. In the meantime, Ed and I had just about collapsed on the beach, laughing;

It again became apparent that Cid was a very intelligent dog. One summer Ed and Millie, my wife Nancy and I took an 'RV' trip to the Midwest. Ed took Cid and J.D. with them, Nancy and I took Cid's mother, Sunshine, with us. All three dogs were good travelers.

We parted company in Salt Lake as Ed and his wife were going to stay there for a few days, visiting kinfolk. My wife and I were going on to Denver to visit relatives in that area. At the conclusion of the two separate visits, we would meet in Taos, New Mexico, about a week later.

We met without incident in Taos and continued after an overnight there on our leisurely return trip for home. Our travel was mostly along "old Route 66" until we deviated to Las Vegas for a two-night stay there to see a casino show or two.

The first night, before leaving for a 'night on the town', we shut Sunshine up in our trailer; Cid and J.D. were put up in Ed's. We had done this many times before without anything unusual happening. Ed and I figured they would act as watchdogs if anyone tried to break in either trailer.

Of course, as Golden Retrievers are really vicious, it wouldn't do a whole lot of good after the barking if someone did try to force entry. J.D. would probably hide under the bed.

On our return, Ed discovered that Cid, in order to get even for being left behind, had mostly eaten Ed's favorite Greek Fisherman's cap. In short order after Ed had discovered this, I thought Cid had breathed his last. Ed got pretty angry. In fact, I had never before seen him so angry. Of course Ed forgave Cid after fifteen minutes or so. Fortunately, Cid never did anything similar to that stunt again.

The next winter, Ed and Millie took the two dogs with them on an extended trip down to Cabo San Lucas, Baja California, Mexico. They were to return in the early spring of the following year.

Ed and Cid spent a lot of time on the beach. Cid would swim, chase waves and pester the sand crab. From the videos I've seen of that trip taken down there, I think Cid had the most fun. He aways had a grin on his face.

Ed was always very good about stopping for Cid to be able to leave his mark where ever they went on journeys. Boy dogs are different from girl dogs in that respect. Girl dogs don't seem to feel the need to leave their mark the way boy dogs are inclined to do. Often when the four of us were traveling together but in separate vehicles, I would feel the need for a stop. So I would call Ed on the C.B. and tell him, "Cid needs to stop." Ed would stop at the next opportunity to comply with my request. That is, Ed would usually stop. Sometimes he wouldn't until I would finally holler on the radio, "Pull over, dangit."

But, back to the Baja trip. On the way home after spending the winter down there, Ed pulled over for a 'Cid stop' and everyone got out and relaxed for a few minutes. I'm told the road was terrible and frequent rest stops were welcome. When everyone loaded back up, they continued north for twenty miles or so. Suddenly Ed noticed Cid was nowhere to be seen. A few miles further were driven before Ed could turn his van and trailer around to return to the area of the last rest stop to look for Cid. When they finally arrived back at the location of the last stop, Cid was sitting very placidly on the side of the road waiting. As soon as the van's door was opened to let him inside, he got in, Giving all a disgusted look, he got up on his usual traveling position on the top of the sink cabinet in the back of the van and went to sleep.

Most every day, Millie would go for an exercise walk, usually taking both dogs on leash with her. Cid was leash broken and easy to take along. J.D. was a more exuberant dog than Cid and even though leash broken he liked to 'do his own thing'. One morning, on Millie's usual walk with both dogs, J.D. managed to break away and was struck and killed by a passing automobile.

Of all the dogs I have been associated with, the Golden Retriever breed seems to be the best family dog of all. This statement is not that of authority by any means. I have come to this conclusion from my own observation and experience over the years. To me, they seem almost human, with the intelligence level of a young human child. I have seen my own Golden Sunshine grin hugely when playing. I have also seen her cry in sympathy on several sad situations.

My Golden Sunshine is not really mine. I belong to her. She accepts all the rest of the family. But I am her sole property.

This was exactly the way Cid regarded Ed. Ed was his sole property. Cid accepted the rest of the family, but Ed belonged to him. Sometimes I have seen Millie or my wife give Ed a hug. It had to be brief though or Cid would root with his nose in order to get between the two to separate them. He just didn't want anyone else to get very close to his Ed.

I swear I have seen that dog read Ed's mind on several occasions. I also have seen and heard Ed countless times talking to Cid; giving him instructions or chastising him gently when needed. Cid would react as if he knew exactly what he was being told, and respond almost exactly as requested. The time of the Greek Fisherman's cap meal was the only time I ever heard Ed raise his voice to that dog. All other times he spoke very softly to Cid.

Cid loved to tease Millie. He would do something he knew would get her goat, then swagger away grinning. This was a usual daily affair.

The older you get, the more precious a pet becomes. It seems to me they are sort of a substitute for a late-life child. A chance to do it all over again.

Cid became listless and seemed to have no energy. Morning mail walks seemed to be a struggle for Cid. Ed took him to his vet and the diagnosis was leukemia. Treatment followed. Expensive treatment. After weeks, the vet gave up and told Ed there was no hope.

One last trip to the vet: Ed brought El Cid home and put him in a space next to a flower bed. I visited Ed the next day. I kept my Sunshine inside the back fenced area; away from Ed. Ed seemed like a broken man. I don't think he ever quite recovered.

I loved Cid. Cid loved me. Some. He always let me kiss the top of his nose. With smiles and tears in remembering, I will miss him.

Ed loved Cid as much as I have ever seen anyone love a dog. And Cid loved Ed. Completely. With no reservations.

I miss them both.

The Chicken Shack

It really was just a shack. It had a wooden floor a foot or so above the ground, a galvanized tin roof with shiplap wooden siding. At this time, the normal sized door in the center of the front of the building had a wooden screen. I am not sure why this was; screens were to keep flies and other insects out but before this time there had been no real reason for it.

The shack had been used for chickens. Complete with a tiered roost and laying nests located underneath. And (as you might suspect) smelled powerfully strong of chickens even though they now lived somewhere in the past. Well, now that you know about the 'Chicken Shack' I'll let you in on the story behind it.

It was a mighty hot day one Texas June a lot of years ago. There wasn't a cloud in the sky; the wind was somewhere else. My fellow classmates and I had just returned from our senior class graduation trip. All of a sudden we were out in the real world, something we all had looked forward to until the ceremony on the last Friday in May. Now the celebration trip had postponed life; the trip was over; life had begun.

On our return to our home town, those of us with any remnants of absorbed education were all of a sudden scared silly. I was pumping gas and fixing flats at a Gulf gasoline service station on the north edge of town. Just exactly right across the highway where our graduation trip started. However the start of the trip had been delayed for a couple of hours. The school bus we were using was parked at the Standard Oil Service Station on the north edge of town. Two of our sponsors, volunteer firemen, felt the need to answer a sudden fire alarm leaving us and the bus we were using for the trip sitting there parked at the station in the early morning hot sun.

But…back to pumping gas. At that time, gas was twenty-five cents a gallon for real regular. I was making a whole fifty cents an hour. And, I was working for a really nice old guy; that made some difference. At that time, I didn't have much else to do except worry about starting college in the fall which I really did not want to do. I just wasn't ready in my head. Fact was, I really didn't know what I wanted to do. Korea was going on; I had thought some about joining a branch of the service. Maybe the Navy. But as I was a few weeks shy of eighteen there wasn't a whole lot I could do about that. Yet. As long as I could, though, I decided to stick my head in the sand and maybe that way I would never have to decide what I wanted to do.

This dusty late model Ford pickup drove up to a gas pump. I walked out to tend to his needs; filled him up with gas, checked the oil and wiped the mess of grasshopper stuff off the windshield. He paid me for the gas, then said he was "Looking for a couple or three farm hands 'till boll-pulling time. Fifty dollars a week, room and board included, Sundays off. Did I know of anybody?"

I hollered at Mac, my co-worker and told him what the guy had said. Mac came out of the grease room wiping his hands; "How about me and you?" I thought for about an instant, looked at the farmer and said 'How about it?" to which he asked "If you wouldn't be doing the station owner a bad turn if we left right now; that he needed hands today?"

Mac told him we would call a couple guys we knew who would take our place. We would be ready to leave in a couple hours: "How did we get there?"

As soon as the new station hands arrived, off we went to pick up the third guy, Ron, all our clothes and whatever else we deemed necessary at that time. We'd burnt our bridges, so to speak. Ron's mother had been screaming at him "You come back here" as we drove off.

We were in my pride and joy, a used up 1938 Chevrolet Master Delux four-door sedan. It was mostly black, and mostly had some upholstery covered with wool blankets, but it did have a really good engine.

We drove west until we were almost in New Mexico and arrived at the farm. This is where we met the chicken shack.

It was painted white and about twenty by thirty feet, and as I mentioned it had a good screen door on the front and only doorway. But its floor had about six inches of chicken you know what on it. It really didn't smell too bad; it was dry. And, with the tin roof on it you wouldn't need a cookstove to fry eggs, just put them in a skillet and set it inside. Over easy or whatever they'd be done in five minutes or less.

Buddy, the farmer, handed us a couple of shovels and a straw broom. He told us to use the windmill tank water to wash it out after we finished shoveling. I looked up at the fair-sized water tank and hoped it was full; like I said, the wind was somewhere else this day.

I grabbed a shovel, Mac took the broom. Ron just stood there. Mac told Ron to go string out the water hose. We started in on the floor of the shack. Pretty soon Buddy's wife came out of the farmhouse and asked us to spread the 'stuff' on her garden. We did as she asked. It was a pretty nice looking garden but after a few days it looked a little sick, that 'stuff' was so rich. We started in on watering it pretty well, though, and it finally recovered and really looked as good as the pictures in the seed catalogues.

We finished shoveling and started scrubbing the place out with water and Lysol. The walls were bare 2x4's so all they needed was rinsing off. All in all, it turned out pretty good. The smell was mostly gone, and it looked really clean. Buddy gave us some new army cots, sheets, each a blanket and pillow. Then he told us it was time for supper, to wash ourselves up at the windmill and come on up to the house. We sat down to milk, potatoes, green beans and steak. All summer that was what she fed us for lunch and supper. Breakfast was steak, eggs, toast and milk. But, we needed to eat like that.

Buddy and his wife were young, had a couple of small kids, and the three of us felt worried about his making it as a farmer. So we really worked our tails off. Whatever needed to be done, we did. We cleaned the irrigation ditches with a tractor and ditch blade. We hoed and pulled weeds by hand. We flood irrigated over a thousand acres of cotton 'round the clock. The two six-cylinder truck engines driving the pumps never shut down while we were there. We bathed in the ice-cold deepwell water, clothes and all, and took turns sleeping in the chicken shack.

In the daytime, that shack was hot. It did have electricity in it, so Buddy gave us a fan to move the air. We were always so worn out at the end of our work time; I guess we probably could have slept in the heat without the fan.

In the course of that summer, I killed one huge rattlesnake. Cut the rattles off his tail and stuck them in my pocket.

All of us killed many coyotes, a couple of skunks and one rabid dog.

The day the cotton bolls were full and ready to burst, we shut the irrigation engines down and walked out of the field for the last time. We packed our gear in my old Chevie, Buddy paid us our due, and we said goodbye.

As we drove off, the three of us looked at our former home, the Chicken Shack. Nobody said anything at all.

The three of us went on to college that fall. I guess we were the better for the summer. We didn't seem to want to goof off the way we had before. We three took college seriously and did our best to justify being there. Other students joined fraternities and went on the obligatory panty raids. We didn't. We worked at college as if it was a cotton field that needed tending. Seems like watching that cotton grow day by day was just like the growth of our own future. That our future would grow day by day; the use of each of those days was up to us.

Over fifty years later, I still have that snake's rattles.

My Dog Does Not Snore

The whole thing occurred a few years ago. I don't know why Sunshine took that long to start, we had her about seven years by then. And she never gave us any indication she would eventually pick up the habit of snoring…or affliction, whatever the case may be. However, things happen. Things change.

Probably about the same time, Sunshine developed a mild form of arthritis in her rear leg joints. This is not uncommon in the Golden Retriever breed; sometimes the arthritis advances into 'hip-dysplasia' which makes it very difficult for the affected dog to do much walking.

For years, my wife and I have enjoyed taking frequent short trips; occasionally a few longer ones. Up until the time that Sunshine developed arthritis, we would board her at a kennel near where we lived at that time during the time of the trips. We did continue boarding her for a time after we had started given her morning and evening prescription pills to help her contend with the arthritis. Soon I became concerned that at the kennel she might not always get the medication, especially in the evenings. So, my wife and I decided to take her with us on our trips and let her sleep either in the back of the truck inside the pickup top or on her special rug inside the trailer with us.

As it turned out, having her with us in the trailer each night made it simpler to feed her in the mornings and give her the medication. It became a regular routine. Only problem was, when it rains and she gets wet; then she smells wet. And she does enjoy getting wet as she is a retriever. Then it becomes necessary to dry her with towels or my wife's hair dryer.

I mentioned she loves to get wet…any puddle will do. Lawn sprinklers? Right there she is, playing in the sprinkler spray. Baths? Forget it. She sees me assembling the bath things at home and she disappears.

Even with a drawback or two, she is a pleasure to take on trips. She rarely lets it be known she has a need for us to stop. Girl dogs have big radiators. Also they don't have the need to mark their territory like boy dogs. Heh.

While on one trip to Colorado to visit my parents, my wife and I noticed Sunshine had started to snore but only during night's deepest sleep. No snoring was observed during daytime naps. In the trailer with us at night she generally slept near my side of the bed. So, if her snoring woke me up, I was able to extend a leg and gently push her with my foot bringing her to a momentary semi-wakefulness. This usually stopped the snoring. At least, for a short while.

As she grew a little older, we started the habit of allowing Sunshine in the house on winter evenings to nap on her special rug in front of the fireplace stove insert. It wasn't long before she started snoring right there in front of the fireplace. If it became too bothersome, I would extend my booted foot and gently push her; this would interrupt her snoring cycle for a short while.

A few weeks after these initial snoring incidents we were notified of the date of the planned annual reunion of a group of our old friends to be held at one of the participant's home a few miles east of Merced in the hills. We decided to attend and, of course, take Sunshine with us.

On our arrival, it turned out beds in the house for this particular four-day reunion turned out to be a little scarce. We volunteered to change our R/V trailer dinette table into a bed in order to accommodate another couple.

The first night Sunshine's soft snoring kept waking the female half of the couple; she would poke her husband periodically in the back with her elbow and grumble for him to shutup. She never quite woke up enough to realize it wasn't her husband snoring. Sunshine was sleeping at the other end of the trailer on the far side of the bed so the lady did not connect the snoring with Sunshine.

The next morning, she said not a word about it to either my wife or me. However, I heard her giving her husband heck over his protest of denials. I didn't really connect all the dots together at that time. Sunshine's snoring was a fact but it did not really bother my wife or me; we had grown kind of used to it and besides, she did not snore really loud.

The snoring complaints between the two guests sleeping on our dinette table continued throughout the rest of the days of our stay. The reunion visit ended with no one, not even me, being the wiser.

A few weeks later, much the same group was together again at the same place for another celebration of some sort…I forget now what for. Same situation, same lack of beds. Same couple sleeping on our dinette table/bed. It was really comfortable, used as a bed. Same dog softly snoring. Same elbow-poking in the husband's back.

The next night, activities in the house kept most everyone occupied until fairly late. Our female guest decided to call it an early night and go out to the R/V and to bed before her husband. As she approached and entered the R/V, empty except for our sleeping Sunshine on her personal rug, snores were heard very plainly. Suspicious now, she started investigating for the source of the snores and found Sunshine lying on her rug. Snoring. Very definitely, very audibly snoring.

The next morning at breakfast she jumped me out the very first thing, making sure everyone there understood that the responsibility for the bruises on her long-suffering husband's back, shoulder and arm was all mine. That I was a master of deceit. I looked at her and told her in a very subdued voice "My dog does not snore, she growls in her sleep." On her part, she attempted some further discussion of the subject. I very pointedly, yet politely, pretended not to hear.

A few weeks after the reunion, Sunshine, my wife and I were on an extended trip. As is our usual custom, we selected several post cards to send to our closest friends. I sent one to our former female R/V guest. I worked it simply: "My dog does not snore. She growls in her sleep." I did not address it as 'Dear so and so' nor did I sign it. Naturally, she later complained laughingly to me she got the point.

On this particular cool spring evening, our R/V is parked in front of a friend's house in San Jose. It is late, my wife had gone to bed and to sleep a couple of hours ago.

Not yet sleepy enough to go to bed, I am busy writing this declarative tale; Sunshine is nearby lying on her personal red fuzzy rug, sound asleep.

She is softly growling in her sleep each time she breathes. Ever one in a while, I reach out a booted toe and gently poke her. Lovingly. Just for the heck of it. Her gentle sounds do not bother me.

My dog does not snore.

Ditchin' Bobby

I reckon I need to give a little background information about me, my best buddy Charlie, our schoolmate Bobby, and some about the rest of the small town kids in order for a reader to fully appreciate the humor of the whole darn thing. I guess a little irony took place along with the humor. But, at the time, it was all really serious.

This incident happened just a short time ago or so it seems. Back when we were all much younger. And a lot dumber. At the time, it was of major significance to Charlie and me. But, nobody else who knew of it really cared. The whole incident was Bobby's fault. And, as far as I remember, he never even knew about it. Like I said, it was all his fault.

Now, about me and my buddy Charlie: It was the summer before we were both to be seniors in high school. Both of us worked at the local drive-ion movie theater located a mile or so south of town and had been since the place was built and open for business a couple or so years earlier.

We had been taking nightly turns running the big twin Monarch carbon pencil arc film projectors about a year before this Ditchin' Bobby took place. On the off-night, the other of us would patrol the grounds and sort of act like an indoor movie theater usher. During the day, we both cleaned the snack bar and restrooms, and picked up the paper cups and pop-corn boxes along with anything else that was scattered around that didn't belong on the ground.

Now about Bobby (God please rest his soul): He was a different kid. His parents were financially better off than most. Or, at least, it appeared that way. The summer before we were all promoted to the senior class, his folks gave him a fairly new '51 Ford Crown Victoria.

That car was Ford's sporty two-door hard-top model sedan with no center door/window post. The roof was black orange-peel textured vinyl, one of the first such roof coverings. The body color was vivid chartreuse. A very unique automobile. It was a standout. That was part of the trouble. A real standout. Back then, you could hardly miss it.

As I mentioned, that vehicle and its driver, Bobby, were responsible for the whole embarrassing incident.

You might say we were pretty responsible citizens for our young and tender age. I guess we were. But we weren't any different from the rest of the young people back in that day and time. All of us, growing up, worked at just about anything you could imagine in a small farming community. We had to. The work needed to be done; it just seemed that was what we were supposed to do. For instance, during the fall harvest season, school turned out for two or three weeks in order for the older kids could work in the harvest of crops: Mostly cotton. Those years, no mechanical pickers. John Deere had just begun to think about them.

Us kids did it all. At a penny a pound, if the cotton wasn't too heavy with sand. Really easy work. You try dragging a ten-foot long yard wide tube-shaped muslin sack full of a hundred pounds or so of sand-laden cotton bolls down a sandy field furrow. For a penny a pound. Try it sometime. Try it all day, like we did. Sunup to sundown with a short break at noon. With some of those days having to squint so you could barely see, trying to keep the sideways wind from blowing sand in your eyes.

So, from that example, I would say we were, for the most part, hardworking fairly decent kids. For the most part. But, when we played, we played pretty hard. Compared to farm work, football was like a Maypole dance. We even played tackle football during recess on hard bare ground with no shoulder or hip pads. So, some of us occasionally broke a collar bone or such. Back then, it was part of growing up. And, sort of a badge of honor. Ouch.

For my personal transportation, I had a 1938 black Chevrolet Master Delux four-door sedan. It certainly wasn't the best a kid could have be any means. For instance, think about Bobby's Ford. I personally bought mine with my own money. No super gift there. It ran, it was all mine and I could go anywhere I wanted within reason in it. I had put a used '48 Chevie hi-torque truck engine in it, so it was pretty fast for an old car. But, it smoked.

Charlie wasn't as fortunate as I. He had a mostly red really used second-hand Cushman motor scooter. It and my car had one thing in common besides being second hand. They both exhausted smoke. Plenty.

Charlie and I went a lot of places together. Most of the time we rode together out to the drive-in. We went out there daily in either the theater company's '37 Ford pickup truck or in my Chevie. If it was time for movie film change, we drove the theater Ford pickup hauling the five or six good-sized heavy steel film cans. On these change nights, we hauled the previous night's movie cans to town and placed on the sidewalk in front of the in-town movie theater. The next morning, we loaded the newly delivered movie cans into the pickup and then back out to the drive-in for the next couple of nights showing.

On one such film-change night after the show we closed up the drive-in, went to town with the previous nights' movie in cans and parked the pickup in front of the indoor movie theater. We unloaded the film cans from the pickup bed and stacked them in front of the box-office for collection by the pickup-delivery company early that next morning. We parked the theater pickup in its usual spot close to the front of the theater. Then we got in my car which had been parked in front of the theater, and started our usual nightly practice, sort of just riding around town. It was then that we saw Bobby in his chartreuse-colored Ford messing around just as we were. Our fate was sealed.

He appeared to be alone. So, being sort of smart-alecky, I honked at him, blinked my lights a couple of times and took off leaving a cloud of dust and smoke. Mostly smoke. Charlie, looking to the rear and observing Bobby, told me the chase was on; Bobby had taken the bait.

We sped off, turned and dodged parked cars, fences and trashcans. Blocks later, he was still behind us. So, I took a route toward the only real refuge I could think of: The block ice plant. As soon as we got there I turned a corner and dodged around into the alley behind the plant. I turned all my car's lights off, scooted around another corner into the street and parked by two or three other old cars similar to mine in front of a house. We both scrunched down into the seat trying to stay out of sight.

Bobby's headlights went on straight and we saw we were home free. Now tomorrow we could brag to any of our peer we happened to see that we had ditched Bobby in his new car. Heh. Real heroes, we were.

The next day, we did plenty of gloating to ourselves as we drove around town. As I remember, though, we didn't seem to run into anyone who would be even remotely interested in our accomplishment of the night before.

All too soon, it was time to go back to the indoor theater to pick up the new movie and go out to the drive-in. There we would patch in the film trailer advertisements, newsreel and comedy with the main feature's film. To get all ready for the night's show.

We parked in front of the indoor theater and went inside. The town constable, Olan Heath, was standing there, big and tall and wearing his grey Stetson hat. Talking to his wife, who was busy making popcorn and coffee for the afternoon indoor movie program. Charlie and I started to say "Howdy" to Olan but as we looked at him, we could see he wasn't wearing his usual friendly smile under his big hat. He looked at us. He sure-nuff wasn't grinning.

He spoke. Words I don't think I will ever forget: "If you two boys ever pull that crap like last night on me again I will take you both to your daddies and I expect that will involve a visit to the woodshed." Charlie and I just stood there, mouths open wide. Plenty wide.

One really big thing we had forgotten. Constable Heath owned a car exactly like Bobby's. Only one minor difference: Constable Heath's car had a spotlight mounted outside on the driver's door just in front of the side rear view mirror. At night it would have been really hard to see the difference. But he never used his car on town patrol. We hardly ever saw him driving his own car. He always drove a sheriff's car. Well, almost always.

So it had been Constable Heath we ditched instead of Bobby. Both Charlie and I yessired him and promised never to do it again. We picked up the patching instruction papers for that night's movie film, loaded the new movie film cans in the old pickup's bed and left. In a big hurry. Sweating, we were.

I never played "Ditchin'" with anyone else again. And, Charlie and I never referred to that night again. In fact, I had not thought of it in years. Until a few months ago, that is. Occasionally I have a telephone conversation with Willie, one of my old high school classmates. Getting all the 'back home' news and other things about our classmates. During this conversation, he told me Bobby had dropped dead of a heart attack a few days earlier. Shortly after that bit of news was mentioned, we ended our conversation.

I moved outside on my deck and sat there for a while, looking at all my beautiful fruit trees. Thinking about old times when we were all younger and had the world by the tail.

Then I remembered about the two chartreuse Fords. And, Ditchin' Bobby.

No Savvy

Years ago, the steam-electric generation plant where I worked in the operations department temporarily transferred a replacement janitor on the retirement of the regular permanent employee. The janitor's only responsibilities were the office areas for the plant personnel and engineering departments. We operations personnel cleaned the remaining greater portion of the plant.

The replacement was an American Indian. What tribe, I do not recall if I ever knew. He was a retired U. S. Army tech sergeant and, as far as we could tell, he spoke little English. Any time any of us would see him and say anything at all to him he would reply "No Savvy."

Consequently he gradually became known by the nickname "No Savvy." Actually, we never knew his real name, but we had to call him something.

The nickname "No Savvy" really did not suit him. He carried himself with dignity...part soldier, part Indian. We really should have called him 'Chief." Sergeant Chief, that is.

Most of us, after detailed and thorough discussion, came to the conclusion that his standard reply of "No Savvy" to any question or comment was his way of ignoring any request for cleanup not included in his regular responsibilities with no repercussions. How could you fault someone who didn't understand the language? Savvy?

This apparent inability of No Savvy to communicate with the outside world made absolutely no difference to any of the operations crews except he was required to clean the operations restrooms. Other than that, his area of responsibility had nothing to do with us. Everything else in the outside plant equipment area cleanup was the responsibility of the operations personnel.

When our shift rotation changed to swingshift we saw No Savvy regularly as that was his permanent shift. He moved about, cleaning the various offices stuck here and there throughout the plant. Each of us would exchange a sort of greeting with him as our paths crossed in the performance of our individual duties. His response was usually some sort of grunt. This pattern of association continued for several years with very little change. Somewhere along the way, No Savvy's job status changed from temporary to permanent almost unnoticed.

Then, almost without warning the status of plant operating requirements changed. We began to have to endure weekends of plant shutdown from the end of the Friday evening peak electrical load until the plant generation equipment was restarted on the early Monday morning graveyard shift. This situation created little or no additional duties once the shutdown equipment was 'put to bed' for the weekend. However, we were able to accomplish our normal cleanup duties easier and quicker during this time of plant shutdown.

Consequently, during weekend shutdowns in the cold wet winter time, boredom would set in as we all pretty much stayed indoors out of the weather. Some of the guys worked on personal projects that were easily portable from home to work; others read whatever reading material that was handy. A few played cards. To start off, hearts. Becoming tired of that, poker was initiated. Penny ante, at first. Later…well, penny ante pretty much went by the wayside as some of the pots wound up being pretty fair-sized.

Me, I played hearts. When the game was changed to poker, I dropped out. I was busy trying to raise a family and didn't make enough money to risk losing even spare change playing poker. Another reason I couldn't play: They didn't accept IOU's and I never had more than a dollar or two with me most of the time.

After quite a few weekend poker sessions, the game got serious. There were some real howls of discontent from the losers at the end of each hand. Sometimes as much as twenty or thirty dollars would up in one hand's pot. I began to feel a little uneasy about the change in the whole situation yet nobody seemed to hold any grudge after a weekend of poker bingeing.

During all these weekends, No Savvy cleaned the offices around the noise of the games, seemingly taking no notice. Then, one evening out of a clear blue sky, he slowly went into the office where the poker game was in progress. Pushing a broom ahead of him, he quietly entered as if he was purposefully cleaning the floor even though that office was not part of his scheduled cleanup area.

When I saw No Savvy go inside I moved to one of the office's large windows so I could observe the unfolding situation. A player or two looked up, sort of grunted in notice of No Savvy's presence, and went back to concentrating on the game.

No Savvy silently watched the game in progress, leaning on the handle of his broom and occasionally taking a drag on the barely lit stub of a cigar he held between his teeth. Me? I continued to watch him.

After a little while, No Savvy turned and walked out of the office dragging his broom behind him. As he came out of the door and moved toward where I was standing he smiled at me and shook his head. His actions made me thing he was sizing up the whole situation. Setting up some sort of conspiracy.

Next evening...same thing, different game, different money. No Savvy waked into the office, again aimlessly pushing the broom in front of him. He stood and watched for a while, puffing sporadically on a different (I guess) cigar stub. After a few minutes, Richard, the shift supervisor and instigator of the poker games, looked up and indicated questioningly to No Savvy if he would like to join the game. No Savvy gave a short laugh, grinned and shook his head no, saying 'No Savvy." He then turned and walked out pushing his broom.

The following Saturday evening as the games progressed, No Savvy came into the plant area a little earlier than his usual custom. He hardly paid anyone any attention; he simply waked straight into the office cardparlor.

He didn't say anything, he just pulled out a few folded bills and a handful of change, grunting toward the group and indicating he would like to play.

Seeing strange fresh money, not matter how small the bankroll seemed, the group very noisily made No Savvy welcome. He had the usual cigar butt between his teeth. The first hand was dwelt. It hurt me to watch the uncaring card sharks with this seemingly gentle lamb, but I was transfixed. Then, as I suspected, No Savvy lost. He lost hand after hand, as if he didn't even know what he was supposed t do. When some of the pots grew large fairly early he didn't stay but threw in after a couple of raise sessions. It wasn't long before he was broke. He gestured toward the desk being used as a card table by throwing both hands toward it as he turned and left the office. Broke. He lost all the money he had placed on the table at the start.

The poker games on the next evening, Sunday, were played without an appearance of No Savvy in the plant. He had taken care of the offices earlier that past Friday evening; they required cleaning only once each weekend as they were usually occupied only during the week.

A full month later on our regular Friday swingshift, No Savvy came out into the plant, cleaned the engineering office area and waved to the cardplayers as he passed them both ways; in and out.

However, that next Sunday evening it was a different story. I was again at my usual place, observing the action of the game through the office window. No Savvy came into the plant area in a very determined manner; almost a march. He wasn't pushing a broom this time either. He walked very confidently into the office 'cardroom'; stepped up to an open place at the cardtable desk and laid several bills down.

The players casually looked up at him; they were mostly concentrating on their current poker hands. As soon as the hand was done, the winner, nosily gloating, scrapped in his pot amid the losers' cries of dismay.

Various comments of welcome were made to No Savvy and the new money he was bringing to the game. New hands were immediately dwelt to all around the table.

Hand after hand was played. Each successive hand brought less and less verbal noise. Pretty soon all was quiet. The pile of money grew steadily in front of No Savvy. I had to turn and leave, to find something else to do. I could no longer watch. Somehow, though, I was not surprised.

No Savvy cleaned their plows. Everyone's plow. When he left the office cardroom a much richer man, the players were plenty quiet. Maybe they began to realize they had been had.

I could not help but laugh and think that in their greed, the gamblers overlooked one major point: No Savvy was a graduate of years spent in the U.S. Army. And, any ex-military person knows poker, in times of confinement and waiting, keeps good minds sane.

Yessir. Greed does funny things to people. And, we're not talking about a great deal of money to be greedy over. No Fort Knox here.

What really ticked them off was the very last straw. No Savvy's last work day had been that last Sunday. He retired. The next time we got on swingshift, there was a different janitor. Looked like an ex-pro boxer. Nobody asked her to play cards.

Rustlin' One Calf

Back in the days when the Korean War was winding down, I was in the U. S. Marine Corps with Treasure Island, San Francisco Bay as my home duty station. A cousin of mine (one of twin boys; both in the U.S. Air Force) had graduated from the Air Force Air Police Academy at the old Parks Air Force Base near Livermore, California.

Now, I'm going to let you know his name was Ron, because it really was. I'm not going to give you his last name; but it's different from mine. Not because he is bigger or meaner that me: I'm bigger and I am meaner. That last, thanks to the Marine Corps. But Ron is all you are going to get from me because Samuel Colt made all men equal. That's why. He might read this or some who reads it might tell him about it. Then he and Sam Colt might decide to pay me a visit. And, he might now be a fair shot. I don't know. I haven't seen him face-to-face since we looked at each other across Grandma's casket as all of us grandkids carried her out of the church. Maybe twenty-five years ago.

After the completion of his Air Police training, he was stationed at the Air Base at Albuquerque, New Mexico. As I mentioned, my home duty station was in the U. S. Marine Band barracks at the U.S. Navy Base at Treasure Island.

You should think back, those of us who have been young and in the service of our country. Remember how it was. Remember at the end of the week you were so glad you survived without being transferred to Timbuctoo or some equally dire place, you really felt like celebrating when the weekend arrived. I know I did. I know Ron did also. At the end of duty Friday, trotting right away down to the Non-Com's Club, drinking beer and stacking cans on the table.

Well, one Saturday evening Ron and a few of his buddies (a carful of buddies, as it turned out) got tired of the Non- Com's Club on the base near Albuquerque so they loaded up in someone's car and commenced heading to town…or rather, greener pastures.

On the way, they spotted a lonely doggie (or young calf to you ranch-lingo-deprived folks). Fearing it might get hit and killed by some unwary motorist they decided to give the poor scared lonesome doggie a lift into town. So, they made room and put the doggie in the backseat of the car with the rest of the back seat occupants. Then they resumed heading for town.

I suppose they were feeling really grand about the good deed they were doing, so they were laughing and clowning around, you all know the good time I am writing about. And, in a really big hurry to get into town. Speeding, naturally.

As they passed his patrol car, one of New Mexico's finest decided they appeared to be having too much of a good time. Maybe he wanted to enjoy some of their fun himself. Who knows? Well, anyhow, he gave them the red light and siren. Being law abiding boys and Air Policemen, they stopped.

New Mexico's finest did not think it was very funny, them giving the poor, lonesome doggie a ride. So, he arrested them. For rustling. He also arrested the poor, lonesome doggie. It spent the night inside a jail cell with the good time Air Policemen. Sometimes that's the way they do things out west. But for some reason, New Mexico's finest chose not to notice they all were sort of drunk.

The day they went to court was sort of funny. The judge started laughing right away as soon as they started explaining what the poor lonesome doggie was doing in the backseat of the car to begin with. When he finally stopped laughing, he threw them all out of court. Except the judge kept the poor lonesome doggie, I suppose to get it back to its rightful owner.

Their Air Force commanding took a really dim view of the whole thing. Maybe he was having a bad day for some other reason. Anyhow, the C.O. decided to kick all the rustlers out of the service with a general discharge. Whatever his reasons, he sure had no sense of humor like the civilian court judge did.

Years went by. I sort of forgot about Ron and the rustled doggie. I did hear about him from time to time, and as I mentioned earlier, we did see each other at our grandmother's funeral. During our growing-up years, he, his brother and I were pretty close. We did get in all kinds of adolescent mischief together. Once we grew up, though, our different roads made contact difficult. I later learned that for years he had a job setting up rodeos all around the States for a large sponsoring corporation. Finally, he retired from that and formed his own company which furnished stock to rodeos; both broncos and bulls.

One Saturday evening a few years ago, my wife and I were visiting our good friends, Ed and Millie, in Clear Lake at their home. Ed and I were watching a previously recorded rodeo on a cable television station. The rodeo work reminded me of my cousin and his life-long dedication to rodeo activities. So I started telling my buddy Ed, of this story about my cousin's brush with the law for rustling and his eventual career with rodeo work.

All of a sudden, I stopped talking and sat there with my mouth hanging open. Plumb flabbergasted. There was my cousin Ron, big as life, on the screen right in front of us. I repeat, big as life. Big ten-gallon grey Stetson cocked back on his head. Riding over a big grin was a handle-bar mustache, grey to match his hat. Even his whole name was displayed in big white letters at the bottom of the television screen. Turns out, as we listened, he was a rodeo official. A judge, with the Professional Bull Riders Association. In the continuing course of the rodeo, he was even referred to a couple of times by the announcer.

Just think: Seventy five years ago, the local ranchers would have hung the lot of them, those Air Force boys. Today? Well, one is a rodeo official. Wonder how high up in society the rest have gone? Heck, one of them could have become a governor of New Mexico, or Texas maybe. Or something like that, for all I know.

Raising Ducks
or What Are Friends For

It wasn't and isn't that I am not of reasonable intelligence. I just sort of got my head below the water line, so to speak.

To begin with, I was born on a non-working farm in a simple square woodframe house. With a windmill, an overhead water tank and a few chickens and ducks. Mostly chickens. Oops, I forgot: One milk cow.

The few ducks lived around and roosted (if that's what you call ducks do) on the ground under the water tank platform and played in the small puddle from the overflow pipe stuck into the windmill's overhead water tank. Of course, having webbed feet with almost no toes, ducks can't roost in the trees like chickens can.

They looked really neat, the ducks did, playing around in the puddle. That probably was the start of my later on grown up dumb idea to raise ducks.

Our farm was non-producing because the Great Plains were in the middle of the biggest drought in recorded history. Most of the farms in Kansas passed our farm, born by the northern winds heading for the Gulf of Mexico. In broader terms, there had been no rain for five or six years and things were pretty dry and wind was plentiful.

The farmers had not yet graduated from praying for rain or performing rain dances to developing the technology of irrigation using the extensive underground supply of water called the Ogallala Aquifer. Probably few farmers at that time even knew of the existence of the aquifer. If they had of known of it and how it could be used, it would have delayed losses of many families' farms.

But that's enough background for you to get the picture. I grew up working on farms doing various difficult and dirty jobs so by the time I would up in the Marine Corps boot camp I thought I was on vacation even though it wasn't summer and school was not out. In other words, even though my mother wanted me to be a farmer, I wasn't too stuck on the idea.

Finishing my tour in the Marines, I went to work in a regular job and mostly forgot about farming. Except when I would go home and pal around with all my old buddies. They would talk about how much rain they needed and what kind of bugs or worms were eating their crops this year. And all that was after the development of irrigation techniques and aerial crop spraying had been invented.

Somehow I got the idea I would like to move out of town; back into the open country and buy a small farm. Maybe I'd get a few ducks or geese and let them wander around the farmhouse just like in the movies.

Well, I couldn't afford very much land. I wound up getting four and one-third acres, but I figured that would be enough for most anything I had time to do after I got the house built.

Finally the was house finished, the water well drilled and cased, the septic tank and leach field dug and working. I put up a barbed wire fence around the place with a couple of Oakie gates and I was in the farming business. I bought a horse and saddle as I had wanted my own horse for years.

I wangled an unused brooder from a fellow I knew. It was pretty dirty as it hadn't been used in years. I cleaned it up and ordered four dozen Rhode Island Red hen chicks. I decided on the Reds because of the brown eggs they laid. The brown eggs should be easier to sell because they weren't usually found in stores.

Because it was too cold to put the brooder outside, I stuck it in a corner of the garage. While the little hens were getting to be big hens, I built a big pen with a nice open-faced shed with cross-bars for roosting. I made some nice square boxes and filled them with straw so the hens would have a place for egg laying. I made all this really convenient so it would be easy to care for, clean and maintain once the hens took the place over.

I started riding my horse once a week down to the saloon in the nearby village. I would tie the horse to the hitch rail in the front of the saloon, go inside and have a couple bottles of beer and gab with whoever was in the bar enjoying a break as I was. Then, leaving I would continue exercising the horse.

On one such exercise trip, I mentioned to the lady who owned the saloon and also tended bar that I had a lot of Rhode Island Red laying hens and plenty of brown eggs. Did she have any idea where I could find a market for the eggs? She agreed to sell the eggs for me at fifty percent more than market price. She wound up selling every egg I supplied her with and wanted more.

I figured I had room for a couple dozen more hens, so I ordered the chicks and raised them in the brooder. As soon as the new hens started laying, I delivered the eggs to the saloon where they also quickly sold. The lady who owned the saloon wanted still more eggs but I figured I had enough chickens. I used the money from the sale of the eggs to buy feed.

As all the chickens had now matured, I felt I was doing great as a 'gentleman' farmer. In the part of the country where I had settled, if you played around with farming and also had a regular job, you were allowed to identify yourself in that manner.

But…no ducks. Couldn't even order them. One day I was griping about this to a friend and neighbor of mine who generously volunteered to give me one of his duck hens. I gratefully accepted and went out and built duck facilities next to the chicken shack and pen. I buried a small child's wading pool, watered it up and went to get the duck; now I was halfway home. All I needed now was a drake.

That duck was a really prolific layer. I guess it must have been the chicken feed for laying hens I was feeding her. The eggs weren't much use, though. I tried eating them for breakfast. Too strong a flavor. Couldn't even sell them.

I was saved very soon by another neighbor who had a drake. He offered to give me the drake; of course, I accepted. At the time I noticed he had only the one drake with a dozen or so duck hens. No ducklings but I didn't let that small fact bother me. I brought the drake home and he went right to work making, what I hope to be, lots of little ducks. Now I really was in the faming business; a real 'gentleman' farmer.

Days went by. Then weeks. Every so often I would check the eggs the duck laid in her nest. Smelling them and declaring them bad, I would throw them away as they had gone bad instead of hatching.

I finally got tired of this situation and decided I would seek higher authority. I was sure I was doing something wrong. I went to the nearest high school and consulted the Ag teacher. He very obligingly came out to my place, looked at my drake and shook his head. He told me I had a sterile drake; it was a cross between a domestic and a wild duck. Plumb sterile, just like the cross between a male donkey and a female horse. A sterile hybrid: A mule. No little ducks. Ever. Suddenly it made sense why my friend was so quick to give me his only drake. I guess he was tired of feeding an unprofitable critter.

Needless to say I was not very happy at this cloud-opening sunshiny bit of information. A couple of days later, I invited that drake duck to Sunday dinner. He didn't do too well at that, either. He was too tough.

Not many more months went by and I had to move due to a change of job location. So I had to sell the farm. A couple years earlier I had acquired this really stubborn billy goat from another really good friend. I wanted it to keep the Bermuda grass trimmed down. The guy who gave me the sterile drake had seen the goat a while back and expressed his desire to get one for himself to help control the volunteer grass on his place. He had no other large animal to do this so he had to mow the grass himself to prevent it being a fire hazard.

Needing to find homes for all my critters, I gave this friend the goat. What he didn't know and I didn't tell him was that the billy goat hated grass. And hated people, too. All people. So, I finally got even with my friend for the drake. Sort of.

I never did have any little ducklings running around any other place I owned. You know, just like in the movies. Not yet, anyway.

The Springfield Watch

O n my forty-fifth birthday, my father gave me a Springfield Illinois pocket watch he had been keeping for me for many years. It originally belonged to my father's oldest brother, my uncle, Federick Cleo. I never knew him. He died as a result of a hunting accident nine years before I was born. My mother had told me I strongly resembled him. Same color of red hair, same grey eyes. Same lean stature and height of body.

You might think the watch is a very nice keepsake. And, you might also think that with all of today's fancy super-accurate electronic watches of practically all sizes, shapes, colors and descriptions, the Springfield is not really an item for day-to-day use in this day and time. Sadly, you would be right. The era of use for that type of watch has been over for decades.

But, consider this: In those early days of its manufacture and use, it was a very valuable instrument. Entire railroads depended on it for the trains to 'be on time'. Only certain of the available pocket watches could be used on the job by the railroad employees. Those watches had to meet certain design and accuracy requirements to be approved for railroad use.

For instance, common pocket watches were not only wound by turning watch stem, setting of the time was also accomplished by pulling this same stem out a fraction of an inch engaging the tiny gear to allow movement of the hands. At this point, twisting the stem in either direction would move the hands as needed in order to set the time.

Watches of this type were never allowed for Railway employee use while on the job. Approved watches had to have a clutch lever accessible only by removal of the crystal watch face lens for the accurate time-set of the hands.

This clutch-assembly was the only type of watch approved for on-the-job use by railroad employees. It prevented inadvertent time change by the employee grasping the top of the watch including the watch stem when removing the watch from the owner's vest pocket. These watches were called 'lever-set' watches. Illinois Springfield watches were of the approved lever-set type.

Once upon a time in our country, being a railroad employee was not just a job. It was a way of life, a profession. Every bit as important as being a lawyer, an engineer, or an architect. The men who ran the trains were as much a part of the trains as the coal and water that fed the engine. Only another railroader could understand the feeling each had for that profession and the love they all shared for the trains.

The railroad jobs were fairly well paid. They were also very hard to get. Usually the males of entire families devoted their life's work to the running of the trains. And, in those days, it was a male-dominated occupation.

Many of my ancestors on both sides of the family were railroad men. One of these was my Great Uncle Frank. He was a railroad employee of many years. It was my own desire when I was very young to follow in those big footsteps. However, as I grew up, the railroad changed. Progress made obsolete the big beautiful, terribly powerful steam locomotives. The last car in the train, the caboose, also disappeared somewhere along the way. Small, dirty, smelly diesel engines took the place of the wonderful locomotive engines. Due to this 'come-down', railroad jobs lost the status of 'profession' and became just another job.

Because of my family connections to the railroad as I was growing up, I was able to get an occasional ride in the cab of steam locomotives with the engineer and fireman. The engineer of course, was my great uncle. I idolized him. But I idolize him in my young years before I even knew what trains were. As I grew, I discovered his being a steam locomotive engineer was a wonderful fringe benefit of our kinship.

As the railroads changed and many of the jobs disappeared, I no longer had an excuse. I had to go to college. My father would have it no other way.

However, Uncle Sam and the U. S. Marine Corps Reserve saw to it that I resigned from college classes and went instead to combat classes. After my service time over, I found employment with a huge power company in California and started really learning what steam power was all about.

I did study steam…The majesty of steam. I guess it really was in my blood. I delighted in learning of the capability of high-pressure superheated steam. The thrill of opening a hot valve and feeling the throbbing power of the rushing velocity of the steam you personally release has an addicting effect on all who are able to do this. I expect the railway engineers felt much the same as they opened the throttle valves allowing steam to pass through the valves into the giant cylinders, pushing against the pistons and starting to move the whole train down the track.

Back to the Springfield watch. My Uncle Cleo was fortunate enough to have kin in powerful places in the Santa Fe Railroad round house in Amarillo, Texas. Through his Uncle Frank, he was able to get a job as a brakeman. His duties were not just those of a brakeman. He had several responsibilities. He would walk the tops of the moving cars looking for hot and smoking bearing grease boxes or any other unusual situations.

As he was a railroad employee looking forward to a long career with the railroad, he purchased the railroad approved 19-jewel Illinois watch manufactured in Springfield, Illinois. It is a very fine watch. Among the finest made. Looking at the watch today, I can almost feel the pleasure he took in the purchase and use of it in his everyday personal and working life. Simply put, it feels good just to hold the smooth golden case in the palm of your hand.

One clear and sunny day in November, 1924, Cleo went down to the county office and bought a resident hunting license costing two dollars. The date on the license was Wednesday, the 25th. Late in the year; winter had yet to get a good grip on the high North Texas Plains.

Very early the next day, Thanksgiving, Cleo, our Uncle Frank and his wife, Erbie, left town traveling south a short way to a lake to try and bag a few geese. Cleo had seen the big birds take flight when they were disturbed by the noise and rushing wind of the railroad cars of the train he had been on as it passed along the lake shore.

Arriving at the lake area, Uncle Frank got out to hunt the west side. Erbie then drove the Dodge coupe on around the south side of the lake to take Cleo up to the east area where he got out. Erbie continued on around to the north side and stopped to wait where she could see both men as they hunted. This had been arranged before the trip and she was in a good spot to watch for a signal from either man.

At that early hour there were no geese in sight. The big birds had not yet returned to the lake from their night feeding grounds.

Cleo loaded his 12 gauge pump exposed hammer type shotgun and started walking over to a bushy area where he would be concealed from the geese as they came in to set on the lake surface.

After waiting for some time and the geese had not returned to the lake, Cleo decided to give up and signaled Erbie to drive around and pick him up.

When Erbie arrived and Cleo started to get in, she accidentally stalled the Dodge's engine. Becoming flustered by her mistake, she could not remember where the engine's starter button was. Before showing her, Cleo sat down on the driver's side fender facing the rear. He cradled the shotgun between his knees, trigger up with the muzzle pointed toward his chest and the butt of the stock resting on the car's running board. He then leaned in the open window to point out the location of the starter button on the dashboard to Erbie. In doing so, somehow he partially cocked and tripped the exposed hammer tang of the upside-down shotgun's breech on the metal facing strip of the running board.

The flipping movement of the hammer, however small, was enough to ignite the primer on the shotgun shell within the breech of the shotgun. The gun discharged and the pellet charge struck him in the upper chest.

When my father gave me the watch, he included a picture of my Uncle Cleo standing up at the driver's controls for a steel-tracked tractor that appears to be a Caterpillar brand. A picture of a good-looking, smiling young man wearing a vest. A vest that probably had the Springfield watch in one pocket with a chain and fob stretching across his chest to the opposite vest pocket. In the manner of railroaders. A picture of a man too young to die. With the watch and picture my father included the hunting license Cleo had bought the day before his death.

A few years ago, my wife and I were traveling through the land of my birth. Previously my father had asked that while we were there, to please stop at the graveyard and take pictures of the tombstones standing over the family gravesites. I did as he had asked. One of the pictures I took was of Cleo's headstone. On that cold grey marble slab cut below his name is the date of his birth: January 27, 1903. Beneath that is November 25, 1924, the date of his death, Thursday, that year, the day of Thanksgiving.

One of the few fringe benefits given to railroad employees and their families back then were free train rides. Cleo got one last ride on the Santa Fe. On the train that brought his coffin home.

The State Bug

After hearing me relate this tale, some friends of mine with sensibilities somewhat more dominant in their lives than those in my life suggested I not write this story. That, perhaps, in doing so, I would be crossing the lines of propriety. Maybe I might insult some of the natives of our newest state.

Well, the whole thing really did happen. Actually, I did not know the complete story for years. I am now going to attempt to relate it as best I can; the whole uncensored tale. If you find I am offending your sensibilities, turn the page. Read something else. However, I will certainly be disappointed if you do not read and enjoy this tale.

After my wife and I were married, we decided to spend our honeymoon with a trip to Hawaii. Specifically, the Island of Kauai. This was several years before the last great hurricane practically destroyed all structures and foliage on the surface of the Island. Truly this was one of God's Garden of Eden. The original, in my feeble capability of understanding, could not have been much better. We first flew to the Island of Oahu as that was the only way you could get to Kauai from the 'Mainland' as the Hawaiian natives call the American continent. I made reservations for us to spend the first night of our trip in the world-famous Royal Hawaiian Hotel, mainly because they had a listed toll-free telephone number in the book I had access to.

The next afternoon, we caught an inter-island flight on a two-engine, sixteen (or so) passenger plane to the town of Lihue on the Island of Kauai. The only really unusual thing of the very short flight occurred as we made the approach to the airport at Lihue. The airplane made a very sudden complete u-turn which ended in the very direct approach to and the touchdown and landing on the runway. I mean, a real u-turn.

This action the pilot kept a big secret until the plane had touched down on the runway and was slowing down. You know, the time when the flight attendants welcome you to wherever you happened to have just landed. Then the pilot told us…heh heh…told us that was a necessary u-turn, the only way to land on the island. After he told us that, I was figuring it must have been about a six-'G' u-turn. I now realize why the seatbelt light stayed lit the entire short trip. Heh heh.

We went to the 'We Try Harder' office in the airport terminal building and rented a Honda Civic. I had never been in a car so small. My vehicle of preference at the time was (and still is) a full-size pickup truck. The tiny car was fairly new, very clean and shiny. A pretty blue. It sat fairly well; it drove fairly well. Couldn't really ask for much more. Away we went to the Beach Boy Hotel and the Coco Palms Plantation where we had reservations courtesy of the people at the Royal Hawaiian Hotel. Remember, they were in my phone book.

As soon as we settled in our very nice hotel room, we decided to give in to jet lag and take a nap. When we awoke, we elected to have supper at the local nightclub within walking distance. Maybe dance a little afterwards.

As I walked into the bathroom-dressing area, I noticed a huge bug on the carpeted corner of the dressing area. I immediately got a piece of tissue, quietly picked the creature up and gave him the deep-six before my wife had a chance to witness the burial at sea. Already in the time I had known her before our marriage, I knew she did not much care for bugs of any kind. The bug was quickly forgotten in the anticipation of the evening ahead.

Later that night back at the hotel, we looked at a brochure with a map of the small island we were on. We decided to journey around to the Polihale State Park Beach area the next day, taking a picnic lunch and spending the day there.

The next morning we took off fairly early on the planned journey as we had pretty well overcome the effects of jet lag. I stopped at the Colonel's place for our picnic lunch and bought two individual boxed chicken dinners. I carefully placed them on the floor behind the driver's seat for the rest of the trip to the beach.

As we continued our journey to the state park beach area, my wife noticed an old, small white church with a visible graveyard to our right just off the road. She requested that we stop to look over the church and grounds. We signed the visitor's registration book inside the open and empty ancient church; afterwards we walked around the neat, quiet grounds and cemetery.

On the completion of our tour, we returned to the Civic and I assisted her into the passenger side of the car. As I approached my side and opened the driver's side door, I spied a big bug on top of one of the lunch boxes. Mentally identifying this critter as a cockroach, I quickly picked the bug up and tossed him down on the ground in front of one of my pointy-toed boots and stepped on him. Just as quickly I picked up and opened the lunch box, greatly relieved to find no other bug. I closed the box and handed it to my wife with the request she hold it as I didn't want to risk spilling it on the curvy road ahead. I opened and inspected the other lunch. Finding no additional bug, I reclosed that box and handed it to my wife for her careful protection.

Before sitting down in the car, I stood back, scratching my head, quietly wondering where the bug had come from as it was on the outside of the box. I kneeled down and looked under the driver's seat. That area was fairly clean with no bug in sight. I carefully raised the edge of the floor carpet behind the driver's seat and observed another carpet...of solid bugs. Saying not a word, I gently lowered the edge of the floor carpet, got in the car and drove on, considering the problem.

We spent a very nice day at the beach area. On the return trip, I drove around Lihue on the guise of sightseeing but actually looking for a hardware store. Finally coming across an open one, I went inside, having told my wife I wanted to get a coffee cup size water heater for instant coffee in the mornings. On my return, I opened one of the two paper bags I had, showing her the two small heating units I had found. The other bag I stuffed behind my seat. We continued on to our hotel, stopping on the way to get a jar of instant coffee.

Arriving at the hotel, we unloaded our odds and ends we had taken with us to the beach. At that time my wife asked me what was in the other paper bag I had returned from the hardware store with. I urged her to come around to my side of the car and I showed her my discovery of the occupants of the underneath side of the floor carpet behind the driver's seat. She was horrified as I knew she would be. I assured her all would be well tomorrow.

Then I showed her the contents of the other paper sack. She did not look convinced. I began to wonder if I would be able to get her back into the car for the next day's journey.

Closing both doors with each window opened slightly I opened the rear hatchback. I took the bug bomb I had bought at the hardware store from the other sack. I set the can on the center of the floor in the rear area, pulled the starter pin and closed the hatchback.

The next morning before we left for the area where the movie "South Pacific" had been filmed, I peeked under the driver's side rear carpet. All those bugs were now upside down, feets up. My wife appeared, still looking as if she was not going to get back into the car. I called her around to show her what I had found. Finally, she agreed to again get in the car.

We had a really wonderful time on that then lovely island. Several years were yet to pass before the terrible hurricane. We both were saddened when we saw the television news reports of the devastation caused by the storm.

By the time our visit had ended and we had returned the rental car, it had begun to smell sort of funny inside.

As our pilot lifted the airplane off the runway for the return to Oahu, he took off straight-away.

No G-forces.

Several years later I related most of this story to a guy on my work crew who happened to be a native Hawaiian. At the conclusion of the tale, he laughed and asked, "Don't you know that the cockroach was and is the state bug of Hawaii? Even before statehood?"

Well, I didn't know then and I don't know now any such thing, even to this day. States have birds, flowers, trees and animals as representatives. Why not a cockroach? But, as Paul Harvey would say: I finally had the "Rest of the Story."

Anyhow, you know what they say about those bugs. That in the event of a nuclear war, they would be the only survivors. Well, now, I wonder: What about hurricanes?

The Royal Hawaiian Band

I 'll bet the title of this story and the name of a band of musicians from yesterday is something people have not thought of in years. Well, the band leader's name was Harry Owens. Years ago, this band gave a weekly Sunday evening concert on radio under the program name "Hawaii Calls" before and after World War II. The program was broadcast live from the garden stage of the Royal Hawaiian Hotel in Honolulu, Hawaii.

Several years after the conclusion of the war and with the nation's developing electronic ability the band gave concerts on black and white television. These program concerts were also broadcast live from the same hotel's garden stage. The program was transmitted live to the 'Mainland' as Hawaiians call the States by coaxial cable. It was a very popular program and was on the air immediately after another extremely popular show, the old Lucky Strike Hit Parade.

I don't know very much about the early radio years. I haven't been able to successfully research this; information concerning Mr. Owens or his band is very limited. I was able to find out he was born stateside in 1902 and was an educated man. He also wrote a dozen or so songs.

Most of this story is from my own memory, and parts are from recollections of friends; some who lived in Hawaii during that time. I really was too young to remember very much. I do know that during the war years and a few afterward, radio reception on the Texas South Plains was pretty limited to not-too-distant stations. It is doubtful during those early years if the 'Hawaii Calls' program was re-broadcast locally for our reception and enjoyment.

I must confess (before people who know me read this and fink on me) in my younger years, my radio listening time was mostly spent on the Louisiana Hayride and the Grand Ole Opry. Mostly, the Hayride. Its airtime was the longer of the two programs.

The broadcasts of the Royal Hawaiian Band from the Island of Oahu were brought front and center into the public's awareness because of the tragedy of Pearl Harbor. Not to belittle the fact that the band was really great on its own. And times were very near to the final curtain closing of the 'Big Band' era, an age of the most golden music ever listened to.

I first became aware of Harry Owens and crew during my tour of duty in the U.S. Marines. After all, when you did get occasional weekend liberty it ended on a Sunday evening. So, I was back in the barracks in time to be able to listen and watch television in the music room of the recreation hall. There was Harry Owens, big as life, and his dreamy, haunting magical music. Just close your eyes and listen. You were there.

The Lucky Strike Hit Parade and Harry Owens were mostly the only programs any of us paid any attention to. Face it, back then nationwide live broadcast television was not only in its infancy, there wasn't a whole lot of experience, knowledge or imagination for the variation of good programmable material. So musical programs were not only very popular, there just wasn't much else.

As faithfully as I could, I listened to and watched Harry Owens and his band. I watched Harry as often as possible as long as his program was on the air. It was indeed magical to me; I suppose it also was to many other people. For its time, the production was lavish. The off-camera overhead view of the opening and closing scenes of the band in the garden with the announcer's captivating phrases added to the nostalgia of the program as well as the mystery of the islands so famous and so far away. A land as real as the Garden of Eden on earth could possibly be. A land far away, in the middle of the blue Pacific waters.

I desperately wanted to go and see all the dreams that the music of Harry Owens and his band had created for me. Just close your eyes and listen.

Several times, I requested a transfer to the Pearl Harbor Naval Station. Several times I was turned down. I stopped requesting the transfer after a fellow Marine and my friend in the same company received an undesired transfer to the Islands. We were both the same rank, same MOS (job classification), and had been active in the Marines the same length of time.

The only difference between the two of us was that he had a year longer to serve. I was on a two-year reserve call-up; he was a three-year enlistee. As I mentioned, I wanted badly to go. He didn't want to go at all. I really envied him.

After my release from active duty and return to the Marine Reserves, I started building my civilian life and working toward finishing my education for a career. Harry and his music took a back seat in the corners of my mind.

Years went by. I married and divorced. I met a nice lady and we started seeing each other on a regular basis.

After a few months our relationship became serious; we began planning for a future together.

My future mother-in-law was making arrangements for a six-week South Seas trip on the old SS Monterey. Her daughter (my bride-to-be), her son and daughter-in-law were going to accompany her. She asked me to go with them; she would pay all the trip expenses. The last scheduled port of call was going to be Honolulu. I didn't have quite six weeks of vacation time on the books. So I asked my boss for the needed extra time. His reply? "You have got to be kidding."

But I was able to schedule a few vacation days so I arranged to meet them in Honolulu near the end of their trip. I was asked to get reservations at a hotel for them as the ship would dock there in couple of days.

You guessed it. Without remembering Harry Owens, I managed to get all the reservations at the Royal Hawaiian Hotel.

The departure day for me finally arrived. I flew over to the Island of Oahu, arriving late that night. My reserved room, I later learned, was in the old original section of the hotel. The other reserved rooms were in the new L-shaped section adjoining the original structure.

The next day I learned the SS *Monterrey* was going to be a couple of days late; a result of mechanical problems that had occurred near New Zealand. So I wandered around the beautiful Island alone.

Later that same afternoon I ventured into the new section of the hotel. From a tenth or eleventh floor balcony, I could see down into the garden stage area of the original hotel. My head swam with realization. I had been in this very spot; I had seen this downward view of the garden in front of me over and over. I had to grip the balcony rail to stay steady on my feet.

Leaving that section of the hotel I was not sure of anything. The sense of having been there before was so strong I felt it somehow was true. Maybe some inherited sense of recollection. I just did not know.

Later that same night I left my room in the original section of the hotel to find a nearby place for supper. When I arrived downstairs I the lobby area, I could hear music coming from the hotel garden area. As I passed the area's entrance portals in the hallway, I stopped to listen. After a minute or two I turned and walked out into the garden. The Island music, the palm trees…long forgotten memories suddenly returned from the corners of my mind. I realized Harry Owens and his Royal Hawaiians had brought me here many times with his dreamy magical music now so many years ago.

Hear the haunting strains of *Sweet Leilani* floating high on the air.

Just close your eyes and listen.

I was there.

Blue Graham

It was a hot summer Sunday afternoon in mid-July. The Seagraves Oilers were playing the Post Millers and the Oilers were ahead 2 to 1. The Oilers were taking their turn at batting in the seventh inning and Blue Graham was up. Blue walked out of the on deck area and up to the batter's box, bat resting on his left shoulder. He paused just outside of the box, kicked the dirt with his spiked shoes and took a look at the pitcher who was busy rubbing powdered alum into the baseball with his sweaty hands.

Shortly after the end of World War II the people of my hometown and the surrounding communities got together and decided to form an amateur baseball league. For want of a better name, it was called the "Oil Belt League." This name was chosen as there had been and still was a considerable amount of oil well drilling occurring in the surrounding areas.

Each town's teams were made up of any and all job-holding adult males who were somewhat capable of playing and had the desire to participate. Games were usually held on Wednesday and Saturday nights and Sunday afternoons. Of course, this was before the discovery of television in these fairly remote areas. So these games were fairly popular with the general public and most always well attended. A modest attendance fee was charged to cover the cost of equipment, lights and pay the umpire's fees.

Our baseball field was created in the existing rodeo grounds. Fences were moved back and reshaped in the form of a ball field and the ground was leveled. A pitcher's mound was constructed and baselines were measured and chalked with anchors placed in the proper places for the base markers. Attendance stands had been built previously for the rodeo attendees. Home plate and the batter's boxes were placed appropriately in the front center of these stands.

I was a dedicated fan. So was most everyone else in the town. The ballplayers were minor heroes in our town. Everyone knew and spoke to them. Sports were the topic of the town over café coffee during each sport's season. Baseball was no exception. Those seldom lost games were played and replayed over hundreds of cups of coffee, each sport in turn.

The stands were full for most ball games. People stood here and there behind the home plate netting and the fences bordering the first and third baseline out-of -bound areas.

All the regular big league rules were observed. Only professional umpires were used. Townspeople swore allegiance to their home team and wore base-ball caps and T-shirts in home team colors not only to the games but also around town. Our home team, the Seagraves Oilers, wore gray uniforms trimmed in Navy blue with Navy blue baseball caps.

The Oiler team was one of the better teams. Usually the players of all the teams rode with their own townspeople in private cars or pickups caravanning to the out-of town games. There was always plenty of transportation. The individual teams were well represented at the out-of-town games.

Three of the Oiler ballplayers, Red Deatheridge, Lefty Faulkner and Blue Graham, worked on the electric utility line crew stationed at my father's office. Red was a very effective catcher; Lefty and Blue were both pitchers. Lefty was obviously left handed according to his name; Blue was the team's best right-hander. Red and Lefty were very close friends. They did everything together, at work and in their time off with their families.

I knew all three of them better than most of the other boys my age. I was often down at the office during the hours they were coming in from their line work. Of course, I didn't know them well, but I did know them. I really admired all the members of the line crew. They were happy hardworking men and seemed to really enjoy their jobs and working with each other. During those early years, the job they each enjoyed so much was a very dangerous job.

A few years later, Lefty was hit in the head and killed by a swinging out-of-control forty-foot utility pole. After this happened, Red, who began to drink hard liquor to help forget the death of his partner in work and play, finally drank his way out of his job. Blue…well, he is the heart and soul of this story.

Blue had a bluish complexion. That earned him the nickname, 'Blue'. I don't recall his real name or even if I ever knew it. Everybody called him Blue.

As I earlier mentioned, the club had two very effective pitchers, Blue and Lefty. Years before, Lefty had successfully tried out for a major league farm club stationed at that time in Fort Worth. He did not accept their contract, as the money earned would not be nearly enough to support him and his family. Lefty was a very effective curve ball pitcher; Blue threw a wicked fastball before anyone connected pitching and the speed of miles per hour. Red was the team's catcher for both. The two pitchers contributed greatly to the winning successes the team had over a good number of years.

Back to the ball game, now in the seventh inning. The Post Millers' pitcher finished preparing the ball and stepped onto the pitcher's rubber pad. Blue stepped into the batter's box and assumed his hitting stance, slightly proffering the bat. The pitcher started working. Blue looked at a couple of pitches and backed out of the box. He was leaning on his bat looking down at the ground. The right side of his face and neck those of us in the stands could see had really turned blue…almost black. He sagged to his knees on the ground and then very slowly fell over. The next batter up, Charley Lawrence, ran over, moved Blue over onto his stomach and started the old fashioned technique of chest compression.

The stand-by ambulance rushed Blue to the town's clinic-hospital. He never recovered. Later, the clinic's on-duty doctor stated that Blue was probably dead before he hit the ground.

Up until that hot afternoon, the ball field had never had a name. Shortly after Blue's death, the city council voted to name it "Graham Field". They erected a high, wide entrance gate and hung a sign across the top of it proclaiming the new name. This sign stayed there for many years, even after television caused the demise of grass-belt league ball clubs.

After that terrible hot afternoon, baseball in my hometown was never the same.

Snowed In

All these years later, I cannot remember exactly what year it took place. It happened in Colorado, and it was during that year's early deer hunting season. I know it was the early season, because I didn't want to go hunting in the late season because of the possibility of bad weather. Too much chance of having to sit the entire time cabin bound due to Colorado's heavy snows which are very likely that late in the year in the area where we planned to hunt.

I am pretty sure it was the fall of '85 or '86 as we were living in Los Banos, California at the time. We had moved there in late '84 and left in the spring of '87 due to a job transfer to Oroville.

Each year since 1980, my brother and my father had invited me to go hunting with them in their home state of Colorado right after Nancy and I had moved to Wyoming. And, each year I had accepted their invitation. My wife, Nancy, would stay and keep my mother company there in Golden while the males of the family journeyed south and west (mostly west) of Craig where we would hunt on BLM land.

As circumstances dictated, this hunt would be the first my brother and I would go on without our father who decided to stay home as our mother was not feeling well. As it turned out, his final hunt would be that of the previous year. This particular year we were going to a different place, one of much higher elevation. Harder country to hunt in but a better chance of bagging one of Colorado's dwindling deer population. This hunt would be in the high forest area of the San Juan Mountains above Creede. Co-incidentally, this hunt would be mine and my brother's last hunt together.

For years, the Fish and Game Department of Colorado had been catering strongly to the vast crowd of out-of-state hunters, taking their $150 license fee across any store counter that would go to the trouble to stock and sell the license. This resulted in an over-population of so many hunters, they were practically stepping on each other's toes and camping almost tent-to-tent. To relieve this situation, the Fish and Game Department decided to split the deer seasons. One in the early fall, the other later in early winter.

This was successful in drawing more hunters so they could step on each other's toes twice a year instead of only once. It also resulted in the decimation of the once great deer herd and the eventual loss of license fees, a great loss in revenue for the state. In short, no out-of-stater goes to Colorado deer hunting anymore. That is, if they are really hungry for venison. There just ain't none no more.

Now, I'm not saying on these hunts we did not have a really good time; successful hunt or not. We did. It is always enjoyable for fathers and sons to get together out in the 'wild' and just sit around the campfire reminiscing about days gone by. Especially late in life, that is.

To get back to the meat of this, my wife Nancy and I (well, I did, anyhow) planned and looked forward to this planned hunt with much expectation. My two hunting rifles were cleaned and sighted in, the ammunition load had been tested and found to be the best I could dream up. My share of the camping gear was loaded into the camper with some of my share of the food. My brother was to go grocery shopping there in Golden for the bulk of the larder. This expense would be shared at some later time. Nancy was to keep our mother company during our father's absence with us on the trip.

A friend of my brother's, John Melby and his wife, Cathy, were going with us. The couple had accompanied us on prior unsuccessful hunts. Unsuccessful, that is, as far as any of the group bringing home any venison.

My wife and I arrived in Golden with a day or two to spare before leaving for the hunting ground my brother had selected. The evening before the hunt, our mother had taken slightly ill, and my father had determined he should stay with her. Nancy decided since her company was no longer needed as planned for my mother she would go with us on the hunt.

Late that night on the end of the regular news cast the weather report indicated a front was expected to come in from the west with possible precipitation for the Golden area. I pointed out to my brother that at the much higher elevation where our hunt was planned, we were sure to be snowed on instead of rained on. My brother insisted after much prodding by me that it never—well, practically never—snowed in Colorado that early in the year.

As my wife was going with us, I decided to drive my own truck with its self-contained camper so we could both stay in it and not have to sleep in one of the tents. As far as I was concerned I really appreciated a firm mattress with sheets and blankets instead of a mattress of air on the ground and a sleeping bag on top of that.

We left before sunrise the next morning with no visible indication for good weather assurance. As a matter of fact when the sun did lighten things up, the clouds definitely looked snowy to me. We stopped at Saguache for lunch at a drive-in where we all ate on an outside table. It was shirtsleeve weather so far.

However, as we arrived at the campground later that afternoon it was a little cooler weather but no rain or snow. Of course, the cooler weather could have been due to the higher elevation of the hunt area. We were at an elevation of almost eleven thousand feet. The area of our proposed campsite was located near Spring Creek Pass. About twice as high as our starting elevation of Golden.

Camp was set up in no time at all. I leveled and blocked our camper; then I assisted the others in setting up their tents. My brother brought an additional tent, one big enough for cooking and a place for the group to eat. Looking back on this whole thing now, I wonder about the cooking tent. We never had one before. I think my brother must have been thinking we might really need the extra large tent in case of rain or something similar.

In any case, the first night we all ate sort of a potluck supper in the big tent. After supper and the dishes were all cleaned and put away, we decided to play some card games and started off with ordinary rummy. Not too long after we started playing cards, we could hear rain pattering on the tent canvas. I got up and looked out through the entrance flap. I felt the raindrops with my outstretched hand. They were really cold. I turned to my brother and again remarked that it was going to snow, at which comment he jokingly disagreed. I turned my attention back to the card game as play resumed. After a few more hands had been played, I noticed that it had become very quiet outside. I commented I could no longer hear rain drops falling on the tent. Remarks came from the rest of the group agreeing that the rain had stopped and they were all glad of it. I replied, "The rain has stopped because it has turned to snow." I got up, and to prove my statement, I again raised a tent flap and observed great big fat flakes of snow silently whispering down from above. I sat back down without saying a word and again directed my attention to my hand of cards.

When bedtime finally came and the card game broke up, someone opened the tent flap to leave and exclaimed there was practically a foot of snow out there. I could not resist. I looked at my brother and gloatingly said, "I told you so."

It snowed all night. Morning came cloudy and threatening more snow; a few wistful flakes still falling. There was well over two feet of snow on the ground. We had to forego any hunt away from camp as the snow was too soft to even try to go anywhere. Finally later that day, the clouds broke up and even with the sun shining it seemed to get colder.

The next day the snow had enough crust for us to get out a ways from the camp. As the days progressed, the snow would melt a little in the day time, then the crust would refreeze at night. The eighth day of our encampment and the sixth day of our hunt, John killed a fair sized elk. So we finally had steaks for supper courtesy of the Melbys.

During all this time, my wife was camper-bound. Because we had not prepared for her to go on the hunting trip to begin with, she had no weatherproof boots or shoes other than the low-cut slipper types. So, she spent the entire time in the camper, going outside only to go back and forth to the cook-tent using a well trampled path.

Day nine we determined that as John and my brother needed to get back to work, we decided to chain-up all four tires on each of the three four-wheel drive pickups and try to get out. We broke camp, packed everything up and hoping for the best started out on the two-rut trail toward the far-off two-lane highway.

Once we got out of the protection of the trees, the snow-covered trail became so sloppy it was unbelievable that we were still able to move. After much careful maneuvering, we finally reached the paved highway, turned east on it and headed for home.

I still visit the state of Colorado although my mother and father are no longer with us. My brother still lives in Golden; it looks like he will finish his life there also. He has raised his grandson from around age 8 and the grandson is now a freshman in the prestigious Colorado School of Mines.

I see John and Cathy Melby occasionally; John is now retired from the geology field and loving it. Even with John's single success on getting that elk, none of us have ever mentioned going hunting again.

Living in Wyoming, I have decided I am going hunting this next year's season. Hunting where we now reside, and where there are plenty of deer to hunt. Where it snows deeper sideways than up and down.

The Gangster Cat

He was really small I thought as I bent over to pick him up. A few seconds earlier, I had heard a small squeak as I started to go out the back garage door to feed the horses and chickens. Stopping, I looked down and there he was at my feet, a small fuzzy black spot in a pile of dirty clothes on the garage floor next to the washer. Picking him up, I stuck him in my vest pocket and walked on out to the small corral. Muttering all the way under my breath at my wife for leaving me, and now him. Leaving without so much as a note, or goodbye; just a half-empty cold house when I got home from work this past midnight. How could she leave something as helpless as a two-week old kitten that apparently no one wanted, as he was coal black instead of silver-blue like his brother and two sisters? How he survived all alone during the cold December night I couldn't figure. Some things have a will to live most of us can't understand.

I threw the horses a flake of hay apiece, filled the chicken and turkey feeders, topped off the water jugs and started back toward the house trying to think what I was going to do with that small still being in my pocket. Nothing I had at home could possibly be used to feed and care for him, so I walked over to the pickup and started for town.

In the local five-and-dime I found a doll's bottle, went over to the grocery store across the way and bought a couple of tins of tuna fish and a couple of cans of condensed milk. When we both got home, I ran some hot water into a pan, punched a hole in the top of one of the cans of milk and heated it some on the stove. I ran hot water over the doll's bottle and filled it about half full of warm water and mixed it with the heated canned milk. All this time the kitten lay quietly in my pocket, not knowing or able to smell the gourmet breakfast I was fixing for him. Finally I eased him out of my pocket and set him down on the cabinet top. He yawned, blinked a couple of times, squeaked a little. Up against his nose went the bottle nipple with a drop of milk on it. He took to that piece of rubber like he really knew what the whole thing was all about. He emptied it as I held it for him, me thinking now what? I had to go to work later that day and what was I going to do with him?

Well, I guess, little buddy, you survived one night all by yourself, I reckon you can another. Here I was calling him a buddy and I didn't even know whether he was a buddy or whatever you call a baby female kitten. So, I fixed a bed in one corner of a fair-sized box and put sand in most of the rest of it, not knowing whether he would even need the sand, much less know what it was supposed to be used for. Then, just before I left for work, I fixed him another meal of the milk and water and on leaving, I hoped for the best. I knew he was still so wobbly on his feet he would be out of harm's way in the box for a few days, anyhow.

Late that night on returning from work, I saw that he was fast asleep until I disturbed him as I reached into the box to pick him up. I played with him for a while, mostly petting, then fed him again wondering about what I was going to do with him. After he finished his bottle, I put him in his bed and me in mine.

This routine kept both of us occupied for the next several days. His eyes began to take on some color other than baby blue. There was as yet no evidence he had used the sand. I figured it was about time for some real chow so maybe he and I both wouldn't be so tied down with his meals. It seemed every time I looked at him he was ready for a bottle. So, I opened a can of tuna fish, took a little of the oil and rubbed it on his nose with my finger. No question about it, month old or no, this kid was ready for a real meal. He licked my finger almost raw with his rough little tongue. Spooning some fish into a saucer under his watchful eyes I pushed it toward him and he promptly put both his front feet into the dish and licked in. When he had finished, he looked up toward me as if to say, "That's all?" Well, I figured we would just wait, see if it all stayed down.

Now everyone knows cats need names. Not that they ever come when summoned, or do they ever admit to even recognizing the same repeated sound that just might maybe belong exclusively to them. Even so, I decided this cat was going to have a name. Picking him up, I investigated him carefully and discovered even at this young tender age he appeared 1) to be a boy, and 2) he didn't have a single hair on his whole carcass that wasn't black. So that seemed to settle it. I would call him Koal whether he liked it or ever recognized it; after all, I was the Boss, wasn't I? Well, Boss maybe for the present. So Koal he became, and when I said it to him over and over to get him used to it, he didn't seem to mind—or care, for that matter. He did sort of rub up to me though, whether I talked to him or not, probably mostly because he was lonesome and I happened to be handy. I also fed him, and you have to stay on the friendly side of the cook, right?

About this time I put the place up for sale, sold the two horses, chickens and turkeys, and moved to a rent house we owned in a nearby town. Here I kept him indoors as there were plenty of loose dogs in the neighborhood. The only time he seemed to mind being shut up was when I would leave for work: He would sit there in front of the glass door looking at me as if to say, "Me, too." I decided to take him with me for errands or when just messing around. He would sit behind me on the top of the seat back facing the window and watch the world go by. This manner of travel he kept up for several weeks until— well, I'm getting ahead of myself.

I had put the rent house we were staying in and one other my soon-to-be ex-wife and I owned up for sale at the same time the country place went on the market. Within a week's time all three of the places sold to different individuals. Now I was really in need of a place to live. I finally found a place closer to my job that didn't ask if I had a cat but did ask if I had a dog. I guess they figured a bachelor might have kids or a dog but not a cat. Or maybe they just didn't care if I had a cat. I found out later there were a few cats around in the apartment complex. So, Koal and I moved in. I had one bedroom, he had the other, or so I thought.

The place had a small patio off the 'master' bedroom, and a sliding glass door gave access to it. The patio was fenced off with concrete blocks about six feet tall. Very handy flowerbeds outlined the concrete deck so I devised a sill block to give Koal continual easy access through the glass door to the nice sandy flowerbeds. This solved one problem but created another I discovered later and the new problem wasn't flies or mosquitoes. I had decided to change his diet to dry cat food, which would solve the problem of him having to depend on me to serve his meals. He really didn't care too much for this at first, but since I was Boss (those days were numbered) he started eating the dry food. Well, it was a Good Brand. The Best Money Could Buy for your cat, according to the TV commercials. Besides, I was getting tired of smelling tuna fish. We even went shopping and bought two nice-sized un-tippable dishes, one for food, the other for water. Both also had high enough sides that weren't handy for putting front feet in. Now things were really going great. I kept both dishes filled and he seemed to at least accept the situation. All of a sudden when I would come in from work, he would meet me at the door and I would observe that his food bowl would be empty when I was sure I left it plumb brimful. Now, being born before yesterday, I figured I was feeding at least two cats, and even though Koal was too small to climb the block fence was no sign a larger cat couldn't both get in and out. So, in spite of risking an upset kitten I cut down the amount and fed him mostly when I was there to see him eat it. That seemed to work pretty well.

Shortly it became my "turn in the barrel" at work and my new schedule of dayshifts as relief supervisor began, the first in our new apartment. This brought me quite a surprise. The third morning the alarm went off was the last time the alarm woke me up. I had been feeding Koal as soon as I got up, even before I shaved and all the other morning stuff. The next morning I woke up with sunlight coming in through the glass door and Koal sitting mostly on my chest. I opened one eye to see two looking at me and hearing a very small "meow," I got up and fed him.

This became the normal morning job until I woke up one morning with two black cats in bed with me, one mostly sitting on my chest, the other on one side of the foot of the bed, looking at me with big yellow eyes very cautiously and front paws tucked in. I very carefully got out of bed and started into the kitchen. Both followed me as I expected; both watched me fill the food bowl. I turned, walked out to start my morning stuff. A few minutes later I observed them both eating side by side as if they had been doing it all along. Now I had the reason for the bigger food bill right before my eyes, only the other cat had perfectly formed white spats on each foot.

Later I found he lived upstairs, his mother was a house sitter by occupation, and when she went sitting she kicked him out of the apartment for the two or three days she would be gone. Also, his name was White Socks.

And, even though he was very dignified being an older cat, he would allow Koal to play with him, but he didn't much play back. In the following four months I would have his acquaintance, I fed him many times, allowed him to sleep on my bed many nights, always on that one side at the foot. I was never allowed to get within touching distance, much less petting distance.

I met a very nice lady across the entry from mine who loved cats. We started going around together and found we had a lot in common, both of us recovering from very unsatisfactory marriages; both of us having dated others but with no idea of any desirable future. Things began to look up for us both. We began keeping very regular company and it seemed maybe we had both found good things in each other the other liked and wanted.

Having received my share of the equity checks from the real estate sales I began to house hunt and invited her along, partly for company, partly that if things continued to develop into the serious situation it seemed to be headed for, I didn't want to buy a house that she disliked.

In the meantime, my Koal became mostly her Koal. Now I didn't exactly know what to make of this; she seemed to like the cat at least as much as she seemed to like me. Which I guessed would be alright as long as we did develop into a permanent relationship. As far as Koal seemed to be concerned, that was that. And, as it turned out, that was that. I bought a house.

Because I didn't want Koal to wander like tomcats seem to be wont to do, I decided on making an "it" out of him. He was about five months old now and I was going to rotate back to working shift. The upcoming swingshift seemed to be the right time for the operation. I would be with him in the daytime, his lady would be with him in the evening while I was at work. Then I would be there for him and his buddy to sleep with if Sock's mother was again away from home. So, I made an appointment for the big event.

The only catch was I wouldn't be able to pick him up after the operation. So I asked our mutual lady friend, Nancy, to pick him up the early evening after the operation. I suggested she put him in the trunk of her car for the ride home, as he would be slightly woozy and that way wouldn't be able to distract her as she drove. Now, this was one big mistake-for all of us. Little did we know what this would do to that cat. Never again would he ride peacefully in a vehicle; or even willingly get near one. Due to that one short ride home in the trunk of that car he developed a hate for vehicles that lasted to his next to last day on this earth. He would actually glare at them with huge yellow eyes that displayed nothing but the most sincere dedicated form of hate. Later on, I even observed him spray the car; cats supposedly can no longer do this after being neutered. When I saw him do this, I thought to myself: "Now, that is dedicated hate." Real, dyed in the wool, "Dedicated Hate."

Soon after Koal returned home a new (read different) cat, Nancy and I married and moved into our new home. Koal stayed shut up in the house for a week or so in order for Nancy to be sure he would recognize his new home and know to return after he was permitted to roam freely. During this period of incarceration he seemed to believe it was completely my fault; instead of sleeping on my side of the bed, he moved to hers; instead of waking me in the mornings, he woke her. He still tolerated me, but barely. Quite often during the wintertime when I would be on the graveyard shift and Nancy would be working during the week, he would sleep with me; it really wasn't out of desire to be with me as it was to be on a nice warm electric blanket. Now sleeping in the daytime for a human isn't really easy; for a cat it's routine. And the vibrating motor lying against your leg almost tickles, making it even more difficult to drop off to sleep. Then, once the sandman does come, the darn cat leaves and you wake up due to the loss of the warm spot by your leg and the lack of vibration. Sometimes it really is difficult to be human, a shiftworker, and belong to a very stubborn cat.

Also, a very smart cat. I had installed a pet door for Koal in the kitchen door. This made it easier for us to take off on occasional weekend trips and not have to worry about his sanitation problems. As his diet was normally dried food we would put out an ample supply for him; he never seemed to overeat. The pet door worked as well for us as it did for him.

One afternoon on the way home from work, I stopped off at a neighborhood bar for a bottle of beer or two. One of my bird-hunting acquaintances was there; he had just returned from an unsuccessful quail hunt. Blaming the dry haul on his dog, he stated he was going to "Git rid of that darn dog". Now I knew the dog, and would like to have her for myself. I had never seen him so disgusted. I knew the dog's problem was his master; he had on more than one occasion hit the dog with the butt of his shotgun; faulting the dog for not being able to read his master's mind. So, I told him I'd take the dog as I had several times before. This time, he surprised me by saying "She's yours. Let's go get her right now". The dog, Lady Bridgett Rhett III, acquired a new owner. A few days later I ran into him and he told me, "By the way, that dog hates cats." However, when she had arrived at her new home that dog accepted Koal a whole lot better than Koal accepted the dog. In fact, from the very first meeting, that cat had that dog completely buffaloed. And that never changed.

Koal was now about two years old, and had mostly attained his full growth: He weighed seventeen pounds and had no fear of man nor beast. My father, on seeing Koal, said he grew so large due to the loss of his masculinity, or whatever you want to call it that male cats lose when they are neutered; that we should have waited until he was about a year old.

Behind our house was a concrete lined irrigation ditch about two feet wide; beyond that was an open field. Koal would jump the ditch and hunt in the field. On the occasion when he would be lucky and capture prey, the pet door opening into the back yard would present a problem for him. The fenced backyard was occupied by Bridgett and my son's Irish Setter. We had somehow graciously volunteered to keep the Setter during my son's initial training session for state service in the newly formed California Conservation Corps. Koal was not about to bring any of his prizes into the back yard and risk sharing it with the setter, ignoring Bridgett completely. So he would bypass the back and go around to the protected area of the front door.

On one of his particularly successful hunts I had worked graveyard and was asleep in the bedroom; it must have been a weekend as Nancy was home. She heard Koal growling at the front door in his Siamese drawl for assistance in getting in that door. Koal, knowing somehow Nancy was not about to let him and any monster he might have gain entry into the house, had placed his prey down below the doorsill out of sight and held it with both front paws on it. Nancy opened the door; Koal reached down, grabbed his monster in his tusks (that cat had no eye teeth, just huge tusks) and jumped through the open door into the house. Nancy reacted with a scream that brought me on a run in my undies toting my shotgun, certain the natives had invaded. Koal had dropped a full grown mole into the living room floor and continued to frolic with it, almost allowing freedom, then recapturing the way fun loving cats do. I calmly took the shotgun back into the bedroom and pulled my pants on while my wife continued hysterics in the living room. I went out to the shop, put on a pair of heavy lineman's gauntlet gloves, took the mole away from the cat and outside to throw it back across the canal from whence it came. Back in the house, we now had one mad cat.

You would think that Nancy would have learned from that episode, and maybe she did. But a month or so would go by, and it would be a small mostly live snake, a bird; once a gopher. Once or twice on our return from an overnight trip, we would find a few feathers scattered around, somehow smuggled past the Irish Setter. As I recall we never found any significant beast or parts thereof.

I received a job offer in Wyoming that promised a substantial increase in salary, company transportation, and best of all, straight days. So we decided to move to Wyoming, and, after a couple of trips out there we sold our house in California and bought one in Wyoming.

We had not counted on the trip out there as being particularly significant. Nancy would drive the car; I would follow with the truck and camper. As we had two dogs and the cat, we would spend the trip nights in the camper instead of in a motel.

I had a CB radio in the truck and I bought another and installed it in the car so we could communicate on the road. This turned out to be a very useful tool, the ability to talk to each other at any time: Except for one drawback. Koal. Every time Nancy responded to my call, I could hear that cat's Siamese growl. Not just occasionally; constantly. His hatred of vehicles was now right up front. As long as the car was moving, that cat growled. I insisted to Nancy that we put the cat in the camper where neither one of us would have to hear him. Absolutely no dice. So the cat continued to announce his hate of vehicles. For two days, sunup to sundown, he did this. You would think he would have worn his vocal cords out, or got laryngitis. Before this trip, he rarely ever used his voice, but you paid attention when he did. It was as overgrown as he was.

With the new house we discovered we had a problem. The back door was sliding glass with no way to put in a pet door. The ground level floor exited into the garage; I didn't want to put a pet door in it and also one in one of the big garage doors. So Koal would go to the front door or the glass doors and expect to immediately be let out. He never seemed to wake us up in the night, though. So in that he was very thoughtful.

The first time Koal saw snow was hilarious. He, unknowing, went to the front door. Nancy went over to let him out. The snow had piled up against the door about a foot high; it stayed that way when she opened the door. Koal started his usual quick jump out the door and suddenly stopped the preparations when he saw the stacked up snow. He turned his head and looked up at Nancy who simply stood there. Finally he jumped over the drift. As he landed he picked each foot up out of the snow, shaking each in turn. Every step he took, he shook each foot—all the way to the mailbox. Same thing on the way back. In the four years we lived in Wyoming, he never got used to the snow.

About this time we discovered he would stalk passing dogs as if they were prey. What is really funny about this is the dogs took that cat seriously. Very seriously. One spring day, Nancy was pulling weeds from the front lawn. She had the dog lying near her; not to be outdone, jealous Koal was also out there with her. Three or four men were riding on bicycles up the street followed by several dogs, one a standard poodle. Koal went into stalk mode creeping toward the street. As soon as the group passed Koal's mid-point line of sight, he charged. The dogs saw him, started yelping and took off running in all directions. One of the riders started laughing; laughed so hard he almost fell off his bike.

A few days later I was working at the side of the house on a backyard fence we had started. I observed a couple of loose midsized black poodles having a great time across the street in a cul-de-sac. They had sneaked out of their home's open side-yard gate and were really tickled to be free. I went back to fencing, and suddenly the dogs started yipping. Looking up, I saw Koal chasing them back toward the gate. The dogs, both just smaller than Koal, went through the side gate back into the yard, and so did Koal. He stopped only when they took refuge on the side porch, then turned around and swaggered—I mean, swaggered— out of the gate and toward home. Now I thought that cat is nothing short of a gangster. No mercy whatsoever.

All of this really did a lot for Koal's ego. He now would sit in a chair beneath the dining room table and take a sudden swat at Bridgett when she walked by. Poor Bridgett. She would always be unsuspecting on her way out the opened patio deck door and Koal would win again. It proceeded to be so bad that Bridgett wouldn't come onto the deck from the yard if she saw

Koal sitting at the top of the deck stairs. But she always forgot about the dining room chair.

One summer our side neighbor's grandchildren came to stay for a while with their grandparents. They brought along a small fox-terrier puppy. As the fence had not been completed we kept Bridgett on a chain in the back yard when the weather was nice enough for her to be outside. It wasn't long before the pup was coming over to see Bridgett; they became fast friends. That is, until Koal happened to see the pup in our back yard. He sat growling at the patio door to be let out. Well, I didn't pay any attention to occupants of the back yard; I just let Koal out. The poor pup never came back after that.

Our front entryway opened onto a stair landing; as you walked up you entered the living room, the down stairs led into the lower section of the house. The living room had a cathedral ceiling so the entry way overhead was a good ten feet in altitude. The edge of the living room near the entryway was separated from the stairwell by a banister. Over the entry door was amber-colored opaque glass all the way to the ceiling. Due to the decor on the outside of the glass there was an area birds could seek shelter. Quite often Koal would sit on the banister and watch the birds.

Once temptation overcame brains and Koal jumped up at the shadow of the birds—I don't know how he did it, but he managed to hook his front claws at the very top of the glass. As soon as this happened, reason took back over, or maybe panic. He realized he could not get down. So he started a sort of wail, asking for assistance, I guess. I took pity on him, and with the aid of a ladder from the garage, rescued him. Once back down on the floor, he acted like it never happened, just sauntered away as if he had made a neat conquest.

Friends of ours from Craig, Colorado, came to visit one summer. They brought with them a Chihuahua dog that was used to being around cats. They had a Persian cat that the dog played and slept with. As soon as Yoda, the dog, saw Koal, he went up to introduce himself in a very friendly manner. Koal promptly knocked Yoda completely off his feet with one very positive swat. Poor Yoda scrambled away, fast as lightning as we all sat there and watched sort of dumfounded. Poor Yoda. He not only never trusted cats after that; the rest of his life he stayed away from his former friend, the Persian.

Several years before back in California, it had been Nancy's habit when she was working to eat cold cereal for breakfast. It had become a habit with Koal to immediately stop whatever he was doing and join Nancy in the dining room for this ritual. When she would finish, there would be a spoonful or so of milk and a few grains of sugar left in the bottom of the bowl. It had become a habit with Koal to closely observe her consume the "meal" and upon completion, she would set the bowl on the floor and Koal would very carefully and deliberately lap up the residue.

Nancy's elderly mother, Elsie, had visited us at least twice before here in Wyoming; she really liked the area. When it became apparent she was no longer able to live alone, we suggested she come and live with us, which she agreed to. Now Koal was plenty happy to see her as she was another warm body to curl up to when he wanted to nap; that was all right with Elsie. Koal soon found out that cold cereal for breakfast was also a habit of Elsie's. So he would attend her morning ritual and accept the leavings just as he did with Nancy. But...one morning there was no milk. Elsie, being a retired registered nurse, was a very resourceful person. So she used orange juice on her cereal. And, without thinking, when she finished, she sat the bowl down as usual for Koal. He got at least two tonguefuls down before he realized the bowl contained residue of something other than milk. He backed off, shook his head, and glared at Elsie with huge yellow eyes.

It was several days before he again trusted any bowl sat down before him. Even then, he would carefully sniff the bowl's contents before lapping.

Pre-employment recruiting promises made to me had not come to pass in Wyoming. Instead of working normal daytime hours, I was placed on shift as a first-level supervisor to "Get the feel of the plant." Shortly after my employment my fellow shift supervisors and I were placed on twelve hour shifts to determine if longer work hours resulting in fewer days at work and less travel time would benefit the union employees who were considering twelve-hour shifts. So we lower level management employees were used as guinea pigs. Travel time consisted of a one hundred mile round trip each workday; two hours minimum in good weather. All of a sudden we were working fourteen-hour days. This, at my age of forty-six resulted in an ulcer and uncontrollable high-low blood pressure. Our family physician notified me I was to keep my life insurance current or change my field of endeavor.

So we decided to move back to California where I would attend a computer science school.

We listed the house with a local company; it sold very quickly. Too quickly. We still had not really come to terms with the fact of leaving. Preparations for moving began as soon as I had determined which school to attend. I had made a quick trip to California, passed an admittance test and enrolled in a reputable computer science school. We contracted with a moving company and they soon come out to the house and began packing our household.

The night before they were to load, Nancy and I were in the living room watching a program on television. We were both very sad at leaving; we loved Wyoming and especially the town we lived in. Koal often would sit on a lamp table and look out the front window. Probably watching for his special enemy: Dogs. This night the lamp was packed away; so was the glass tabletop. Only the frame of the lamp table remained in its usual spot. Koal jumped up to sit on the glass and fell completely through, landing on the lower table shelf. This time, having again made a fool of himself, he seemed to realize it as he sneaked away without looking at either of us.

This trip I was able to convince Nancy Koal should ride in the camper in his carry-cage. Now Koal hated this cage about as much as he hated vehicles; it was associated with trips to the vet for yearly shots. He had to be wrapped in a towel and forced in the cage each use. But into the cage he would go; we intended to let him out each night. As it turned out, during the first few hours of the trip he managed to pop open the cage door and take refuge somewhere in the stacked boxes inside the camper.

Each morning, I would change his water and fill his food bowl. We didn't see him from the time he was put into the camper until we unloaded in Alameda, California three days later. But I could hear him. Every time I stopped for a traffic light; every time I slowed down. I could hear him. That darn cat growled for 1200 miles, stopping only for breath or when I shut the engine off. Later we learned the vets have tranquilizers for this; we were ignorant of it at the time. Knowing him as I did, I'm sure they wouldn't have worked even if we had known of and used them. If I hadn't known his mother I would have sworn he was a pygmy black panther. He was the most un-natural cat, the most unusual cat I have ever known. Outside of traveling he rarely ever used his voice. Only in desperation when he wanted outside and no one noticed. For a time, when he was young, I wasn't even sure he had a voice.

Perhaps the return trip to the land of his birth aged him. He stayed closer to home. In Alameda the canine population is pretty much leash and yard-bound by law. He did spend quite a bit of his time lying on the front porch in the sun watching the street. Maybe in hope a dog would wander by. For all of his life up to now, we had never heard him purr. You could feel him purr; I mentioned that before. But you couldn't HEAR him. All of a sudden we both noticed that Koal could now be heard purring. Loud. If he put his mind to it, you could hear him purr six feet or so away. In the middle of the night you could wake up and he'd be lying near you on the bed—purring.

After a year of schooling, I accepted employment in California's central valley, and we set up a new home. The same problem of a pet door that we had in Wyoming occurred in the layout of our new home: Glass patio doors, and a back door leading into the garage. So we determined to simply open the door for him. Knowing from our life in Wyoming he would come to the bedroom window and growl if we were asleep and he wanted in. When awake, we would see him at the patio door. And Nancy wouldn't have to worry about strange critters in the house as long as she looked before opening the door for him.

This lack of his having personal access also had its drawbacks—if we went away for an overnight, he would have to be shut inside. This required dealing with cat sand on a fairly regular basis as we both liked to travel on days off.

One tragic thing occurred soon after we moved. Tragic and traumatic for Koal. We left for three days over a New Year's. We put out more than sufficient food, water and sand for Koal before leaving. It was Nancy's habit to keep the door to her sewing room closed except when she was in it. This trip, however, Koal must have been lying on the windowsill, asleep in the sun in the sewing room. As soon as we returned from our trip, Koal didn't meet us at the door as he usually did. Immediately we feared the worst, and started looking through the house. Nancy found him on lying on the daybed in her sewing room. No food, no water, no sandbox. And, no mess. The poor cat had endured almost seventy-two hours without food, water or sandbox. We not only couldn't believe he survived: But no mess. From that day on, we made certain he was free in the living room before leaving.

Soon after moving to our new home, we discovered the neighbors to our west raised small English Bulldogs. At any given time they had a dozen in their ordinary-sized residential back yard. Certainly this was illegal, but as our bedroom was on the far side it really wasn't too much of a problem. They kept the yard fairly clean, an easy problem since the dogs kept the grass worn down. For Koal this was heaven. He had all those dogs to torment. He would bait and tease the dogs through the knotholes in the fence. They would be enraged—or dumb enough, to stick their noses close enough to the knothole for Koal to draw blood. Koal would infuriate them to the point of the dogs charging the fence, slamming into it very forcefully. Those dogs were dumb. They never did learn. When Koal tired of swatting, he would jump onto the fence and parade back and forth. He wouldn't even flinch when they jumped at him; I guess he knew somehow there was no way they could reach him. I would tire of the racket pretty quick and go out and chase him off the fence. I also was afraid the force of the dog's charges would break the fence boards.

Almost before we really settled in our new home, I was transferred to Northern California in the western foothills of the Sierra. A much more beautiful place than the Southern Central Valley. Our new home had a quarter acre yard, all fenced. And, at that time, no nearby dogs for Koal to torment. But in the summer, it was hot. Too hot for an old man like Koal, and he began to show his age of ten years.

Our new neighbors had a female cat. When she would come in season, she would come over into our yard, rub around Koal, purr and meow. Somehow she seemed to sense he was supposed to be a male. Poor Koal; he would just simply look at her very curiously, him setting upright with just the tip of his tail slightly waving. It seemed she never gave up; each of her "seasons" it was the same old thing. He sat there, looking at her, and waving the very tip of his tail.

Our new house had a twelve-foot wide deck that ran the length of the house, some sixty feet. One end of the deck was enclosed with trellis and climbing grape vines, well protected. In the enclosed area sat a spa with a hardtop cover. As the heat from the water kept this cover fairly warm, Koal would sun there; quite often Nancy and I would have morning coffee there with him as the spa set right out-side our bedroom's double glass doors.

A couple we had known from down south came up for a visit one summer. As we had a spa that came with our new house and they had none, they were invited to use it. I dropped the blinds for their privacy, and opened the cover. We were all sitting on the deck, watching the sun go down and talking.

Now, they were both cat people, and Koal knew it. He was running around, jumping here and there; generally showing off. All of a sudden, he ran the length of the deck, jumped up on the deck railing, and jumped into the spa not realizing the cover was off. We heard a splash-then one more splash and a thump as his feet hit the deck. The first splash brought total silence from us: Like waiting for the other shoe to drop. After the second splash and thump, Koal came stalking—and I mean stalking—back the way he came. His yellow eyes were as big as silver dollars; he was soaking wet and furious. At that point we all looked at him and started laughing, making Koal all the more furious, if that were possible. He disappeared around the corner of the house. Nancy told me to go get him and dry him with a towel. So I followed Koal's wet tracks on the stone walk into the garage, captured him and dried him off.

It was several months before Koal again sunned on the spa top. One morning he saw Nancy set her coffee cup down on it; then he ventured back onto it.

Just before we had received our transfer orders to move to Northern California we had Bridgett put to sleep. She was about fifteen years old, mostly blind and totally deaf. I really missed her, so I coerced Nancy into us obtaining a Golden Retriever puppy. Koal did seem to miss Bridgett a little. But he sure didn't care for our new puppy, Sunshine, as we named her. Lady Golden Sunshine. AKA added an "X"; I guess there must have been another Lady Golden Sunshine somewhere in California. Pretty soon the pup learned to stay out of harm's way with Koal. And Koal seemed resigned to accept Sunshine.

At the age of three, we bred Sunshine. Well, I'll never go through that again. It's one thing, the old dog having a litter of pups down at the barn. This was an entirely different situation. Sunshine had eleven pups; two still born, ten live. One she smothered the second day. She was too young, or too many pups. She lost track of it and somehow it wound up under her back and died. Pretty soon Koal heard the pups and went into the garage to investigate. Sunshine became one irate mother—she growled and charged at Koal. The old man backed up; sure nuff a first. I thought I'd never have lived to see that day. Later, after all the pups were gone, Koal even tolerated Sunshine. And Sunshine was no longer scared of Koal.

We planned a three-week trip to the Midwest to see my family and attend my graduating class' twenty-fifth reunion in my hometown. Due to the length of time we were to be gone, we put Koal and Sunshine in a kennel that had a cat "hotel." It was a very nice clean place; the cats were in individual cages inside an air-conditioned building. Koal had been on a special diet for some time as he was not as active as he used to be and had tended to put on weight. He still was around seventeen pounds, but now he had a gray hair or two. When we delivered him to the kennel, we also took enough of his special food to more than last him while we were gone.

Immediately on our return from the trip, I went to the kennel and picked up both Koal and Sunshine. The young lady who served me was new; I had not seen her before. I took Koal home in his carry-cage, opened the garage door, set the cage on the floor and let him out. Without any of his usual complaining, he followed me into the kitchen and went immediately to his food dish. He didn't eat any, but drank some water. He looked really bad; his fur seemed unkempt. I reached down and picked him up.

I don't think he weighed ten pounds. Nancy had a very strange look on her face as I commented of Koal's condition to her. I called the kennel and asked for the owner. She told me Koal would hardly eat while we were gone; they had ended up feeding him mostly tuna fish and he hadn't eaten a lot of that. I immediately called the vet and we took the old man down to the office.

The vet's examination revealed two bad open ulcers in Koal's mouth and a large tumor in his throat. She told us she could operate on him, but he was pretty far gone. I realized in our haste to get him to the office Nancy had carried him in her arms, and in the truck he had not complained. As I held him on the examination table I realized he was purring. I took my hands from Koal, turned away and told the doctor to put him to sleep. I then left; went out to the pickup and waited for Nancy. In a little while she came out and asked me if I was sure. I told her I was. She went back inside. By the time I had smoked two cigarettes she was back. The vet came with her in order to bring us Koal. I could hardly see to drive. We both cried all the way home.

Later that day, I put Koal to rest in a protected shady spot in the back yard.

Years have passed since that lonely afternoon. It still hurts. I never told him goodbye.

* * * * * * *

CPSIA information can be obtained at www.ICGtesting.com
Printed in the USA
LVOW03*0311140815

450111LV00008B/41/P